PLEASURE &PROFIT

Robert W. Shippee

PLEASURE &PROFIT

100 LESSONS
FOR BUILDING AND SELLING
A COLLECTION OF RARE COINS

Robert W. Shippee
Foreword by Q. David Bowers

Whitman
Publishing, LLC
PUBLISHING SINCE 1934

www.whitman.com

Pleasure and Profit: 100 Lessons for Building and Selling a Collection of Rare Coins

www.whitman.com

© 2014 Whitman Publishing, LLC

3101 Clairmont Road • Suite G • Atlanta, GA 30329

Correspondence concerning this book may be directed to Whitman Publishing, Attn: Pleasure and Profit, at the address above.

ISBN: 0794842437

Printed in China

For a complete catalog of numismatic reference books, supplies, and storage products, visit Whitman Publishing online at www.Whitman.com.

Contents

Foreword

Congratulations! If you are an active buyer of rare coins, you are about to read one of the most *useful* books in American numismatics.

When I first read through the manuscript of *Pleasure and Profit* I imagined myself following Bob Shippee at conventions and auctions, on the bourse floor, exploring Web sites, and otherwise immersing himself in the rare-coin market. I've known Bob as a friend and client for many years, but only now do I appreciate the full depth of knowledge, enthusiasm, and connoisseurship that guided him on this Grand Tour of numismatics.

Q. David Bowers

His quest was to build a collection of each design type from half cents to $20 gold double eagles, from 1793 to the present day. Such a pursuit is hardly new. In fact, it is one of the most popular ways to collect. Rather than seeking to acquire one of each date and mintmark of a coin design or denomination, the idea is to buy just a single example of each motif. This has several advantages. The most obvious is cost. A complete collection of, for example, every double eagle date and variety from 1850 to 1933 comprises slightly more than 200 coins. Even if you had an unlimited budget your display could not be complete, as the last year of issue is for all practical purposes unobtainable. (The single legally held example of the 1933 double eagle crossed the auction block at over $7,000,000 in 2002 and has been off the market ever since.) Obtaining all of the others in high grades would probably exceed $10,000,000.

Continuing the double eagle example, what Bob Shippee did was to stop, think, and carefully consider buying a choice example of each of the six major motifs—a beautiful exhibit. His total cost was $27,712. When his holdings, titled the Waccabuc Collection, crossed the auction block at our sale of November 13, 2007, these $20 gold coins sold for $35,182, giving a profit of $7,470 or 25%. (Actually, the performance of his double eagles is rather on the *low* side. The stellar performer among denominations was his set of silver dollars, which cost $64,290 and sold for $116,602, yielding a profit of $52,512 or 82%.)

In terms of spectacular success, his top five winners gained 88%, 177%, 216%, 342%, and 571%. "When my accountant saw these results, he rejoiced," Bob states. "When I sold the Waccabuc Collection I received net proceeds, after commissions, of $1,405,136. This represented a total gain of 39.4% and an annual compounded return of 10.2%."

While Bob, a "semi-retired" (as he puts it) international banker, is a whiz at mathematics and financial analysis, this is not a book that concentrates on how to *invest* in coins (although few investment guides are better). Instead Bob shares, coin by coin, his *thinking*. You will follow how he decided which coin to pick to represent a given type, what he thought of the design and other aspects, what grade to seek, and how to go about making a wise purchase. Sometimes in the passion of an auction sale he made a bad decision. He tells you how he learned from such experiences.

Judging from the many side references, it's clear that Bob assembled an impressive numismatic library. Building a working library is considered ideal by many coin buyers, but reality is that only a small percentage do so. It is curious that, say, $1,000 to $2,000 spent on a shelf of useful books will repay its cost many times over, but most buyers would rather spend the money, and quickly, on a $1,000 or $2,000 coin. Knowledge is the key to success. Time and again this comes to the fore in Bob's compelling narrative.

His reading of relevant books and catalogs gave him the advantage of being very well informed, in advance, of aspects of nearly all of the items on his "want list." Beyond that he carefully viewed nearly all coins before bidding on or purchasing them. He did not rely on certified holders when buying, but tells of many instances in which such holders helped sell his coins for excellent prices when they crossed the auction block. The Waccabuc Collection ranked high as a PCGS Registry Set.

Bob always sought high quality, but at the same time had an eye out for *value*. This is contrarian thinking to what most buyers do: for them, the higher the grade, the better. Because of this, many "top of the population reports" coins are overpriced. Reflective of his strategy is this comment: "My 1814 is the most common date (among 1808–1814 Classic Head cents), and the About Uncirculated grade seemed like a nice compromise between the sometimes unattractive lower-graded coins that are readily available and the much pricier Uncirculated specimens that are very hard to find."

As you will see, Bob spices his already highly readable text with lots of humor, and irreverent (but never irrelevant) comments. By the time he started the Waccabuc Collection he had already been collecting and studying coins for years. Still, he had to contemplate the modern market, so to speak—the cracking out of coins from their holders, grades such as MS-66 and higher that were not used years earlier, investment hype and sales pitches, movement in the bullion market that affected gold coin prices, and different market conditions.

Bob is accomplished in his other hobby, golfing. Golf and numismatics have a lot in common, respecting theory and challenge. Throughout the text he comments occasionally on golf, and the parallels are instructional. A "mulligan" or free shot in America is quite unlike one in Great Britain, as you will learn. Bob, by the way, is also a very accomplished world traveler—and he could well emulate the late Temple Fielding and create a uniquely useful travel guide to Europe. If you used the Fielding guide years ago you know it made you want to go to places you'd never heard of!

Pleasure and Profit will make *you* want to emulate Bob as a successful rare-coin collector. I guarantee that as soon as you finish it your buying strategy will be different from what it is now.

This is one of the most interesting books I have ever read and, beyond that, has much useful information not found in any other single text. Join Bob Shippee as he shares his pleasures and his disappointments, his hits and misses—his birdies and eagles as well as his bogies. If you collect rare coins, this is a Grand Tour you don't want to miss.

Q. David Bowers
Wolfeboro, New Hampshire

Q. David Bowers, the "Dean of American Numismatics," started his career as a professional numismatist when he was a teenager in the early 1950s. He has served as president of the American Numismatic Association (1983–1985) and of the Professional Numismatists Guild (1977–1979). He has graded and cataloged many of the finest coin collections ever brought to market. Today Bowers is numismatic director of Whitman Publishing, chairman emeritus of Stack's Bowers Galleries, and research editor of A Guide Book of United States Coins *(the hobby's popular "Red Book").*

Preface

O ver drinks several years ago, a close friend asked me one of those questions that just doesn't have a good answer. He asked me, "Bob, if you had to give up collecting and reading about coins *or* if you had to give up watching and playing golf, which one would you choose?" I took a long sip of my Laphroaig single malt whiskey before answering. "Jim, I can't choose. They're both equally important to me."

Jim was shocked. We both shared a passion for golf, but he had no appreciation at that time of my passion for coins. I started collecting coins when I was nine, and my first swing of a golf club happened not many years later. In my early teens, I looked through $50 bags of cents for fun, and I had just as much fun walking barefoot on the plush fairways of a nearby course after school, toting five old clubs and a couple of scarred balls. I love to read stories about coin hoards, sunken treasures, and new numismatic discoveries, and I love to watch the best golfers execute (or muff, just often enough for us to feel empathy) difficult shots on beautiful courses around the world.

Few people know it, but coins and golf have much in common. For example, many golfers use a coin as a ball marker. Most coins are round, as are most golf balls and the holes into which we try to sink them. A great score on a hole of golf (two under par) is called an *eagle*, which is the same name given to our highest denomination gold coin when production of $10 gold pieces began in Philadelphia in 1795. Two years after gold became plentiful, following the fabled discovery at Sutter's Mill in California in 1848, the U.S. Mint began production of $20 gold pieces. These were called double eagles, a term that, for golfers, brings to mind Gene Sarazen and "the shot heard 'round the world"—a 235-yard 4-wood second shot that went into the cup at the par-5 15th hole during the Masters Tournament at the Augusta National Golf Course in Augusta, Georgia. The story of Sarazen's 1935 double eagle is certainly compelling, but no more so than the story of the 1933 double eagle that was once owned by King Farouk of Egypt and was then, decades later, confiscated by the U.S. Secret Service before being sold at auction for $7.59 million. (Alison Frankel's meticulously researched book, *Double Eagle: The Epic Story of the World's Most Valuable Coin*, tells the engrossing tale. It is a pleasure to read, whether you're a collector or a golfer.)

Okay, okay. I know I'm stretching a point. The game of golf and the science of numismatics don't *really* have that many points of intersection outside of my psyche. Though I love both pursuits, I'm a more proficient coin person than I am a golfer. I'd immodestly assign myself a numismatic handicap of 2—hardly a professional, but certainly an enlightened amateur—whereas my more-or-less-real golf handicap of 13 qualifies me only as a strong duffer. Therefore, since I'm the one holding the pen, I'll be focusing primarily on my experiences in acquiring and selling rare coins, but I'll occasionally be tempted to provide some leavening in the form of golfing references and stories.

． ． ．

Beginning almost 20 years ago, I began to get serious about building a meaningful coin collection. I started going to auctions, buying coins, and buying books (sadly, in that order). I didn't yet have a grand vision of what kind of collection I wanted to build. But there were *so* many interesting coins, and the catalog descriptions were *so* compelling, and bidding on (and winning) coins at live auctions was such a rush, that I just couldn't help but have fun.

I also made mistakes. . . bogies, double bogies, and even a snowman or two.[1] While the financial results from the sale of the collection described in this book were very satisfying, a number of my early purchases, and even a few of my more recent acquisitions, were not great successes. I paid too much for some common coins. I didn't stretch enough for some very special coins. I bought some ugly coins. I bought some overgraded and damaged coins. Of course, these coins were not described as ugly, overgraded, and damaged—I was just learning the hard way.

With the passage of time, I made fewer mistakes. I got around to reading some of the books I'd bought. I subscribed to some numismatic newspapers and magazines, and I joined some coin clubs. I found a few dealers who were patient, generous with their time and knowledge, and extremely helpful to my development as a collector.

With greater knowledge came greater confidence. I unloaded my mistakes. I sold my "widgets" (as well-known New Jersey dealer Laura Sperber is fond of calling ordinary coins). I became more focused when making purchases in the auction room, on the bourse floor (the public area at a coin convention), and from dealers' listings. I was having even more fun than before.

By mid-2007, I'd basically finished building a complete United States type set—one example of each design of all denominations of coins issued by the U.S. Mint, from 1792 to the present—in total, about 150 copper, nickel, silver, and gold coins. I'd taken this particular collection about as far as I could on my budget, so I decided to auction it off to pursue other areas of numismatic interest.

The story that follows will be told through the coins that made up the Waccabuc Collection—the pretentious name I gave to my type set. The story includes my observations and opinions on acquisition strategies, storage choices, and disposition options, supplemented with commentary on grading services, auction houses, dealers, valuations, and financial results.

Most of the book is devoted to the coins themselves. With the kind permission of Stack's Bowers Galleries, I've included that firm's photos and catalog descriptions. For each coin, I've then added commentary and a lesson. These lessons are designed to inform, educate, and, sometimes, amuse. There were many missteps along the way, and I've tried to be honest about both what I did right and what I did wrong. I've disclosed my purchase and sale prices and holding periods so the reader can judge whether my collecting decisions were reasonable investing decisions. I've also included a few golf stories to help illustrate a point here and there.

As I've often heard golf commentators say, "There is no perfect in golf." The same can be said for building a collection of rare coins. Your collecting experience will be different from mine, and neither will be perfect. In describing my own journey, I have three objectives in mind: 1) that serious collectors who are new to the hobby will learn how to avoid some of the mistakes I made; 2) that advanced collectors will enjoy seeing parallels with some of their own experiences; and 3) that my golfing buddies will at least think this is an attractive picture book.

"There is no book so bad that at least some part of it might not be useful."
—Pliny the Elder, as recorded c. 103 AD by Pliny the Younger

CHAPTER

1

The
Waccabuc
Collection

"Golf is, in part, a game; but only in part.
It is also in part a religion,
a fever, a vice, a mirage, a frenzy,
a fear, an abscess, a joy, a thrill,
a pest, a disease, an uplift, a brooding, a melancholy,
a dream of yesterday, and a hope for tomorrow."

This is from the New York Tribune *in 1916. They could have been*
writing about numismatics.

Imagine this. It's Christmas morning. You're 11 years old and a budding numismatist. You haven't yet discovered the joys of golf, but for two years you have been filling those blue Whitman folders with cents and nickels and dimes—treasures found from newspaper delivery tips and glass-bottle returns. The family is gathered around the Christmas tree, and your father hands you the "big" gift, something the size of a framed poster, but too heavy to be just a picture. You tear open the wrapping and stare bug-eyed at a green-felt–covered piece of plywood, on which have been mounted row after row of large cents and Indian Head cents, all in date order.

This is exactly what happened to me in 1959, as I became the fourth generation of the Shippee family to carry on the tradition of collecting coins. According to family lore, my great-grandfather, Elmer W. Shippee of Providence, Rhode Island, began plucking coins from circulation as a youth in the mid-1800s.

Looking at these coins today, this seems about right. The earliest-dated cent—a 1795 (S-74)—is a solid AG-3, while the late-date large cents and most of the small cents are Extremely Fine or better.[2] The key-date 1877 Indian Head cent found its way into a PCGS holder (AU-50), but most of the rest remain as "raw" coins[3]—though now removed from that felt-covered board, since I figured the tacks used to hold the coins in place were not conducive to long-term storage and preservation.

Half a century has passed since that exciting morning, and over the years, my enthusiasm for coins and their stories has remained intact. Of course, other life events (like family, work, travel, and finances) sometimes pushed numismatics onto the back burner, but the passion has always been there.

THE WACCABUC COLLECTION

Waccabuc? Doesn't ring a bell? Well, it's the Indian name given to a hamlet that's part of the town of Lewisboro, in northeastern Westchester County, in the state of New York. Waccabuc is famous for its eponymous lake and its country club. The country club has a very attractive 6,398-yard, par-70 golf course that I've played on a couple of occasions. I still remember the time I was able to hit a 175-yard draw with a 7-wood from a downhill lie in the rough onto the green at the 390-yard 17th hole while playing in a Member-Guest tournament. As I recall, my host and I each won an attractive cloth carry bag. But I digress.

In the late 1990s, my wife and I bought a weekend retreat in South Salem, another Lewisboro hamlet. Seeking an escape from Connecticut suburbia, we acquired a six-acre remnant of a 19th-century dairy farm, with an old house, a couple of beautiful barns, two paddocks, an area of phlox-filled swamp, *and* several hundred feet of the mighty Waccabuc River. It's a river that I would call a stream and others might call a brook.

Around that time, I was looking for a name for my coin collection. Did it need a name? Well, maybe not, since my holdings back then were still relatively modest. But I decided to record my collection on the PCGS Set Registry system, and that system asked for a name. I thought the Shippee Collection was too unimaginative, so I chose the more mysterious and evocative Waccabuc name instead.

On November 13, 2007, the Waccabuc Collection was sold for $1.5 million at a public auction in Baltimore conducted by Stack's, one of the oldest and most-respected coin dealers and auction houses in the United States. The Waccabuc name was one of the two collections featured on the cover of the 540-page catalog, even though the 138 lots comprising my collection were able to be presented on just 40 pages of the thick book. Page 11 of the catalog breathlessly announced that the Waccabuc Collection ranked as the "third finest current (and fourth finest all-time) United States type set on the PCGS Set Registry." I wrote the blurb.

MODEST BEGINNINGS

The collection I sold in November 2007 wasn't the collection that I set out to build in the 1990s. When I was young, I focused primarily on Lincoln cents, Buffalo and Jefferson nickels, and Mercury and Roosevelt dimes. These were the things you could still collect from circulation. One of my great treasures was a 1914-D[4] cent—one of the key dates in the Lincoln cent series. I found it in a $50 bag of cents I'd been given as a present for Christmas. That coin alone was worth about $30, even with the scratch that some knucklehead had inscribed in the obverse field. I also had 20 or so silver dollars that I'd gotten from a local bank—they were still available at face value in the early 1960s. I couldn't afford to collect silver dollars by date and mintmark back then, so I only kept the better dates I came across. My best find was an 1879-CC, which listed for $25 in Extremely Fine in the 1963 *Red Book*, though my coin didn't quite measure up to that grade.

Over the ensuing years, I bought a few coins here and there—such as the 1909-S, 1909-S V.D.B., and 1931-S cents that I'd never found in circulation despite years of searching. I also purchased a 1950-D Jefferson nickel for $8.00. This wasn't an especially rare coin (more than 2.6 million were minted), but it was extensively hoarded at the time of issue because its mintage was tiny in comparison with other dates in the series. Very few collectors were able to find an example in circulation. Speculative interest pushed the cost of that coin upwards for a few years, but like anything else that is not fundamentally rare, the price eventually collapsed. That coin is still worth about $8.00 today.

I had coin collecting in my blood, but I didn't yet have a focus on any particular specialty.

SMUGGLING GOLD

While travelling in Europe as a college student in the late 1960s, I expanded my collection in two countries. In Switzerland I discovered that I could buy old U.S. double eagles ($20 gold pieces) at little more than their intrinsic value. With gold trading at around $40 per ounce, I acquired two common-date double eagles—one of the Liberty Head style for $45 and one of the Saint-Gaudens type for $50. The only problem was the order issued by President Franklin Roosevelt on April 5, 1933—it prohibited (or so I thought) my carrying these common gold coins into the United States. Figuring that I could plead youth and ignorance, I stuffed the coins into my duffle bag and smuggled them in through Kennedy airport. Only much later did I learn that I could have imported these pre-1934 gold coins legally with a little paperwork. Fortunately, all restrictions on gold ownership by U.S. citizens were lifted in 1975, and I'm hoping the statute of limitations has now passed.

On the same trip, a friend and I spent two weeks in England. One week was devoted to a bicycle trip from London to the seaside resort of Bognor Regis and back to London. In the arcade at Bognor Regis I found dozens of penny and halfpenny machines.

These pre-computer-game contraptions were addictive. You launched a penny or halfpenny down a chute and tried to pick the strategic moment when the penny would land cleanly on the moving metal platform. Once there, it might push an accumulated pile of other pennies over a ledge and into a bucket near your knees. If you were successful, you could win five or ten pennies for each penny invested. More often, though, your penny was just pushed into the pile, or sometimes it caused part of the pile to tumble over the left or right side into a losing bin.

I soon noticed that many of the coins visible in these gaming machines were old. Although Elizabeth II had been queen since 1952, a number of these coppers had portraits of George VI (1936–1952), George V (1910–1936), and even Edward VII (1901–1910). I started playing only those machines that had old coins in the part of the pile that would soon fall into the winning bin. After many hours of amusement (and without the expenditure of much money), I had collected every large penny from 1901 through 1967 except for four: 1919-KH (made by the Kings Norton Metal Co., Ltd., under contract from the Royal Mint), 1950, 1951, and 1953. I didn't play the ha'penny machines as much but was still able to find most dates from 1910 through 1967.

NUMISMATIC HIBERNATION

My banking career took me on assignments to Hong Kong and Tokyo and London. Over these years, from the late 1970s to the early 1990s, I'd occasionally buy a coin or a medal in a flea market or a bazaar, but I had no specific plan or program.

On a trip to Bangkok in 1979, I was very excited to find a beautiful example of a silver one-yen coin from Japan dated 1912—the end of the Meiji Era. I bought it for just $10. Only later did I discover it was a fake when I sent the coin to PCGS for grading. They returned the coin in a "body bag" (a plastic envelope rather than one of their coveted holders). I had greater success on the Royal Bangkok Golf and Country Club, where my friend Pin Chakkaphak and I teed off at 7:00 am to avoid the worst of the mid-day heat. Our caddies were women dressed in white robes, with large hats to provide shade. They seemed extremely happy to receive a tip of 100 baht (about $5 at the time) for their arduous duties over the course of four hours.

Japanese yen.

Another instance of my numismatic dabbling occurred in Chipping Campden, Gloucestershire, to the west of London, in 1989. At an outdoor Sunday market, I asked a vendor of general merchandise if he had any old coins for sale. He handed me a tattered round leather case.

Opening the tiny clasp, I found inside a 35 mm silver medal—slightly smaller than a U.S. silver dollar—with highly reflective fields and light champagne and azure toning. I bought it for £25 based on its "look."

Later I did some research and found that it was an "awarded" school medal from the Christ's Hospital School, founded in 1552 in Newgate, London, for the education of poor children under a charter granted by King Edward VI. A high-relief portrait of a youthful Edward appears on the obverse, while a Bible, opened to Exodus, dominates the reverse. The medal was designed by Thomas Pingo (1714–1776), assistant engraver at the Royal Mint and a founding member of the Royal Academy in 1768. The name of the recipient (Thomas Hilder) and the date (1844) appear on the edge.

In the seventh edition of *A Brief History of Christ's Hospital* by John Iliff Wilson, published in 1842, the author writes about Examination Day on page 65:

> Half yearly examinations are instituted, and prizes adjudicated to the Classical, Mathematical, and Drawing-schools; and in the Writing-school likewise, two gold and four silver medals are awarded to the six boys who evince the greatest proficiency in arithmetic.
>
> Prize pieces in penmanship are also exhibited; and the Treasurer awards silver gilt pens to the two best writers; and the other boys who write prize pieces have each a small silver medal.

I don't know who Thomas Hilder was, and I have no idea if he won this medal for his writing or math skills. But this 170-year-old medal and its history are interesting to contemplate, and it now enjoys a comfortable place in my somewhat expanded medal collection.

WHAT SHOULD I COLLECT?

One of the great joys of coin collecting is that there are no rules telling you what to collect. The possibilities are almost endless, and there is no right or wrong way.

You might start with a coin you were given—perhaps a Morgan silver dollar—and then decide to collect the rest of that series. Or you might be flipping through a coin catalog or dealer newsletter and see something that catches your fancy. This happened to me when I bought my first trade dollar from Bowers and Merena in the early 1990s. It was an attractively toned coin dated 1879 and grading PCGS PF-62. (Later it magically became a PCGS PF-63, which lent credence to B&M's claim that it only bought coins for its inventory that were superior within the context of their stated grades.) I expanded that collection to about a dozen different dates and mintmark varieties before branching off in a different direction.

An easy way to get inspiration is to flip through the pages of a copy of *A Guide Book of United States Coins*, better known as the *Red Book* (see the bibliography). Your eye might be caught by the section on Connecticut coppers, minted in large quantities between 1785 and 1788. Walter Breen lists 145 varieties in his *Encyclopedia*, and someone must have had a sense of humor as certain of these varieties bear curious names such as African Head, Hercules Head, and Muttonhead. (My small collection of colonial coins includes an example of the Laughing Head variety.)

A significant number of collectors have fallen in love with the broad range of dates, designs, and varieties of large cents, minted from 1793 through 1857. An even larger number of collectors focus on Morgan dollars (minted from 1878 through 1921), either endeavoring to obtain one example of every date and mintmark (97 coins, excluding varieties) or, perhaps, narrowing their goal to collecting each of the dollars produced at the storied branch mint in Carson City, Nevada (13 coins).

For a very modest financial investment, you can build an impressive collection of modern commemoratives or a complete collection of State quarters. For a very immodest investment, you can try to obtain the four varieties of $4 gold pieces (known as Stellas, for the large, five-pointed star that adorns the reverse of these rare coins) minted in 1879 and 1880, or you can be the only person on your block (or, likely, your city or state) aiming to collect each of the 49 dates of Proof Liberty Head double eagles. Or if you're truly rich and truly compulsive, you could even emulate the feat accomplished only by Louis

Eliasberg (1896–1976) and attempt to collect an example of every date and mintmark of every denomination of coin ever minted in the United States.

The Professional Coin Grading Service's "PCGS Set Registry" and the Numismatic Guaranty Corporation of America's "NGC Registry" include many hundreds of types of collections that are being formed by collectors around the world. The PCGS Set Registry included more than 70,000 separate registered collections as of late 2014. You can browse through the PCGS site for information and inspiration and see what other collectors have chosen to devote their energies to.

I took many false steps (all of them enjoyable) before deciding to try to form a complete type set. I experimented with $3 gold pieces for a time before moving on to trade dollars. I acquired a few colonial coins and continue to find this specialty of great interest. I bought a copper pattern dollar (specifically, the Pickle Puss variety, Judd-1283) that appeared in a Teletrade auction in 1996 and have since expanded that collection to a couple of dozen pieces. I am still working on collections of territorial gold pieces and ancient Greek coins—both fields offering vast opportunities for variety, study, and interest.

Eventually, however, I was drawn to the span of history and variety of designs that are represented in a comprehensive type collection. The PCGS Set Registry has decided that 137 coins are needed to complete this particular collection. All denominations are represented, from the half cent through the $20 double eagle. All significant design changes are included, whether on the obverse, the reverse, or the edge of the coin.

While some may disagree about exactly what belongs in a complete type set (for example, is the Coiled Hair Stella a regular-issue coin or a pattern?), there's no dispute that this kind of collection is a worthy challenge and offers a massive opportunity for education and enjoyment. Every item in a dealer's inventory might be the right piece for your type collection, and every page of an auction catalog offers an opportunity to fill a hole in your collection or improve upon one of the coins you already own. Every specialist book and numismatic article has some relevance when you're trying to complete a type collection. It took me about a decade to complete the Waccabuc Collection, and I enjoyed every minute devoted to this pursuit.

Out on the Course: Buying Rare Coins

My wife bought me a doormat that reads, "A golfer and a normal person live here." I've suggested to the American Numismatic Association that they offer a doormat in their online store reading, "A numismatist and a normal person live here." It would be a big seller.

Wow, is it ever easy to buy rare coins—certainly much easier than hitting a golf ball! All you have to do is sit down at your computer and enter "rare coins" into Google. I just tried it and found 7,930,000 sources in 0.11 seconds. That kind of information overload might serve to scare off a curious non-collector, but it has made the life of the addicted numismatist much easier.

What does an aspiring golfer do when he or she decides to take up the game? One approach is to head out to the local municipal course, tee up the ball, and take a lusty swing. The results will be disastrous: your assigned playing partners will think you're an idiot, the group behind you will fume over the slow pace of play, and your frustration will escalate as the 80-year-old codger in your group whips you on every hole. It's more sensible to get lessons from a professional and spend some hours on the range and the putting green. These efforts will be rewarded by the satisfaction of hitting at least a few real golf shots when you later decide to venture out onto the course.

Similarly, it would be foolhardy to pick a random "rare coins" link on the Internet and start buying whatever coins happened to be on offer. Instead, buy some books. *A Guide Book of United States Coins*, by R.S. Yeoman, commonly referred to as the *Red Book*, is a good place to start, and the bibliography offers several other suggestions. Introduce yourself to some coin dealers. They are almost invariably honest—I've only been really cheated on a coin purchase once in 50 years, and if I'd bought the right book first, even that incident could have been avoided. Many dealers are friendly and helpful—indeed, most are more than happy to assist collectors in getting started, since a motivated collector is their best customer. And before you hand over any serious money to buy a coin, look at as many real coins as possible (not just photos) to get a sense of designs and denominations and grades. A coin convention is a perfect place to do this—you can see several thousand coins in a couple of hours, handle many of them, and get a great education in the process.

Once you've built a small numismatic library, befriended a couple of responsive dealers, and spent enough hours looking through boxes and trays of coins to have decided on the area of coin collecting you want to pursue, then you're ready to start building your own collection. You may, with the passage of time, change your focus—in fact, this is the rule rather than the exception—but at least your purchases will have a purpose and be backed by some knowledge. Knowledge is the key to both enjoyment of this hobby and financial success when it comes time to sell your collection.

BUYING FROM DEALERS

Coin dealers and auction houses try to make it very easy for you to part with your money. Many dealers carry extensive inventories of coins that you can browse through on their Web sites.

Most coins of any significant value will be thoroughly described, and color photos of the obverse and reverse are usually available. Dealers will be delighted to add your name to their distribution lists. These "fixed-price lists" used to be *mailed* to clients—and sometimes still are—but the more common delivery method now is via a link or attachment in an email. If you see something that interests you, the dealer will usually be willing to send it to you with full, no-questions-asked return privileges if you decide for any reason not to keep the coin.

One caution, however: coin descriptions written by dealers to introduce you to the coins in their inventory are far more one-sided than auction-catalog descriptions. You will rarely see commentary on weak strikes, unattractive toning, spots, fingerprints, etc. You'll need to make up your own mind when it comes to deciding if a particular coin is right for you.

IS THE PRICE FAIR?

When you find a coin you like and that fits in the collection you're trying to build, the obvious question you must deal with is how much to pay for it. The dealer will quote you a price, and in all likelihood, this price will be in the realm of reasonableness. They are not going to offer you a genuine 1909-S V.D.B. cent graded MS-65 Red for $700 ($7,000 would be more like it), nor are they going to try to gouge you for $500 for a 1909 V.D.B. cent (from Philadelphia rather than San Francisco) graded MS-65 Red when the right price is more like $125.

Nevertheless, I do not recommend that you put your complete trust in the prices offered by any dealer, no matter how trustworthy they may be. Do a little research and make up your own mind on what a coin should cost. There is a wide range of sources for you to consult to learn about the prices of coins.

The *Red Book* and the Red Book Online (Whitman.com/redbook) are certainly places to start to get a general idea of retail selling prices. The *PCGS Price Guide*, available for free on the pcgs.com Web site, is an excellent resource. I would also suggest that you sign up with Heritage Auction Galleries to gain access to that company's online Past Auction Archives. Here not only can you find the prices paid for more than a million rare coins sold at Heritage auctions over the past decade or so, but you can also see high-quality photos of these coins and compare them with the coins you're interested in acquiring. For several years, I subscribed to the *Coin Dealer Newsletter*, known in the trade as the *Grey Sheet* (for exactly the reason you would imagine). It's a wonderfully detailed pricing resource, and for an additional fee you can buy "graph books" that provide historical pricing trends in a variety of grades over the past 25 years for individual coins in all the popular series.

Armed with some knowledge, you can now make an intelligent purchase decision. If you think the dealer's price is a little high, there's no harm in asking if a discount is available. One friendly dealer, from whom I bought a number of coins, offered me unsolicited discounts on several occasions. A little gentle haggling will sometimes save you a few dollars, but most dealers operate on sufficiently slim margins that they won't, in my experience, be able to offer large discounts from their stated prices.

WANT LISTS

If you're looking for a specific coin or a range of coins in a particular series, your favorite coin dealer will probably be happy to help. Most dealers offer a "want list" service. Although there may be differences in how this service is delivered from one dealer to another, the basic rules are similar. You tell the dealer what coins you are looking for and the dealer will tell you when he's found them. If you're a good client, you may get the first call when a dealer acquires a coin that's on your want list. The Heritage Auctions Web site offers an interesting want-list service that will automatically notify you when a coin on your list is included in one of its auctions or becomes available on its fixed-price list.

One note of caution is in order about the usage of want lists. It's probably not a great idea to ask more than one or two dealers at a time to look for a specific rare coin. You don't want to have too many people scurrying around a coin-convention floor looking for the same coin or, worse, bidding against each other at an auction. You'll probably have better luck, and develop closer relationships, by working with one or a small number of dealers who will come to know your budget, tastes, and the kind of coins you'll like.

BUYING AT AUCTIONS

Besides buying coins directly from dealers—either in person, on their Web site, or at a convention—the other principal way that you are likely to build your collection is by buying coins at public auctions. The rules and traditions that apply in the auction room, whether real or virtual, are different from those that govern direct purchases. To be a successful buyer at auction, it's critical you understand how the system works.

MY FIRST AUCTION

On the Ides of March in 1994, I went to my first public coin auction. I didn't go to the lot viewing in advance. I hadn't even looked at the catalog before showing up in the auction room. The event was in a hotel conference room in midtown New York, and I had a little time on my hands following a business meeting. (If truth be told, I'd arranged to have a little time on my hands after my business meeting.) I picked up a catalog at the door and registered for a bidding number, just in case. I sat in the back of the room and followed the action for a while.

The bidding went very quickly—not at all like some art auctions I'd seen in movies, where each piece is wheeled out for bidders to gape at before the auctioneer begins the process of eliciting one bid after another from smartly dressed men and women who convey their intentions with subtle eye blinks and ear tugs.

The coin crowd was far more casually dressed, and there were no more than two or three women in the room. The coins were not on display in the auction room for the simple reason that no one would have been able to see them from their chairs. The auctioneer didn't even describe what was being bid on—he just announced the lot number. So the action was fast, with most lots opening and closing within 10 or 15 seconds. There was no ambiguity about who was bidding on any particular item—hands shot up high in the air, or people shouted out if the auctioneer wasn't recognizing them.

It was great fun to watch, and I was surprised to see the relatively modest prices that many nice coins were going for. I was hardly an expert on coin values, but I had a copy of my trusty 1989 *Red Book* with me (remember, it was now 1994), and I noticed that many coins were selling for amounts significantly below those shown in that guide, excluding the 10% buyer's fee (which today is more commonly a 15% or 17.5% fee). The *Red Book* was first published in 1946 (with a cover date of 1947) and has been issued annually since then. It lists retail values for coins in a variety of grades. I quickly guessed that most of the bidders at this auction were probably dealers who were buying at wholesale prices. I smelled opportunity.

I flipped a few pages ahead in the catalog and spotted a coin I had long coveted: the 1955 doubled-die cent. Although not a date or mintmark variety, this coin is often included in a complete set of Lincoln cents. In my years of searching through tens of thousands of coins, I had seen many hundreds of 1955-dated cents, but never one with the prominent doubling of the date and the legends that can be seen on the 1955 doubled die.

The catalog described this coin as "medium brown" in color and "retaining much original luster." The grade was given as Mint State-63 Brown (MS-63BN). The black-and-white photo was consistent with the description, and I decided I had to own this coin.

The catalog also said the coin was housed in an "ANACS cache." I had no idea what that was, so I turned to the guy next to me and asked. He explained that an ANACS (pronounced "an axe") cache was a plastic coin holder produced by the American Numismatic Association Certification Service. (ANACS still certifies coins today, but it is no longer associated with the ANA.) He added that having a valuable coin in a certified holder was not a bad thing.

A few minutes later, when lot #2316—the 1955 doubled die—came up for bidding, I noticed that my pulse had quickened and my hands were sweaty. The auctioneer opened the bidding by saying he had a bid of $450, and who would give him $500? I hoisted my arm high up in the air, and the auctioneer said, "I have $500 in the back of the room." Someone else bid $550, so I stuck my hand up again, and I became the high bidder at $600. The room was silent for a few seconds, and then the auctioneer tapped his gavel and said, "Sold to bidder number 553 at $600."

So just like that, without ever having seen the coin in person and without having done any research other than glancing at my five-year-old *Red Book*, I'd bought a long-coveted $1,200 rare coin for only $660 (including the 10% buyer's fee). I was feeling pretty smug!

What was I thinking? Did I do any research on the current market value of this coin? No. If I had, I would have discovered that its retail value had dropped by the mid-1990s to around $900. (Yes, coin prices can go down as well as up.) Did I look closely at the actual coin in the ANACS holder rather than just relying on the grade stated in the catalog? No. If I had, I might have detected the slight rub on Lincoln's cheek that would later cause PCGS to re-grade this coin as About Uncirculated-58 (AU-58). Did I think I was smarter than all the experienced coin dealers in the auction room? Yes, but I was wrong.

Almost exactly five years later, I bought a finer 1955 doubled-die cent and sold my PCGS AU-58 example for $598. I'd enjoyed owning this nice coin, but I was disappointed to have lost almost 10% on my original investment after a five-year holding period. This was my first, but hardly my worst, bungle—

many more will be described in the chapters ahead. But I was learning, and the process was exciting and fun, if not exactly profitable.

THE AUCTION PROCESS

At its core, the auction process is simple. One, or several, collectors decide to sell their coins. They consign them to an auction firm. The auction firm describes and photographs the coins, prepares and distributes a catalog, and conducts the auction. Prospective buyers bid for the coins at the auction. The auction firm collects money from the winning bidders and delivers the coins to them, and then sends the money, less a fee, to the consigners. The devil, as they say, is in the details.

Auctions are governed by a set of terms and conditions spelled out, usually in small type, in the catalog and on the auctioneer's Web site. You should, at least once, read through this material since, by bidding at an auction, you are accepting and agreeing to be bound by these terms. The terms and conditions used by different auctions houses will vary to some extent, but all address certain common themes. Let's take a look at these.

Registration: You must register with the auction firm in advance of the auction to be able to place a bid. The auction firm may ask for credit references and may perform a credit check in order to establish a bidding limit for you. The auctioneer will normally reserve the right, at its sole discretion, to exclude anyone from its auction and can disqualify any bidder before, during, or after the auction. Be sure to register a few days before you intend to place a bid. Once you've registered with an auction firm, you will normally not need to re-register for subsequent auctions conducted by that firm as long as you have paid for your earlier purchases.

Buyer's Premium: For most coin and currency auctions conducted by the leading auction houses in today's market, the buyer's premium is 17.5%. This means that 17.5% will be added to the final "hammer price" to arrive at the total cost to the successful bidder. *Since the early to mid-1990s*, the buyer's premium has grown from 10 to 15 to the present 17.5%. At the same time, the seller's commission has shrunk from 10 to 5%, and sometimes this fee can be negotiated even lower.

The buyer's premium of 17.5% is retained by the auction house to pay for its research, catalog-production costs, advertising, and other expenses. Occasionally, the buyer's premium will be something other than 17.5%—either higher or lower. Be sure you know before you place a bid. Also see chapter 21 for a discussion of seller's fees.

Bidding: There are many different ways to place a bid. You can, of course, be in the auction room and participate "in person" as the live auction is taking place. This is the most exciting way to bid, and you can meet people and observe the bidding strategies used by other collectors and dealers by being in the room where the action is. All serious collectors should spend some time at live auctions.

Often, however, physical attendance at an auction is impractical, so other methods of bidding are available. The terms and conditions of most auction firms will generally state that they accept mail bids, fax bids, telephone bids (by prior arrangement), and Internet bids. Regardless of the method of delivery, your bid is a commitment by you to purchase the lot you are bidding on. Auctions are not sales on approval—you do not have a right to return a coin you win at an auction just because you decide you don't like the coin when you receive it.

Bidding Increments: Auction catalogs will specify the bidding increments that are allowed after the opening bid is announced. These are normally 5 to 10% above the immediately preceding bid.

Cut Bids: If someone else has bid $2,000 for a coin, and the auctioneer has asked for a new bid of $2,200 (10% higher than the existing bid), you can jump in with a bid of $2,100 (a cut bid) by making a horizontal slashing motion with your upraised hand or by shouting "Cut." However, the terms and conditions limit you to one cut bid per lot, so you should generally use this option only if you're near the upper limit you've established for yourself for that lot.

Returns: Coins may be returned to the auction firm if they are not genuine. If there is a gross cataloging error, the auction firm may consider a written request for a refund, but only if you did not attend the lot viewing prior to the auction and did not bid on the coin on the auction floor. (I successfully used this provision once with an un-photographed coin that had a deep gash on its reverse. The auction firm agreed that the omission of this feature from its catalog description was a gross error on its part and refunded my purchase price.)

Returns are not permitted based on a disagreement with the stated grade or toning of a coin. In this regard, you should be aware that even with the excellent photo technology available on the Internet today, the color of a photographed coin will often differ, sometimes markedly, from the color you see when you view the coin in natural light. There is simply no substitute for holding a coin in hand and viewing it in person. For this reason, among others, you should try to attend lot viewing prior to the auction or arrange for someone you trust to look at the coin for you. Return privileges for auctions conducted solely via the Internet are typically somewhat more liberal than for auctions that offer an opportunity for lot viewing.

Other Terms: The terms and conditions of most auction firms will contain many additional paragraphs dealing with subjects such as arbitration in the event of a dispute, the absence of any expressed or implied warranty with respect to the lot descriptions, protection for the auctioneer from all claims for consequential or other damages, and other provisions. Most of these additional terms can be considered boilerplate language and will rarely be relevant in practice. Nevertheless, as mentioned above, you should thoroughly read a major firm's terms and conditions at least once to ensure you have a reasonable sense of what you're agreeing to when you place a bid at an auction.

LOT VIEWING

Live auctions always offer an opportunity to attend the lot-viewing sessions that are open to bidders for several days before the auction. These free events are a perfect way to see many coins, hone your grading skills, compare actual coins to the photographs appearing in the catalog, and learn from the auction-firm representatives and dealers in the room. Even if you're not intending to bid on any coins in the auction, it is instructive and fun to go to the lot viewing.

ALL COLORS OF THE RAINBOW

Auction-catalog descriptions always contain useful information and often reflect serious research conducted by the cataloger. When it comes to describing the physical attributes of a coin, however, the text morphs into a unique form of literature. You may be forgiven if you sometimes feel as if you're being told about a bouquet of flowers or a fine wine. I get a real kick out of reading them. Here's a small sample of coin descriptions from some recent auction catalogs:

> Generous glimpses of iridescent sunset-orange, sage, and saffron grace both sides. . . .
>
> The golden hues deepen near the rims into cinnamon and russet. . . .
>
> Even almond-tan patina with good field-device contrast appears on both sides. . . .
>
> Richly lustrous surfaces are deeply patinated in shades of blue and purple. . . .
>
> Tinges of olive-green and gray-gold greet the viewer. . . .

> The fields are quicksilver and brightly mirrored, while arctic mint
>   frost cleanly covers both the central devices and the peripheral
>   legends. . . .
> The peripheries show occasional dappled shades of champagne,
>   amber, and ice-blue. . . .
> Both sides display lovely oil-slick iridescence beneath the
>   dominant brown patina. . . .
> A mélange of dynamic gold, lavender, aqua-blue, mint-green, and
>   gray patination resides on the lustrous surfaces. . . .
> Copious quantities of coruscating luster cascade across the clean
>   surfaces. . . .

I haven't yet seen the words *amaranthine*, *heliotrope*, *purpurescent*, or *violaceous* used to describe the color of a coin, but I'm sure it's only a matter of time.

AUCTIONEER'S CONFLICT OF INTEREST

All auction firms have an inherent conflict of interest between their duty to do the best possible job of selling the coins consigned to them and their duty to describe these coins accurately for the benefit of their buyers. As you read through a catalog, you'll notice that the strengths of the coin (rarity, luster, toning, strike, whatever) are generally described first and at length, while the shortcomings are noted in fewer words and are sometimes excused or mitigated ("the black spot will serve as a pedigree marker," "the scratches are barely noticeable except under a loupe," etc.). In my view, most firms strike a fair balance between their competing obligations to the buyer and the seller, but as with any other important purchase decision, *caveat emptor* is good advice. Use the catalog description as an introduction, but make up your own mind about the coin before buying it.

GRADING SERVICES

Coin collecting experienced a period of strong growth in the 1960s. This growth attracted some unethical characters to the market to take advantage of new collectors. Counterfeit coins and coins that had been altered were appearing in the market with troubling frequency. Silver dollars, especially, and certain other coins were being "whizzed," a process that creates the impression of luster by polishing a lightly circulated coin with a motorized wire brush.

In order to address these problems, the American Numismatic Association started an authentication service known as the American Numismatic Association Certification Service (ANACS). This two-person operation, located in Washington, D.C., certified its first coin as "genuine" on June 15, 1972. ANACS moved to Colorado Springs, Colorado, in 1976, and three years later began to assign grades and issue photo certificates.

In 1986, the Professional Coin Grading Service (PCGS) was established, followed a year later by the Numismatic Guaranty Corporation of America (NGC). Both companies sought to meet the growing demand for better, more consistent grading standards. They introduced the practice of encapsulating coins in sonically sealed, tamper-evident plastic holders (often referred to as slabs). ANACS discontinued its photo certificates in 1989 and adopted the new industry standard of slabbing coins.

Over the ensuing years, a virtual alphabet soup of other grading firms entered the market, including Independent Coin Grading Company (ICG), Dominion Grading Service (DGS), National Coin Grading Service (NCGS), Sovereign Entities Grading Service (SEGS), Photo Certification Institute Coin Grading Service (PCI), American Coin Grading Service (ACGS), Star Grading Services (SGS), International Coin Certification Service (ICCS), and the Ancient Coin Certification Service (ACCS), among many others. By one observer's count, there were 56 coin-grading services operating in 2007, most with dedicated Web sites.

With the passage of time, PCGS and NGC have come to be recognized as the two leading third-party grading services. These two companies have excellent Web sites, consistent grading standards, worthwhile guarantees, and set-registry programs. They are somewhat more expensive than other grading services, but coins housed in their holders are more easily bought by (and sold to) experienced collectors than raw coins or coins in holders of other companies. If you're going to be spending thousands, or many thousands, of dollars per coin, you would be well advised to stick to coins in PCGS or NGC slabs.

All of the coins in the Waccabuc Collection were housed in PCGS holders. Years ago I read in a coin newspaper that some experienced collectors felt PCGS had stricter standards than NGC. I found this status appealing—I suspected that any future sale would be easier if my coins were housed in holders of the service with the tightest grading principles. In addition, I preferred the look of the clear plastic used by PCGS to the white plastic used by NGC. Today, the standards used by both firms are very similar, in my opinion. You'll find great rarities graded by both PCGS and NGC, and many collectors are happy to have a mix of PCGS and NGC slabs in their collections. In the end, a collector's choice about acquiring coins only in one holder or the other might be as much about the collector's desire for consistency in the packaging, storage boxes, and the like, as about the perceived quality of either service.

WHAT ABOUT CAC?

In recent years, a number of collectors and dealers have voiced concerns about the loosening of grading standards by the third-party grading services. These concerns were not limited to just the less well-known grading services, but included the leading graders, PCGS and NGC.

In response to this market development, in 2007 a group of prominent members of the numismatic community, led by John Albanese, founded a company called Collectors Acceptance Corporation (CAC). According to its Web site, CAC's purpose is to verify coins already graded by PCGS and NGC and award its green oval sticker only to those coins that meet its standard for strict quality within the grade stated on the holder. As of this writing, slightly fewer than half of the 350,000 coins reviewed by CAC were awarded its imprimatur. CAC will also very occasionally award a gold label for coins that it feels could warrant an upgrade. Some studies have shown that CAC-stickered coins sell for a premium as compared with equivalent coins without the "green bean."

In my view, there's nothing wrong, per se, with CAC. Its sticker serves to confirm the grade and adds a bit of attractive color to the slab. However, once you've gained experience in grading and selecting coins for your collection, you should not hesitate to pass on a CAC'ed coin that doesn't meet your standards (for example, with respect to strike or eye appeal), nor should you waver when you find a coin you like that doesn't sport the green bean (at least in part because there's a good chance it's never been reviewed by CAC). Parenthetically, with all the stories about counterfeiting (see below), I can imagine that some enterprising scoundrel will someday create a fake green sticker to affix to coin holders, if this has not happened already.

PCGS and NGC have not complained publicly about CAC putting stickers on some of their holders, but I doubt they are happy about it. Perhaps with a view to making CAC obsolete, and certainly with a view to increasing their profits, the two leading grading companies announced in March 2010 that they would begin adding a "+" symbol to certain coins in the EF-45 to MS-68 range, except for coins in the MS-60 and MS-61 categories. Thus, a high-end MS-63 could become an MS-63+ coin (for an additional fee, of course). The grading services state that this development will unlock value for collectors.

For those who thought 11 gradations of Uncirculated coins (from MS-60 through MS-70) were already too many, the new standard of 18 gradations (including the seven half-steps from MS-62 through MS-68) cannot be a welcome development. Not wanting to fall into irrelevance, CAC is now adding its sticker to coins graded with a "plus" sign when they agree with this enhanced grade. This means that there could be as many as four gradations within most of the Mint State grades—for example, MS-63, MS-63 CAC, MS-63+, and MS-63+ CAC. Time will tell how this all works out. Personally, I'm unimpressed with this excess of opinions. My approach is to continue to look closely at the coins I buy and make up my own mind.

MORE THAN JUST A NUMERICAL GRADE

The "Four C's" used to assess the quality and weight of a diamond are cut, clarity, color, and carat. Without extensive training and experience, it is extremely difficult for a consumer to make an independent judgment about the brilliance of the cut, the inclusions and blemishes that determine clarity, the degree of color, and the weight of the diamond in carats. The vast majority of us who have ever purchased a diamond just have to trust the jeweler or rely on a certification from a third party.

With coins, on the other hand, there are many resources available to help collectors make up their own minds about a coin's condition, luster, strike, and toning. All of these factors have an impact on a coin's value, but they are not all captured in a coin's numerical grade.

CONDITION

A coin's condition, or extent of wear, is generally expressed in words (Good, Fine, About Uncirculated, Mint State, etc.) with a modifying number, on a scale of 1 to 70. Poor-1 is used for a coin that is worn virtually smooth but is identifiable, while Mint State-70 is reserved for completely pristine coins that show no evidence of surface disturbance whatsoever under 10x magnification. Circulated coins—coins that show some evidence of wear or handling—are assigned grades up through AU-59 (usually stopping at AU-58). Coins that show no signs of circulation, but which may well have some hairlines from improper cleaning or minor nicks and marks from storage and handling at the mint, are given grades from MS-60 through MS-70. In practice, many coins grading AU-58 will have a nicer appearance or "eye-appeal" than a similar coin grading MS-60 or MS-61.

Despite many efforts to make coin grading more scientific and less subjective, establishing the grade of a coin remains a matter of opinion, not fact. PCGS and NGC provide grading opinions that are backed by guarantees, and it's therefore understandable why these firms have become popular and successful. However, two coins of the same date and mintmark that have been assigned the same grade by a leading grading service will often sell for very different prices. Understanding the reasons for this will both increase your enjoyment of the hobby and help you make better investing decisions.

LUSTER

Luster, which is the glistening appearance that you see on a newly minted coin, is created via metal flow at the moment a coin is struck by the dies. A coin blank, or planchet, will typically have a matte-like surface with myriad tiny marks. When the coin dies come together and exert great pressure on the planchet, the metal near the surface of the blank will flow into the crevices of the design on the dies. The marks on the planchet will disappear, and the flow of metal across the fields of the coin (which are the high points of the die) will leave a clean, lustrous finish. If the dies are highly polished, as is the case for many Proof coins, the result can be an appealing contrast between the mirror-like fields and the non-reflecting devices. Such coins may be designated as Cameo or Ultra-Cameo (after the similar contrasting effect seen on antique shell cameo pins popular in the second half of the 19th century), and usually command a premium.

Luster is an important factor in establishing the numerical grade of an Uncirculated coin. Mint State coins that have "subdued" luster will generally not grade above MS-63 or so, even if they have almost no evidence of bag marks or hairlines. Conversely, Mint State coins with "booming" luster can attract a grade of, say, MS-65 even though they may show a number of light scuffs. These features are, perhaps, most obvious in the larger (and highly popular) denominations, such as the Morgan dollar and the Liberty Head and Saint-Gaudens double eagles. As you gain experience by looking at lots of different coins, you will soon notice and appreciate the difference between a highly lustrous gem and a muted low-end Uncirculated coin. Luster is often still visible on lightly circulated coins, particularly in protected areas of the fields.

STRIKE

Unlike a coin's physical condition and its luster, both of which features have an important impact on the numerical grade, the quality of a coin's strike is only infrequently factored into a coin's grade. Because of this, collectors who develop an ability to differentiate between a fully struck coin and another that might display an average or weak strike will have a distinct advantage when it comes to selecting a coin from among several available examples.

The quality of a coin's strike is primarily determined by how well the mint did its job. If new dies are set up completely parallel to one another, are spaced apart correctly, and are brought together with the proper force, the resulting coin will pick up all the details from the dies and will possess a full strike. Often, however, the dies are not set up properly, either through carelessness or, sometimes, deliberately, as when dies are purposely set slightly too far apart to prolong the life of the dies. When this happens, some design details in the dies are not imparted to the coin, and the strike will be considered average or weak.

The grading services have acknowledged the importance of strike quality for only a few coin series. Some Franklin half dollars are graded as having "Full Bell Lines" on the often weakly struck Liberty Bell on the reverse. Some Standing Liberty quarters are singled out by the grading services for having a "Full Head," though experienced collectors will often additionally look for a complete set of rivets in the shield. There are a few other examples, but for the most part, you are on your own when it comes to assessing the quality of a coin's strike. Learn more about what to look for, and you'll have a distinct advantage over other collectors.

TONING

When copper and silver coins are freshly minted, their colors are bright orange (called "Red" in the trade) and sparkling silver (called "White"), respectively. With the passage of time and exposure to air, both metals darken, sometimes uniformly and other times in a mottled pattern. This process is called "tarnishing" in most of the world and "toning" (much less pejorative, don't you think?) in numismatics.

As you might expect, toning can be highly attractive or downright ugly. Coins with unattractive toning are almost always priced below equivalent examples that sport average or attractive toning. Don't be tempted—the savings are almost guaranteed to be illusory. You won't enjoy owning an ugly coin, and you are very unlikely to make any money when it comes time to sell.

Buying toned coins is a matter of personal preference. Some buyers of silver coins only want "blast white" examples. They don't seem to be bothered by the virtual certainty that such coins have been dipped in a coin cleaner (such as E-Z-Est, formerly known as Jeweluster). Do they really think that these coins have retained their original silvery hue 100 years or more after they were produced? Many other collectors are attracted to the genuine "natural" look of an attractively toned coin—one that has the appearance you would expect for a well-cared-for 100-year-old coin. I'm in the latter camp, and you'll find many examples of what I consider attractive toning in the following chapters.

As years and decades pass, copper coins generally lose their original mint "red." A partially toned copper coin is often called "red-brown" (RB on coin slabs), while a fully toned copper is classified as "brown" (BN on slabs). Red coppers command a significant premium in the marketplace, but they often are seen with some very unattractive dark spots. My personal preference is for evenly toned red-brown coins and light-chocolate-brown coins.

EYE APPEAL

Although not explicitly noted on third-party grading service holders, eye appeal is nevertheless a critical part of the grading and buying decision. Along the lines of Justice Potter Stewart's celebrated 1964 definition of pornography, eye appeal is difficult to describe, but you will know it when you see it.

Does the coin you're looking at appear original, or has it been fooled with? Is the overall color balanced or uneven? Are there any obvious distractions, such as spots or streaks? Is the surface dull or full of "life"? Many sellers will claim their coins have strong eye appeal, but you need to be the final arbiter. One of the best pieces of advice I received from a numismatic mentor was to trust your own judgment: if you like the look of the coin, then chances are others will, too, when it's time to sell.

ARTIFICIAL TONING

A few members of the numismatic fraternity with more ambition than scruples have taken to reading chemistry texts and have devised ways to create artificial toning. Iodine, sulfur, and ammonia are among the elements in their bag of tricks. The grading services do their best to avoid slabbing artificially toned coins, but sometimes it is difficult to distinguish the natural from the unnatural.

Take a close look at lot 1035 in chapter 7 and try to imagine how the colors on the surface of that coin were acquired. Did the rainbow hues appear after years of storage in an old sulfur-laden cardboard album, or did some numismatic chemist have his way with this war-time nickel? I don't know where the truth lies, but I loved the look of the coin, and so I bought it, despite my doubts. The next owner liked it almost as much as I did, based on the price he paid.

COIN DOCTORING

Artificially adding toning to a coin is just one form of altering the appearance to make it more appealing to unsuspecting collectors. The Professional Numismatists Guild (PNG), reacting to complaints from collectors, dealers, and the grading services, has tightened its regulations by explicitly prohibiting coin doctoring in its bylaws. The PNG's definition of doctoring, as adopted in 2012, gives examples including "plugging, whizzing, polishing, engraving, 'lasering,' and adding or removing mint marks." An earlier draft of the PNG's coin-doctoring definition included an instructive laundry list of the illicit approaches employed by certain coin people I have not met, and hope I never will:

> Among the practices defined as doctoring are effacing hairlines by polishing or manipulating the surfaces of Proof coins, applying substances to the surface of coins to hide marks and defects, hiding marks or otherwise changing the appearance of a coin by adding toning, adding chemicals or otherwise manipulating the surfaces to create "cameo" frost on the devices of Proof coins, and making a coin appear more fully struck by re-engraving portions of the devices, such as re-engraving bands on the reverse of a Mercury dime or adding head detail to a Standing Liberty quarter.
>
> Altering dates or mintmarks or other struck portions of a coin to make it appear to be from a mint, date, or type other than that of origin, and altering business strike coins to make them resemble Proof issues are also examples of coin doctoring. This definition is not intended to be all-inclusive, but only illustrative of forms of coin doctoring.

Similarly, the PCGS agreement with its dealers has an informative definition of coin doctoring. It says, in part:

> Coin doctoring . . . may involve, among other things, adding substances to coins (such as, among other things, putty, wax, facial oils, petroleum jelly or varnish); treating coins with chemicals (such as among other things, potash, sulfur, cyanide, iodine or bleach); heat treating coins in any way to alter their appearance; re-matting ("skinning") Proof gold; "tapping" and "spooning" (i.e., physically moving surface metal to hide marks); filing rim nicks; or repairing coins (re-tooling metal).

The leading grading services have been burned by doctored coins. When, despite their best efforts, they mistakenly certify a coin that has been doctored, they become liable to repurchase that coin for its (unaltered) market value if the alteration is later discovered. The two- or three-figure grading fees earned by the grading services will quickly be overwhelmed by five- or six-figure buy-backs if they make mistakes too often. I recall seeing in an auction catalog a rare early dime in the holder of a leading grading service. The cataloger correctly identified the coin as one that had had a hole in it when the auction firm had last handled it. The hole had been expertly filled before it was submitted for grading.

To combat embarrassing and expensive problems like this, PCGS filed a lawsuit in May 2010 claiming that six named defendants and ten John Does (unnamed defendants to be added to the suit later) had submitted doctored coins for grading. Among the seven counts is a claim that the defendants violated RICO—the Racketeer Influenced and Corrupt Organizations Act, which, after its enactment in 1970, was intended to be used to prosecute the Mafia. It's sad that our hobby has come to this, though at the same time it's heartening that one of the leading institutions is trying to fight back.

COUNTERFEITS

Counterfeiting has almost certainly been a fact of life ever since the first coins were produced more than two-and-a half millennia ago, probably in Lydia, Asia Minor (current-day Turkey). Governments have always taken a dim view of counterfeiters and those who clipped or shaved genuine precious-metal coins, since these activities were often viewed not simply as petty crime but rather as treasonous attacks on the state itself.

As an example, in 1690, two individuals were apprehended in England for the crime of shaving silver from the edges of coins. According to the Proceedings of the Old Bailey, London's Central Criminal Court (available at the wonderful Web site, oldbaileyonline.org),

> Thomas Rogers and Anne Rogers were tried for Clipping 40 pieces of Silver. The Evidence swore, That there were Shears, and Rubbers to rub Money, and a File and some Clippings, &c. found in the Prisoners' House in Ealing Parish, near Acton; all [of] which were produced in Court, in Testimony against them, as also a Parcel of clipt Money, which was found in the bottom of

a Chest. The Prisoner [argued], That he found the clipt Money, and they both denied it stiffly, and that they never used the Tools, neither did they hide them from any Body, using several extenuating Arguments to stifle their horrid Crime; which came to no good Effect, for they were both found Guilty of High Treason. Thomas Rogers was ordered to be Drawn upon a Sledge to the place of Execution, to be hanged by the Neck, cut down alive, his Bowels burnt, his body quartered, and to be disposed of at their Majesties' pleasure. And Anne Rogers was ordered to be burnt alive.

Not long after Mr. and Mrs. Rogers were put to death, Isaac Newton, better known for his accomplishments in physics, mathematics, and astronomy, was appointed as warden of the Royal Mint. Three years later, in 1699, he became Master of the Mint, a position he held until his death in 1727. He mounted a major campaign against counterfeiting and caused several men to be sent to their deaths on the gallows for manufacturing fake coins.

Counterfeits have been part of the American economy since colonial times. Indeed, contemporary counterfeit colonial coins are actively collected alongside their genuine counterparts. During the American Revolution, both the states and the Continental Congress issued paper money, and very quickly a shadow industry of businessmen with printing presses came into existence. Stephen Mihm, an assistant professor of history at the University of Georgia, has written an excellent book on early counterfeit currency. Titled *A Nation of Counterfeiters—Capitalists, Con Men, and the Making of the United States*, it tells the fascinating tale of the generally unsuccessful battle to eliminate fake currency in the United States in the years between the Revolution and the Civil War.

In modern times, governments continue to devote substantial resources to battling individuals and groups that produce fake money—principally paper currency. Many millions of dollars are spent on changing designs and adding security devices to our paper money to make it more difficult for deceptive copies to be made.

For numismatists, unfortunately, much less attention is paid by governmental authorities to the problem of forgeries of rare coins. With the quarter being the highest-denomination coin in general circulation in the United States today (when was the last time you received a dollar or half dollar coin in change?), it hardly makes economic sense for a counterfeiter to produce U.S. coins for a profit. The situation is different in the United Kingdom, however, where it has been estimated that fully 3% of the £1 coins (worth about $1.70 at the time of this writing) in circulation are fakes.

For many decades, numismatists have been plagued by deceptive copies of rare coins. The temptations to the unscrupulous are obvious: if you can spend $10 for a circulated 1909 V.D.B. cent and turn it into a 1909-S V.D.B. worth 100 times as much, you can make yourself a tidy profit. Similarly, many 1944-D cents, worth very little, have become 1914-D rarities after some minor re-engraving. There are dozens of comparable examples. Fortunately, the leading grading services have done an excellent job of detecting these and other, more subtle, fakes.

The latest wave of counterfeit coins has come from China. Under the provisions of the Hobby Protection Act of 1973, all imitation numismatic items are required to be plainly marked with the word COPY, but this regulation has not always been enforced. The policy applied by online auction site eBay has evolved gradually. For many years, it permitted the sale of replica coins that complied with the Hobby Protection Act but did not monitor the coins that were actually delivered by sellers. A number of Chinese minters were happy to deliver replica coins without the word COPY on them, and the best of these coins are extremely realistic. To address this problem, eBay's current (2014) policy does not permit the sale of replica coins, but I just typed "replica coins" into eBay's search function and found 908 listings.

Even more troubling, some counterfeiters have devised ways to put fake coins into imitation slabs to make them look like products of the third-party grading services. In a variation on this theme, some genuine coins have been put into fake slabs with higher grades stated on the fake insert than the coins warrant.

The grading services are fighting back by providing a certificate-verification service (which gives collectors a way to check the certificate number on a slab against the grading service's master database of valid certificate numbers) and by digitally photographing each coin they review. For collectors, the best defense against Chinese fakes is to buy only from reputable dealers. Experienced dealers know what they're doing, and they will work with you if there's a problem. Unless you're building a reference collection of counterfeit coins, do not purchase U.S. coins from sellers based in China: there's a high probability that these coins will not be genuine.

BOOKS, CLUBS, AND OTHER RESOURCES

It's completely possible to participate in numismatics without ever buying a coin. There are thousands of books to read, hundreds of clubs to join, and numerous other resources that contribute to enjoyment of the hobby.

Every collector should own a copy of the *Red Book*, join the American Numismatic Association (www.money.org), and subscribe to one or both of the weekly numismatic newspapers (*Coin World* and *Numismatic News*). As stated earlier, you should sign up (for free) on the Web site of Heritage Auction Galleries, www.ha.com, to gain access to that firm's Past Auction Archives, as well as Stacks.com (for the archives of Stack's Bowers Galleries), and other dealers' and auctioneers' sites. These resources are invaluable for researching coin values and comparing potential purchases with previously sold examples of the same coin. Their photographs are excellent.

If you decide to specialize in a particular series of coins, there will be at least one book (and usually several) that will focus on your area of interest. In all likelihood, there will also be a specialist club you can join. If, like me, you decide to build a type set, there are many books (including those listed in the bibliography) that cover numismatics in breadth rather than in depth.

If you're interested in building a numismatic library, join the Numismatic Bibliomania Society (www.coinbooks.org) and subscribe to its online publication, *The E-Sylum*. For scholarly pursuits, join the American Numismatic Society (www.numismatics.org) and read the articles that appear in that organization's *American Journal of Numismatics*. For history and pleasure, there are many books that recount the tales of sunken treasure ships and coin hoards. The choices are almost endless. I now have several hundred books and catalogs in my own library, and they provide both information and enjoyment.

• • •

This chapter has been designed to give you an introduction to the topic of buying rare coins. However, as noted, the best way to gain real knowledge is to look at specific coins and learn about grading standards, strike quality, toning, rarity, and value. In the chapters that follow, I will discuss each of the coins that made up the Waccabuc Collection and explain why they were good purchases or lousy decisions. I want to share these lessons with others because I know I would love to have learned them two decades ago, before I got serious about building a real collection myself.

The Coins of the
Waccabuc
Collection

Half Cents

It was a sunny Saturday morning. Dick was taking his stance and visualizing his upcoming golf shot. Suddenly, a voice came from the clubhouse loudspeaker. "Would the gentleman on the ladies' tee please back up to the men's tee."

Dick was still deep into his pre-shot routine and ignored the interruption.

Again the announcement: "Would the man on the women's tee kindly back up to the men's tee."

Dick had had enough. He shouted, "Would the announcer in the clubhouse kindly shut up and let me play my second shot."

A s all golfers know, there will be errors. The key is to put them behind you and move on to the next shot. You will make mistakes as you build your collection, but they'll generally be less painful if they occur in the lower-denomination minor coins. Three of my six half cent purchases, all discussed below, yielded only tiny financial gains after many years of ownership, while the other three generated very satisfying returns—all said, an excellent outcome. All six coins were a pleasure to study and own. To read about some of my most egregious missteps, you'll have to venture more deeply into this book.

This chapter discusses half cents, which were minted from 1793 through 1857. There are six basic designs of half cents, only one of which is difficult to acquire—the Liberty-facing-left type, which was minted in limited quantities in the single year of 1793.

Using a format that will also be employed in the following 17 chapters, this section includes auction-lot descriptions, photos, and commentary. A learning opportunity is included at the end of each lot. These lessons relate to the specific coins under discussion but are designed to have more general applicability to other series and denominations. Financial results are shown for each coin. The accumulated financial results are shown and discussed in the back of the book.

HALF CENT—LIBERTY CAP, HEAD FACING LEFT (1793)

Lot 1001.
1793. VF-20.
C-3, B-3. Rarity-3. PCGS #001000.

Auction description: Deep chocolate brown with lighter tan high points. Nice design elements present, rims far from all devices as should be on a half cent of the date in the VF range. Surfaces faintly granular in places when viewed under low magnification, no serious marks present and choice as such to the unaided eye. A distinct one-year-only design type, with Miss Liberty and her flowing tresses facing left; the other Flowing Hair Liberty Cap half cents (1794–97) all have the head of Liberty facing to the viewer's right. An exceptional coin for the grade, free of unsightly marks as noted, and a specimen that is ideally suited for the first coin in an expanded U.S. type set.

From the Waccabuc Collection. Earlier from the William Walser Collection; Bowers and Merena's Rarities Sale, July 2002, Lot 12.

There's plenty of demand for the 1793 half cent—from half cent collectors, type collectors, first-year-of-issue collectors, and collectors who admire the similarity of this design to that of the beautiful and famous Libertas Americana medal. That medal was commissioned by Benjamin Franklin in 1782 and designed by Augustin Dupré. The 1793 half cent was modeled, probably by Joseph Wright, on the Dupré design.

Roughly 500 coins from the original mintage of 35,334 have found their way into PCGS or NGC holders, so you'll have regular opportunities to bid for one that suits your taste and budget. But you'll have lots of competition from other bidders, and you'll need to pay a price reflecting this reality. Even this darkish, moderately worn, and modestly corroded example realized almost $10,000 when I sold it. You will need to pay much more for a specimen with "hard," glossy surfaces and light or medium brown color.

Lesson 1: When considering the purchase of early copper coins, you may want to seek an example with a little more surviving detail by compromising on surface quality, unless, of course, money is no object. However, never, under any circumstances, should you compromise on eye appeal.

Financials: Half cent, Liberty Cap, Head Facing Left, 1793

Cost	Sale Price	Gain/Loss	Holding Period
$4,370	$9,775	+124%	5.3 years

HALF CENT—LIBERTY CAP, HEAD FACING RIGHT (1794)

Lot 1002.
1794. EF-45.
C-1a, B-1a. Rarity-3. PCGS #001003.

Auction description: Deep golden tan with some lightness on the high points. Mark-free to the unaided eye, though we note tiny scattered marks under low magnification. Choice for the grade with regard to both sharpness and eye appeal. Struck from clashed dies with evidence plain on both sides. Definitely choice for the assigned grade.

From the Waccabuc Collection. Acquired from Bowers and Merena, February 2002.

Joseph Wright is thought to have designed the 1793 half cent. In 1794 Robert Scot came up with a new design, perhaps by looking at a 1793 specimen in a mirror. The new version has the head of Liberty facing to the right rather than the left. The reverse was modified only slightly.

The cataloger twice describes this coin as "choice for the grade." Perhaps. But by the stricter standards of the Early American Coppers Club, I suspect this coin would warrant a grade of VF-30 or so. I was attracted by the eye appeal and the clear evidence of die clashing[5] on both sides of this coin, though this feature only rarely can be seen in photographs.

Lesson 2: When you have an opportunity to choose among several similar coins, look for one that has something special to set it apart from others, such as attractive color or sharp strike or, as in this case, the evidence of clashed dies, which are interesting to study and contemplate.

Financials: Half cent, Liberty Cap, Head Facing Right, 1794

Cost	Sale Price	Gain/Loss	Holding Period
$3,345	$8,050	+141%	5.8 years

HALF CENT—LIBERTY CAP, HEAD FACING RIGHT (1795–1797)

Lot 1003.
1795, Punctuated Date, Lettered Edge. AU-55.
C-2a, B-2a. Rarity-3. PCGS #001009.

Auction description: Medium golden tan with some olive overtones. No appreciable marks noted to the unaided eye, though careful scrutiny under low magnification reveals some trivial, well-hidden tics. Central striking weakness on the reverse, typical for the issue. The popular "punctuated date" variety, so-named owing to a die defect resembling a comma between the 1 and the 7 of the date. Pleasing for the grade.

From the Waccabuc Collection. Earlier from ANR's sale of the Medio / Da Costa Gomez collections, June 2004, Lot 2080.

What to include in a type set is sometimes a matter of judgment, and it is PCGS's judgment that the 1795–1797 half cent is a separate and distinct design from the half cent of 1794. In fact, both designs are essentially the same, though the size of the head of Liberty with her liberty cap is noticeably smaller on the coins issued after 1794. I didn't really want to buy a "small head" variety, but I had to for set-registry purposes. I chose one of the distinctive *Guide Book* varieties,[6] with the punctuated (1,795) date. It's an attractive and curious coin, but not a financial investment that you'd want to write home about.

The cataloger mentions "central striking weakness on the reverse." Note how indistinct the denomination HALF CENT is. This is not the result of wear. Rather, the dies were positioned too far apart to bring up the full details, particularly where the wording on the reverse corresponds with the face of Liberty on the obverse. Where the legends do not oppose the portrait on the opposite side, the strike is much stronger.

Lesson 3: When trying to complete a Set Registry collection, you may sometimes be faced with the need to buy a coin you don't much care about. In such cases, demand (and value) can remain flat for long periods of time since other collectors may feel the same way. If you do decide to buy a coin just because you need it for set-registry purposes, keep your expectations for financial gain low . . . they will probably be realized.

Financials: Half cent, Liberty Cap, Head Facing Right, 1795, Punctuated Date, Lettered Edge

Cost	Sale Price	Gain/Loss	Holding Period
$8,050	$9,200	+14%	3.4 years

HALF CENT—DRAPED BUST (1800–1808)

Lot 1004.
1800. MS-62 RB.
C-1, B-1b. Rarity-2. PCGS #001052.

1800 marked the first year of the attractive (to my eye) Draped Bust style of half cent, designed by Robert Scot. The original mintage was generous (slightly more than 200,000), and a couple of hoards of this date were discovered in the first half of the 20th century. My example could well have come from one of these stashes. I loved the look of this particular example—already more than 200 years old when I bought it but still with a very fresh appearance. I almost certainly overpaid for it, as the modest return after more than six years of ownership suggests. On the other hand, a different (but also appealing) MS-62 RB example graded by PCGS was sold at a Heritage auction in March 2009 and garnered the same price that I received in November 2007, so maybe this is just one of those coins that trades in a narrow range over a period of many years.

Lesson 4: Certain series of American coins, including early half cents, are rarely bought by capricious coin investors, but rather are accumulated gradually over time by true collectors. As a result, price volatility is often lower, and price appreciation over time is likely to be unspectacular (except, perhaps, for especially rare dates and the finest-quality examples). Manage your expectations accordingly.

Financials: Half cent, Draped Bust, 1800

Cost	Sale Price	Gain/Loss	Holding Period
$3,910	$4,600	+18%	6.7 years

HALF CENT—CLASSIC HEAD (1809–1836)

Lot 1005.
1809. MS-63 BN.
C-3, B-4. Rarity-3. PCGS #001123.

Auction description: Lustrous dark chocolate brown with some lighter golden areas. Nicely struck with no serious surface marks and no breaks in the luster on the high points. A lovely specimen that would do justice to virtually any half cent collection or U.S. type collection currently being formed.

From the Waccabuc Collection. Earlier from ANR's Classics Sale, December 2003, Lot 373.

The talented German engraver Johann Matthias (John) Reich immigrated to America in 1800 and was the designer of several of our higher-denomination coins beginning in 1807. By 1809, he got around to the little half cent, copying the design he'd used a year earlier on the large cent. The resulting Classic Head type was minted intermittently through 1836.

By late 2003, I had been looking for an attractive first-year-of-issue example of a Classic Head half cent for quite some time. This one fit the bill perfectly, except for one thing. It was housed in an NGC holder, and I was collecting only PCGS coins. I thought I was getting a bargain when I paid $1,495 for this NGC MS-65 coin. Instead I got a big surprise when I sent it in to PCGS for re-grading and learned that they felt the coin only deserved a grade of MS-63. I would not be shocked to learn that this coin resides today in a holder with a grade of MS-64 or higher.

Lesson 5: Do **not** assume that the grade opinion of one grading service will be shared by another service. Though I got away without financial damage in this case (because the coin itself was attractive and desirable), mistakes like mine with this coin can be very costly. For example, see Lesson 49. And do not assume that this can only happen when an NGC coin is crossed over to a PCGS holder. Downgrades have occasionally occurred when coins are transferred from PCGS holders to NGC holders.

Financials: Half cent, Classic Head, 1809

Cost	Sale Price	Gain/Loss	Holding Period
$1,495	$1,610	+8%	3.9 years

HALF CENT—BRAIDED HAIR (1840–1857)

Lot 1006.
1849. MS-65 BN.
C-1, B-4. Rarity-2-. PCGS #001218.

Auction description: Tied for finest BN certified by PCGS. Deep golden tan with some deepening highlights in the protected areas. A sharply struck and aesthetically appealing example of this popular low-mintage issue, a date that saw a production run of just 39,864 pieces intended for general circulation. PCGS Population: 3; none finer within the designation.

From the Waccabuc Collection. Earlier from Heritage's Baltimore Sale, July 2003, Lot 5131.

The highly regarded designer Christian Gobrecht conceived a new "Braided Hair" rendition of Miss Liberty for the half cent, with production beginning in 1840. In my opinion, all of the earlier designs from 1793 onward were superior, but that's just my view. Only Proofs were issued through 1848, so my 1849 example is the first year of issue for circulating coins. Although the mintage of 1849 half cents was modest (fewer than 40,000), and my example is among the finest known, this series is not widely collected, so the price is less than one might expect.

Lesson 6: Many collectors seek un-toned "red" examples of copper coins and pay a significant premium for this color designation. You can often achieve much better value by seeking out brown or red-brown coins, and in many cases, these less-costly coins will look more attractive than pricier "red" coins that sometimes come with mottled coloring or dark spots.

Financials: Half cent, Braided Hair, 1849

Cost	Sale Price	Gain/Loss	Holding Period
$1,553	$2,645	+70%	4.7 years

Cents

Playing as a single at Saint Andrews, a committed golfer named Frank was teamed up with a twosome. After a few holes, the twosome finally asked why he was playing such a beautiful course all by himself. Frank replied that he and his wife had played the course every year— for more than 20 years—but this year she had passed away, and he had kept the tee time in her memory. The twosome commented that they thought certainly someone would have been willing to take her spot. "So did I," Frank said, "but they all wanted to go to the funeral."

Frank's commitment to golf has many parallels in the world of numismatics. Among the most committed of coin collectors are those who build date sets of cents, particularly the large cents that were among the first coins minted by our country in the late-18th century. Even a type set of large cents is a challenge to assemble, as you will read below.

Dr. William H. Sheldon, devotee of large cents, author of *Early American Cents*, and, perhaps, an aspiring golfer himself, wrote the following in the epilogue of his seminal work:

> Trying to perfect a collection of the early cents [i.e., those minted from 1793 through 1814] has in it much of that quality of elusive difficulty that endears the game of golf to many. Golf offers a measurable sense of progress toward an ultimate perfection which remains beautifully unattainable. The perfect golf score is imaginable, and definable, but is never realized. It is the same with the perfect cent score. For the 301 collectibles, such a score would be 301 x 70, or 21,070. That would be the score for the 295 known varieties and the 6 sub-varieties all in perfect Mint State. No golfer seriously aspires to tour a course in 18 strokes, and no student of early cents expects to reach the total score of 21,350 [*sic*]. Golfers do aspire to move from the nineties to the eighties, however, and a follower of the early cents can dream of advancing from the 2000 level toward the 2500 level.

Large cents were minted in every year from 1793 through 1857, except for 1815 when no coin blanks were available. As hard as it may be for a noncollector to imagine, there are many numismatists who seek to build collections of large cents by date and variety. The much narrower *type* set of large cents needs just eight coins to represent completion, with three of them dated 1793. These eight are described below.

In 1857 the small cent was introduced. The 2,000 or so small-format Flying Eagle cents dated 1856 (see below) are generally considered to be presentation pieces or patterns. The very attractive Flying Eagle variety lasted only until 1858. Indian Head cents were produced in each year from 1859 through 1909, and just three minor variations are needed for a type set. Since the 1909 centennial of Abraham Lincoln's birth, the Lincoln cent has been produced, and it is the series that many of us first collected. For the first 50 years the design was basically unchanged, though the metallic composition was modified to zinc-coated steel in the war year of 1943. In 1959 (the sesquicentennial of Lincoln's birth), the reverse of the Lincoln cent was changed, for the worse in my view, with the substitution of a depiction of the Lincoln Memorial for the original elegant wheat-ears reverse. All these varieties are discussed in more detail below.

LARGE CENT—FLOWING HAIR, CHAIN REVERSE (1793)

Lot 1007.
1793, Chain Reverse. VF-25.
S-2. Rarity-4+. PCGS #001341.

Auction description: Desirable 1793 Chain AMERICA Cent. A True American Classic. Deep chocolate brown verging on olive with golden tan highlights. Fully delineated devices on both sides, especially sharp at the central reverse where the all-important chain motif is found. Absolutely free of noticeable contact marks even when examined carefully under low magnification. We do note some minor granularity, mostly hidden to the unaided eye. All told, this is an outstanding coin for the grade with sharpness that easily meets the grade's criteria, and with eye appeal that places it apart from many Chain cents currently available in similar grades. An exceptional coin that will see unbridled bidding enthusiasm.

From the Waccabuc Collection.

I bought this famous coin at the Bowers and Merena Rarities Sale held in New York City in late July 2002. It was being sold on behalf of William Walser, a prominent collector whose now-disbursed complete U.S. type set ranked as the fifth finest on the PCGS set registry. The purchase felt to me like a bit of a stretch at the time—almost $10,000 for a slightly corroded "penny"—but it turned out to be one of my best buys.

I was attracted by the crisp design elements and attractive overall "look" of the coin. Most Chain cents are, well, just plain ugly. The B&M cataloger in 2002 was mostly positive in his assessment of this coin, calling it "impressive" and "extremely sharp," and speculating that the "combination of sharpness and visual appeal will surely bring out the competitors." He noted, however, that the surfaces showed "the sort of fine corrosion associated with burial." The Stack's description is also enthusiastic about this coin, but in contrast only notes "minor corrosion," without guessing as to its origin. I wasn't deterred by the thought that this cent might have spent some time in the dirt—I just thought its appearance was very attractive. Good decision on my part, and I bet the new owner is also happy with his purchase. It wouldn't surprise me if this coin finds its way into a new holder with a higher numerical grade some-day, and perhaps that thought influenced the buyer's strong bid.

Lesson 7: Learn how to grade coins. This large cent is better than VF-25 in terms of wear, and the eye appeal is excellent. PCGS probably assigned a "net" grade—deducting some points to account for the corrosion. This situation can represent an opportunity for the astute buyer.

Financials: Large cent, Flowing Hair, Chain Reverse, 1793

Cost	Sale Price	Gain/Loss	Holding Period
$9,775	$34,500	+253%	5.3 years

LARGE CENT—FLOWING HAIR, WREATH REVERSE (1793)

Lot 1008.
1793, Wreath Reverse, Vine and Bars Edge. EF-40.
S-9. Rarity-2. PCGS #001350.

Auction description: Nice EF 1793 Wreath Cent. Medium olive-brown with some golden brown high points. Faint granularity in certain areas of the coin, some faint, old circulation scratches near the date and the point of Liberty's bust, a few other scattered marks noted, none readily obvious to the unaided eye. As for the overall quality, surprisingly PCGS has certified just a baker's dozen of the type at a finer grade than offered here. The present example certainly fills the bill for anyone looking for a nice, lightly circulated example of this popular scarcity.

From the Waccabuc Collection. Earlier from Heritage's New York Sale, July 2002, Lot 5838.

The Wreath cent is the most common of the three 1793 types, and this S-9 is the most common of the Sheldon varieties. The two leading grading services have slabbed more than 600 Wreath cents, though this number undoubtedly includes some resubmissions. Nevertheless, all collectors of American coins would love to own a first-year-of-issue large cent, so demand and prices have been strong for many years.

When I bought this coin at a Heritage sale in 2002, the PCGS holder described the edge as "Lettered" (a scarcer variety), even though all S-9s have a Vine and Bars edge. I had the coin reholdered before selling it. The Stack's description (quoted above) suggests that only 13 finer examples have been graded by PCGS. The real number is closer to 100.

Lesson 8: Mistakes are made, even by superlative firms like PCGS and Stack's. While the old Poe adage ("Believe nothing you hear, and only one half that you see") may be a trifle extreme, don't forget to look carefully at the coins you're considering buying to be certain that what you see is consistent with the information on the holder and in the catalog or price list.

Financials: Large cent, Flowing Hair, Wreath Reverse, 1793, Vine and Bars Edge

Cost	Sale Price	Gain/Loss	Holding Period
$5,290	$10,925	+107%	5.3 years

LARGE CENT—LIBERTY CAP (1793)

Lot 1009.
1793. VF-20.
S-13. Rarity-4-. PCGS #001359.

Auction description: Important 1793 Liberty Cap Cent Rarity. A pleasing olive-brown example of the most desirable of all 1793 large cent varieties, the Liberty cap style of Joseph Wright. Nicely centered on both sides, full beaded border on planchet, some faint old brush marks and few scattered, light planchet marks can be seen under low magnification, though the coin holds up well to scrutiny. Obviously hand selected for quality within the assigned grade, we suggest the present piece is probably among the nicest VF-20 Liberty Cap cents to come under our examination in recent times.

From the Waccabuc Collection. Earlier from the Denis W. Loring Collection; Heritage's sale of the Wes Rasmussen Collection, January 2005, Lot 3016; PCGS holder marked "Troy Wiseman Collection."

The Liberty Cap design is by far the rarest among the three types of large cents dated 1793. It's an extremely difficult coin to acquire, whether you're trying to build a large-cent collection or working on a type collection. Why? Because it's expensive in all grades, and most of the examples that appear in auctions are so worn down that they're barely recognizable. I looked at several dozen examples over the last decade and (sadly) passed on a couple of other acceptable ones, because I thought they were over-priced. When I saw this piece being offered by Heritage in 2005, I decided I *had* to get it. I had grown frustrated in not being able to get a 1793 Cap, and this one was a decent companion for my two other 1793 cents in terms of appearance and condition. I kept my hand up in the air for longer than I wanted to, but at the end of the auction, the coin was mine. (I wasn't actually in the auction room—I bid on this via the Internet—but you get the idea.) The price appreciation over the next two years was modest, and indeed I lost a little money after the juice. However, I think the new owner made a very good purchase if he has at least a medium-term investment horizon. This is a very tough coin.

Lesson 9: Genuinely rare coins, like this one, will always be expensive. When you find one that fits the set you're building (in terms of grade and eye appeal), you should stretch to buy it. If you have a medium- or long-term investment horizon, you are unlikely to regret your purchase. And in the meantime, you will own something that most other collectors will covet but not possess.

Financials: Large cent, Liberty Cap, 1793

Cost	Sale Price	Gain/Loss	Holding Period
$46,000	$48,300	+5%	2.2 years

LARGE CENT—LIBERTY CAP, DENTICLES (1794–1796)

Lot 1010.
1794, Head of 1794. AU-53.
S-22. Rarity-1. PCGS #901374.

Auction description: Choice AU 1794 Cent. Head of 1794. Somewhat glossy golden tan with attractive highlights in the protected areas. Surfaces mainly hard and glossy with a bit of metal flow stress seen on both sides, a small diagonal mark near Miss Liberty's nose, no other appreciable marks present on either side. A choice and pleasing example of the date and grade.

From the Waccabuc Collection. Earlier from Superior's May 2003 Sale, Lot 363.

The Liberty Cap design was continued from 1794 through 1796, but the border design was changed from beads (which are clearly visible in the preceding photo) to denticles (which are somewhat less visible in this photo). This distinction was enough for PCGS to include the 1794–1796 cents as a separate type.

With three years to choose from (not to mention close to 80 Sheldon varieties of the 1794 cent alone), there will be many opportunities to fill this slot in your type collection. One of the 1794 varieties is especially famous and desirable—the so-called Starred Reverse (S-48), which has 94 tiny stars situated around the reverse among the 83 reverse denticles. A barely discernible example will cost you around $10,000, while the finest known (graded AU-50 by PCGS) sold for more than $600,000 in early 2008.

Lesson 10: If money is no object, then go for it: buy the best and most unusual coins. There will always be a market for these. For the rest of us, buy something that appeals to you. It will likely appeal to someone else when the time comes to sell.

Financials: Large cent, Liberty Cap, Denticles, 1794, Head of 1794

Cost	Sale Price	Gain/Loss	Holding Period
$3,450	$5,060	+47%	4.5 years

LARGE CENT—DRAPED BUST (1796–1807)

Lot 1011.
1796, Reverse of 1797. AU-58.
S-119. Rarity-3. PCGS #001407.

Auction description: Choice AU 1796 Draped Bust Cent. Solitary PCGS AU-58. Deep olive-brown with some chestnut highlights. No serious marks are evident to the unaided eye, though low magnification reveals scattered tiny marks, many of them in the planchet when struck. Obverse die state with heavy crack at date and lowest curl. An exceptional example of the date and grade.

From the Waccabuc Collection. Earlier from Heritage's Pittsburgh Sale, August 2004, Lot 5098.

As a design, the Draped Bust is one of my personal favorites. As an investment, this Damned Bust was one of my worst. After owning it for over three years in a strong coin market, I realized a loss of more than 30% after fees. Why? Maybe the right buyers weren't at this auction, though this seems unlikely. Maybe I just overpaid for the coin in the first place. But I choose to think the real reason is that there are just too many Uncirculated Nichols Find examples around, making my "exceptional" About Uncirculated example just not good enough.

The Nichols Find was an accumulation of Mint State 1796 and 1797 large cents that were, reportedly, purchased by Benjamin Goodhue of Salem, Massachusetts, directly from the Mint. The coins, probably 1,000 in total, descended in the family and were eventually acquired by David Nichols of Gallows Hill, Massachusetts. By 1863, all pieces had been dispersed. You can read more about this and scores of other coin hoards in Dave Bowers's delightful book, *American Coin Treasures and Hoards* (see bibliography).

Lesson 11: The stories, history, and charm of old coins can assuage the pain of the occasional lousy financial investment. I still like this particular coin, and the new owner has acquired it at an excellent cost basis.

Financials: Large cent, Draped Bust, 1796, Reverse of 1797

Cost	Sale Price	Gain/Loss	Holding Period
$8,625	$6,038	-30%	3.3 years

LARGE CENT—CLASSIC HEAD (1808–1814)

Lot 1012.
1814. AU-58.
S-294. Rarity-1. Crosslet 4.

Auction description: Choice AU 1814 Cent. Crosslet 4. Glossy chestnut brown with some lighter chestnut regions in the protected areas. Strong underlying luster bolsters the already fulfilling eye appeal. An old diagonal contact mark on Liberty's cheek is the only mark of merit, careful scrutiny reveals fairly hard surfaces overall. Choice and appealing.

From the Waccabuc Collection. Earlier from ANR's sale of the Kennywood Collection, January 2005, Lot 78.

After 12 years of coining Robert Scot's eye-catching Draped Bust cent, the Mint switched to John Reich's Classic Head design in 1808. This seven-year type has no great rarities. My 1814 is the most common date, and the About Uncirculated grade seemed like a nice compromise between the sometimes unattractive lower-graded coins that are readily available and the much pricier Uncirculated specimens that are very hard to find.

The copper used to mint Classic Head large cents was purer, and therefore softer, than the metal used for the preceding and succeeding designs. Therefore, the coins wore more easily, with the result that it is difficult to find choice examples today.

Lesson 12: My favorite grade for early coins is AU-58. You can see all design details as conceived by the engraver. Wear is minimal, and original luster and color are often evident. Marks and scuffs are usually fewer than on coins graded MS-60 and MS-61. Once in a while you can get an upgrade (see lot 1061). And, the cost is normally much more reasonable than for coins in Uncirculated grades. My AU-58 1814 cent had most of these positive attributes, except for the cheek gash, which was probably sufficiently nasty to deter many prospective buyers. Beyond that, this was a fine coin. ("And, otherwise, Mrs. Lincoln, how did you like the play?")

Financials: Large cent, Classic Head, 1814

Cost	Sale Price	Gain/Loss	Holding Period
$3,220	$2,990	-7%	2.8 years

LARGE CENT—LIBERTY HEAD, MATRON HEAD (1816–1839)

Lot 1013.
1816. MS-64RB.
N-2. Rarity-1. PCGS #001592.

Auction description: Struck in the first year of the Matron Head design type. A pleasing, highly lustrous golden tan specimen with generous amounts of mint orange and rose in the protected areas. A few well-hidden marks are mentioned for accuracy, though the overall eye appeal is substantial, especially for the grade. Rim crumbling from 2:00 to 3:00 on the obverse. PCGS Population: 8; 1 finer within the designation (MS-65 RB).

From the Waccabuc Collection. Earlier from the William Walser Collection; Bowers and Merena's Rarities Sale, July 2002, Lot 42.

Numismatic art took a step backward, in my view, with the issuance of the Matron Head design in 1816. Gone were the youthful beauties of the Flowing Hair and Draped Bust designs. Gone, too, was the stylish, curly-haired mother figure of the Classic Head design. In their place, the nation was given a stout, glum woman who has always reminded me of a shot-putter on some Soviet-era Olympic team. My opinion is shared by others. Walter Breen anointed this design "spectacularly ugly" and called this version of Miss Liberty a "characterless slattern." William Sheldon said that the portrait "resembled the head of an obese ward boss instead of a lady." Harsh words, but sadly accurate.

More than 60 million Matron Head cents were minted between 1816 and 1839, so obtaining an example is easy. I chose one dated 1816, both because it's the first year of issue and because it's fairly widely available in nice condition. My coin may have come from the famous Randall Hoard, the name given to a wooden keg of 5,000 to 10,000 Uncirculated large cents discovered beneath a railroad platform in Georgia shortly after the end of the Civil War. Most Randall Hoard coins are dated 1818 or 1820. Some researchers do not believe any 1816-dated cents were included in the hoard, and some claim the coins were not hidden under a train platform but were buried in the earth. In any event, enough attractive 1816 cents survive today to suggest that someone (or a number of people) saved these at the time of issue.

Lesson 13: You don't have to love a coin's design to find it appealing and interesting. My 1816 cent has wonderful color, and I enjoyed contemplating the possibility that it was hidden away for many years, and then was forgotten, and later was re-discovered. The 1816 cent is also famous for another reason: it is the only denomination minted in the United States in that year. Thus, by owning this single coin, you will have a complete denomination set for the year 1816. Obviously, the buyer also felt this coin possessed certain attraction, since he (or she) paid almost triple my original cost.

Financials: Large cent, Liberty Head, Matron Head, 1816

Cost	Sale Price	Gain/Loss	Holding Period
$1,265	$3,680	+191%	5.3 years

LARGE CENT—LIBERTY HEAD, BRAIDED HAIR (1839–1857)

Lot 1014.
1855, Upright 55. MS-65 RD.
N-4. Rarity-1. PCGS #001909.

Auction description: Frosty Uncirculated 1855 Large Cent. Upright 55. A satiny, frosty mint orange Gem with delightful, bold cartwheel luster. Sharply struck on both sides, with just a hint of weakness at certain central star radials on the obverse. An exceptional example of a hoard date, this particular specimen is especially devoid of the tiny black specks that typically haunt the issue; we do note one small fleck in the reverse wreath below the first A in AMERICA. Aesthetically and physically worthy of the assigned grade.

From the Waccabuc Collection. Earlier from Heritage's F.U.N. Convention Sale, January 2006, Lot 661.

The Braided Hair cent was minted from 1839 through 1857. The design was changed only slightly from the earlier Matron Head type—note, among other subtle changes, the tightly braided hair beneath the coronet and the removal of the line under the denomination on the reverse. The visage of Miss Liberty appears to me to be a bit younger than on the earlier type, but she seems just as vacuous as her predecessor.

I bought this coin in an old PCGS holder. These holders are smaller and less secure than later models, but some collectors seek out coins in old holders because there is a perception that grading standards were stricter then than they are now. (This perception is almost certainly correct, but this does not mean that all coins in old holders will get higher grades today.)

I decided to have this coin re-holdered, not because I was seeking an upgrade, but because the old holder was badly scratched. To my surprise, PCGS's records showed this as a Red-Brown coin, even though the slab clearly (and correctly) designated the coin as Red. It took me three months and some intervention from Heritage Auction Galleries to get the situation corrected.

Lesson 14: An advantage of developing a personal relationship with reputable dealers is that when you run into a problem, it's likely to be resolved to your satisfaction. In the present case, Mark Borckardt (the best bowler in all of numismatics) and Greg Rohan at Heritage assisted in the communication with PCGS and even offered to repurchase the coin at my cost if PCGS did not re-holder the coin in its original grade.

Financials: Large cent, Liberty Head, Braided Hair, 1855, Upright 55

Cost	Sale Price	Gain/Loss	Holding Period
$2,990	$4,600	+54%	1.8 years

SMALL CENT—FLYING EAGLE (1856)

Lot 1015.
1856. Proof-63.
S-2. PCGS #002037.

Auction description: Ever-Popular 1856 Flying Eagle Cent Rarity. Satiny golden surfaces with pale rose and tan highlights. Prooflike reflectivity on both sides. Nicely struck for the issue, with no serious surface marks present. Always desirable, and perhaps America's most famous and popular small cent issue. One of the rarer varieties identified by Snow as one of the early Pattern issues which are estimated to comprise perhaps as little as a couple percent of the total issue of 1856 Flying Eagle cents. A worthwhile coin that will be a highlight in virtually any numismatic cabinet.

From the Waccabuc Collection.

Everyone who started collecting small cents by trying to fill all the holes in their blue Whitman folders dreamed of one day being able to own an 1856 Flying Eagle cent. Why? Because the "hole" for the 1856 cent was filled in with a cardboard plug, and the word RARE was printed on the plug. I was one of those young tyros who coveted this coin, and it was one of my early targets when I started attending auctions. I soon found I had lots of company. The first one I bought had been cleaned, though that fact wasn't disclosed in the auction catalog, and I didn't have enough experience to tell the difference. I was shocked when I received the coin back from ANACS in a holder marked "genuine," the terminology used at the time to indicate that the coin was real but un-gradable because of improper cleaning or damage. Nevertheless, I was able to sell that coin a year later for a small profit and move on.

I bought the present example at a Bowers and Merena auction in 1997. Comparing it to many I've looked at since then, I consider it to have more eye appeal than most others in PF-63 and PF-64 holders. I speculate that it didn't receive a higher technical grade because there's a tiny area to the left of the date where a small spot seems to have been removed. A hint of a surface disturbance appears in the photograph. This flaw didn't bother me because of the coin's excellent overall "look," but I think it served to limit the final grade.

Lesson 15: Even coins with minor enhancements performed outside the mint can sometimes find their way into leading third-party grading-service holders. Many (some might say most) silver coins in slabs have taken a bath in Jeweluster or a similar product. Take a close look at the coin, not just the grade on the holder, to be sure you like and understand what you're buying.

Financials: Small cent, Flying Eagle, 1856

Cost	Sale Price	Gain/Loss	Holding Period
$6,600	$14,950	+127%	10.7 years

SMALL CENT—FLYING EAGLE (1857–1858)

Lot 1016.
1858, Large Letters. MS-65.
PCGS #002019.

Auction description: Gem Uncirculated 1858 Flying Eagle Cent. Large Letters. A lustrous Gem with bright gold, peach, sky blue, and pale sea green iridescence on both sides. Sharply struck with only a hint of weakness at the eagle's talon on the obverse; the reverse wreath details are all crisp and accounted for. Accompanied by an Eagle Eye Photo Seal certificate.

From the Waccabuc Collection. Earlier from ANR's sale of the Worthington Collection, May 2005, Lot 13.

Flying Eagle cents were minted from 1856 through 1858. James B. Longacre was the designer, though the majestic flying eagle on the obverse is very similar to the one that appeared on the dollar coins of 1836 to 1839 designed by Christian Gobrecht. The metallic composition was changed from pure copper to an alloy of 88% copper and 12% nickel. The reduced diameter and new design were immediately popular with the American public. Sadly, some difficulties with striking the coins may have led to the decision to discontinue the design after only three years.

The catalog description notes that this coin was accompanied by an Eagle Eye Photo Seal (EEPS) certificate. Like the CAC sticker discussed in chapter 2, an EEPS certificate is an external expert's assurance that a particular coin is solid for the grade. The difference is that EEPS's laminated certificates (and the related stickers that are affixed to slabs) are issued only for Flying Eagle and Indian Head cents. The man behind the idea is Rick Snow, the owner of Eagle Eye Rare Coins of Tuscon, Arizona. Rick is the leading authority on Flying Eagle and Indian Head cents, and he was named the ANA's Numismatist of the Year in 2010. His opinion on the quality and grade of coins in his area of specialization is respected throughout the hobby.

Lesson 16: If you can afford one, buy an 1856 Flying Eagle cent—their eternal popularity seems assured. If you can't afford an 1856, or if you are in the camp that considers it to be a pattern rather than a regular Mint issue, then be sure to buy an 1857 or 1858 with a good strike. Look especially at the eagle's head, tail feathers, and talons. These features are opposite the wreath on the reverse, which made full striking challenging.

Financials: Small cent, Flying Eagle, 1858, Large Letters

Cost	Sale Price	Gain/Loss	Holding Period
$2,990	$3,910	+31%	2.5 years

SMALL CENT—INDIAN HEAD, COPPER-NICKEL, LAUREL WREATH REVERSE (1859)

Lot 1017.
1859. MS-65.
PCGS #002052.

Auction description: Gem Mint State 1859 Cent. A frosty golden Gem with intense cartwheel luster on both sides, and with rich rose iridescence in the protected areas. A pleasing example, boldly struck, from the first year of the Indian cent obverse design, and the only year of the series with an unadorned laurel wreath on the reverse; in 1860 through the end of the series in 1909 a wreath of oak and other leaves with a Federal shield at the top was the mainstay of the design.

From the Waccabuc Collection. Acquired from North American Certified Trading, December 2002.

The 1859 cent is a one-year type, distinct from the Indian Head cents of later years primarily because of the laurel wreath adorning the reverse. The Indian Head cents of 1860 to 1909 used an oak wreath instead. The "Indian" on the Indian Head cent is actually a depiction of Miss Liberty wearing a Native American headdress. This curious combination might have been an expression of national guilt over the expulsion of Indians from their vast American lands and the relocation of many to reservations.

Lesson 17: Even though this is a one-year type coin that both Indian Head cent and type collectors need for their collections, it is, in fact, quite common in all grades. There's no need to buy the first example you encounter—another will come along soon enough. Choose one whose strike and color appeal to you.

Financials: Small cent, copper-nickel, Indian Head, Laurel Wreath Reverse, 1859

Cost	Sale Price	Gain/Loss	Holding Period
$2,314	$3,450	+49%	4.9 years

SMALL CENT—INDIAN HEAD, COPPER-NICKEL, OAK WREATH WITH SHIELD REVERSE (1860–1864)

Lot 1018.
1860, Round Bust. MS-65.
PCGS #002058.

Auction description: A frosty golden Gem with exceptional eye appeal and cartwheel luster that just won't quit.

From the Waccabuc Collection. Acquired from David Hall, November 2002.

With just a one-sentence description by the Stack's cataloger, you might guess that this "Gem" cent is not particularly rare, and you would be correct. There are a couple of hundred other gems out there to choose among. The Round Bust variety is more frequently seen by far. Probably fewer than 5 percent of the mintage of 1860 cents had the Pointed Bust that was used on the cents of 1859. A small Union shield was added to the reverse—not a surprise given the state of politics and public discourse in 1860.

Lesson 18: With a little research, you can learn about scarce varieties (such as the Pointed Bust feature of some 1860 cents) and price differentials. For this coin, the Pointed Bust variety is at least 20 times rarer than its Round Bust counterpart, but the price premium is closer to two to four times in high grades. This situation may provide an opportunity for the astute buyer. Note that I did not follow my own advice.

Financials: Small cent, copper-nickel, Indian Head, Oak Wreath With Shield Reverse, 1860, Round Bust

Cost	Sale Price	Gain/Loss	Holding Period
$1,100	$1,150	+5%	5.0 years

SMALL CENT—INDIAN HEAD, BRONZE (1864–1909)

Lot 1019.
1900. Proof-66 RD.
PCGS #002389.

Civil War tokens represent a fascinating subset of American numismatics, with many avenues available for study and collecting. These tokens were in widespread use during the war—so widespread, in fact, that the U.S. government stepped in and banned their production with the Act of April 22, 1864. To compete with, and eventually replace, the tokens in use in daily commerce, the Mint issued huge quantities of a thinner version of the Indian Head cent, composed of 95 percent copper and 5 percent tin and zinc. Almost 75 million bronze cents were made in 1864 and 1865, and close to 1.7 billion were produced by the end of the Indian Head cent series in 1909.

Lesson 19: When you have a vast number of years and varieties to choose among, make your decision carefully in order to avoid being tempted to buy something more interesting at a later date. For example, you might pick the first year of issue (1864, or even better, the 1864 L, showing the last initial of the engraver, James B. Longacre), or one of the rare dates (such as 1877 or 1909-S), or a curious variety (like the 1873 with doubled LIBERTY). I decided on a nice Proof 1900 because this coin fit in both my "complete" type set and in my "20th century" type set. (Note that PCGS subscribes to the theory that the 20th century began in 1900 rather than 1901.)

Financials: Small cent, bronze, Indian Head, 1900

Cost	Sale Price	Gain/Loss	Holding Period
$2,703	$2,300	-15%	3.8 years

SMALL CENT—LINCOLN, WHEAT EARS REVERSE (1909–1958)

Lot 1020.
1909-S, V.D.B. MS-65 RB.
PCGS #002427.

Auction description: Lovely Gem 1909-S V.D.B. Cent. The Eliasberg Specimen. Sparkling golden brown with a generous amount of fiery gold, peach, and crimson iridescence on both sides. A frosty, matte-like Gem with no appreciable surface disturbances. The key to the Lincoln cent series, a date that has grown in popularity and stature virtually since the day of issue. A splendid opportunity to add your name to the illustrious Louis Eliasberg cachet.

From the Waccabuc Collection. Earlier from Bowers and Merena's sale of the Eliasberg Collection, May 1996, Lot 668.

The "S-V.D.B."[7] was the Holy Grail for kids like me looking through change in the 1950s and 1960s. Most of us never found one, so the desire to own one just grew. I've bought and sold several over the last 15 years and have always made a profit—a fact that attests to the ongoing popularity of this particular coin. It's a wonderful choice for a type collection.

The example shown here was once owned by that giant of American numismatics, Louis Eliasberg Sr. Over a 25-year period ending in 1950, Eliasberg was able to acquire an example of every denomination, every date, and every mintmark in the federal series from 1793 to the present. In late 1950, Eliasberg completed his collection with the acquisition of the unique (yes, the only known) specimen of the 1873-CC Liberty Seated dime without arrows. His accomplishment was widely heralded, with exhibitions at the Philadelphia Mint and the Smithsonian (where 1.5 million people viewed the collection), and with full-color feature articles in *Life* and *Look* magazines, among others. Q. David Bowers shares his personal memories of this great numismatist in his book *Coins and Collectors: Golden Anniversary Edition*.

Louis Eliasberg's 1909-S V.D.B. was sold at a fabulous Bowers and Merena auction in May 1996 in New York. The price was $2,530, representing a hammer price of $2,300 plus the (then typical) 10 percent buyer's fee. I was not the buyer. I acquired this coin almost three years later in March 1999 at another Bowers and Merena auction. My cost was $1,840, representing a hammer price of $1,600 plus the (by then typical) 15 percent buyer's fee.

Lesson 20: Buying a coin with a famous provenance adds interest and a certain cachet to any collection. However, buying a pedigreed coin at the original auction for that pedigree comes with the risk that the publicity preceding the event will generate record prices—great for the consignor but not so great for the buyer. I experienced this first-hand when I bought Louis Eliasberg's 1885 Proof dollar for $4,600 and sold it less than two years later for $2,400. My experience was hardly unique. However, it's worth pointing out that in the 11 years since the original Eliasberg sale, his S-V.D.B. eventually tripled from its original price— although I doubt my former 1885 dollar has done as well.

Financials: Small cent, Lincoln, Wheat Ears Reverse, 1909-S V.D.B.

Cost	Sale Price	Gain/Loss	Holding Period
$1,840	$7,475	+306%	8.7 years

SMALL CENT—LINCOLN, WHEAT EARS REVERSE, STEEL (1943)

Lot 1021.
1943-D. MS-68.
PCGS #002714.

Auction description: A superb Gem of the date, a coin that is tied for finest certified by PCGS. Sparkling bright silver gray surfaces with intense cartwheel luster, a needle-sharp strike, and eye appeal that is as vivid and unyielding as the cartwheel luster on both sides. PCGS Population: 121; none finer within the designation.

From the Waccabuc Collection. Earlier from Teletrade's February 2001 Sale, Lot 1027.

The U.S. military needed additional supplies of copper during World War II, so the Treasury Department helped the cause by minting cents in 1943 on steel planchets covered with a thin layer of zinc. Almost 1.1 billion were produced at the Philadelphia, Denver, and San Francisco mints. Most of these became extremely ugly, as the zinc wore off and the steel rusted. But fortunately, many thousands were saved by collectors, so today there is an ample supply of stunning gems to choose among.

Lesson 21: Yes, the 1943-S is a tiny bit scarcer and a bit more expensive than its Philadelphia and Denver counterparts. But don't overlook the fact that more than 191 million pieces were minted. You shouldn't spend your money for a slightly rarer coin when a common coin will do just fine. Save your powder for a genuinely rare coin.

Financials: Small cent, steel, Lincoln, Wheat Ears Reverse, 1943-D

Cost	Sale Price	Gain/Loss	Holding Period
$857	$1,380	+61%	6.8 years

SMALL CENT—LINCOLN, MEMORIAL REVERSE (1959–2008)

Lot 1022.
1956, Proof-67 RD; 1959, Proof-67 RD; 1964, Proof-69 RD; 1983-S, Proof-69 RD.

Auction description: Quartette of PCGS-certified Lincoln cents: * 1956 Proof-67 RD * 1959 Proof-67 RD * 1964 Proof-69 RD * 1983-S Proof-69 RD DCAM. An exceptional group. (Total: 4 pieces)

From the Waccabuc Collection.

I bought these four Lincoln cents because I needed them for inclusion in my 20th-century type set. None qualifies as a rare coin, though all are in much finer condition than normally seen. I have to admit that I got very little excitement from acquiring these coins, and I felt absolutely no seller's remorse when the hammer came down on this lot.

The next time you need a question for a bar quiz, ask what is the most reproduced portrait in the history of the universe. The answer is the portrait of Abraham Lincoln. It has been recreated about 500 *billion* times on the Lincoln cent, and that doesn't even include the tiny sculpture of Lincoln that can just be seen on the reverse of the vast number of cents minted since the change to the Lincoln Memorial reverse in 1959.

Lesson 22: Don't spend a lot of time or money on items you don't care about. Yes, completing the collection of modern issues was somewhat satisfying, but I rarely looked at these coins or showed them to others. This is not to say that collecting modern coins isn't worthwhile. It can be interesting, educational, and fun. Indeed, enough other people had an interest in these Proof cents that I was able to make a reasonable profit on this lot. But they're not rare coins, and seeking an imperceptibly finer example of a common modern coin wasn't something that gave me much of a thrill.

Financials: Small cent, Lincoln, Memorial Reverse, 1956, 1959, 1964, 1983-S

Cost	Sale Price	Gain/Loss	Holding Period
$100	$138	+38%	4.5 years

CHAPTER
5

Two-Cent
Pieces

*For most golfers, the only difference between
a $1 ball and a $4 ball is three dollars.*

For those who don't play golf, you may not know that only accomplished players can feel and appreciate the difference between a high-quality ball and an average ball. The former has a "softer" feel when struck and can be controlled more easily when it comes to shaping a shot (from left to right or right to left) and imparting spin. For most duffers, the $1 ball is perfectly adequate.

The differences between a nice Uncirculated coin and, for example, the "lustrous gem" described below are similarly often not evident to a non-collector. Once you've been bitten by the coin bug, however, you'll soon come to appreciate these differences, and your enjoyment—and financial success—in the hobby will increase commensurately. The familiar advice to buy the best you can afford is usually valid, and the two-cent denomination is one where beautiful specimens are available at reasonable prices. This is one instance where you'll want to buy the "$4 ball."

TWO-CENT PIECE (1864–1873)

Lot 1023.
1864, Large Motto. MS-65 RD.
PCGS #003578.

Auction description: A lustrous Gem with rich mint orange blending warmly with varied rose hues. Intensely lustrous with exceptional eye appeal and a bold strike. Clash marks and a network of rapidly developing die cracks, especially on the reverse. Obverse rim cuds noted at 12:30 and 1:30. An impressive Gem overall.

From the Waccabuc Collection. Acquired from Legend Numismatics, March 2001.

As part of the government's effort to replace privately issued Civil War tokens with federally produced coins, the Mint supplemented its massive production of 1864 bronze cents with a similarly large issuance of 1864 two-cent pieces. Their composition was the same as the cent (95% copper and 5% tin and zinc), and their weight was exactly double that of the cent. Unlike the cent, however, their popularity was limited, and production declined in each year through the end of the series in 1873.

The curious two-cent denomination was chosen as the first U.S. coin to bear the motto IN GOD WE TRUST, which was placed on the ribbon above the shield. Mint Director James Pollock submitted a design for the two-cent coin to Salmon P. Chase, secretary of the Treasury under Abraham Lincoln. Pollock's design included a motto with the words GOD OUR TRUST. According to Walter Breen in his masterful *Complete Encyclopedia of U.S. and Colonial Coins*, Chase's decision to change the motto to IN GOD WE TRUST was "evidently influenced by the motto of Chase's alma mater, Brown University, IN DEO SPERAMUS, 'In God We Hope.'" This is a wonderful story, and as a graduate of Brown (class of 1970), I would love to believe it. However, according to all other sources I've checked, Chase was a graduate of Dartmouth College, class of 1826.

Clash marks (mentioned here in the auction lot description) are imperfections on a working die that are created when obverse and reverse dies come together without a coin blank between them. In extreme cases, you can clear-

ly make out design elements on the obverse of a coin that should only be on the reverse (or vice versa). Mint workers sometimes tried to repair clashed dies by a process called die lapping. This involved abrading the surface of the die with rubbing compounds or files to remove the upper layer of the steel die where the clash marks appear.

Lesson 23: Auctions are fun, easy, and many times the best choice for obtaining unusual, hard-to-locate coins. On the other hand, it often makes sense to buy more "common" rare coins from a reputable dealer. The price will likely be near the average auction result, and you will gain a valuable resource by developing a relationship with the dealer. I bought my 1864 two-cent piece from Legend Numismatics on the bourse floor at the American Numismatic Association convention in Baltimore in March 2001. Over the next several years, I did several more deals with Legend—both purchases and sales—all to my satisfaction. The periodic market reports posted on the Legend Numismatics Web site, usually written by Legend partner Laura Sperber, provide a frank, refreshing, and insightful source of information on the state of the coin market.

Financials: Two-cent piece, 1864, Large Motto

Cost	Sale Price	Gain/Loss	Holding Period
$1,100	$2,530	+130%	6.7 years

Three-Cent
Pieces

*Knowing the swing weight of your club is as indispensable to playing
good golf as knowing the temperature of the grass in the fairway.*

I t is better, in golf, to follow the KISS principle: keep it simple, stupid! But in numismatics, you can multiply your pleasure by learning as much as you can about the history of your coins and the context in which they were produced and used. The curious, in today's monetary framework, three-cent pieces are a case in point. They were first introduced in 1851 in a tiny silver format. In 1865, a larger copper-nickel version made its appearance, and both types continued to be made through 1873, after which the silver coins were discontinued. The copper-nickel type remained in production for another 16 years. The four recognized varieties are described and discussed below.

THREE-CENT PIECE—NICKEL (1865–1889)

Lot 1024.
1881. Proof-67 CAM.
PCGS #083777.

Auction description: An exceptionally lovely cameo Proof of the date, a splendid little coin with heavily frosted motifs and deeply mirrored fields that display faint rose irides- cence. Among the 20 finest CAM designations for the date at PCGS. PCGS Population: 17; 3 finer within the designation (all Proof-68 CAM).

From the Waccabuc Collection. Earlier from Heritage's F.U.N. Convention Sale, January 2006, Lot 1199.

Nickel three-cent pieces (which are 75% copper and 25% nickel) were minted from 1865 through 1889. Silver three-cent pieces had been made since 1851, but they were inconveniently small (some called them "fish scales") and even- tually disappeared from circulation due to hoarding. The nickel version was designed as a more-useful replacement. It also served another purpose. Nickel was removed from the composition of one-cent coins in April 1864. This displeased the nickel-mining interests. To placate them, and to rid the nation of the hated paper three-cent notes known as *shinplasters*, Congress authorized the nickel three-cent piece in March 1865.

With the introduction of nickel five-cent pieces in 1866, the nickel mining interests had an assured use for their production. When U.S. postal rates for a 1/2-ounce letter were reduced from three cents to two cents on October 1, 1883, the final *raison d'être* for the three-cent denomination was eliminated. Nevertheless, for some reason nickel three-cent pieces continued to be produced, in small quantities, through 1889.

As with a number of other denominations, the first year of issue (1865) saw a huge mintage—more than 11 million pieces. In modest accumulations of old coins shown to me over the years by friends and acquaintances, I have almost always found a tired 1865 three-cent piece. If you're looking for a circulation strike for your collection, you'll have lots of nice examples to choose among from the early years of this issue. Many attractive Proof coins are also around, including some with distinct cameo contrast. Even at grades up through Proof-67, the cost is quite reasonable. If you're willing to spend more, then get an 1877. It's one of the very few American coins with a total mintage (Proofs plus circulation strikes) of less than 1,000. The *Red Book* reports a mintage of 900 (all Proofs).

Lesson 24: If you're not strict about having a collection made up entirely of circulation strikes (coins made for use in commerce), there are a number of cases where Proof strikes (coins made on specially prepared dies for sale to collectors) are less expensive than their Mint State counterparts. At an auction conducted by Heritage in March 2009, an 1881 PCGS MS-67 nickel three-cent piece sold for $4,025. At the same auction, you could have become the owner of an 1881 PCGS PF-67 nickel three-cent piece for almost $3,000 less.

Financials: Three-cent piece, nickel, 1881

Cost	Sale Price	Gain/Loss	Holding Period
$1,208	$1,495	+24%	1.8 years

THREE-CENT PIECE—SILVER TRIME, VARIETY 1 (1851–1853)

Lot 1025.
1851. MS-66.
PCGS #003664.

Auction description: An exceptional Gem from the first year of the design type and denomination. Boldly struck on both sides with just a hint of weakness at one pair of vertical shield stripes on the obverse. A high degree of luster supports pale rose and champagne toning on both sides. A beautiful coin that practically defines the assigned grade.

From the Waccabuc Collection. Acquired from Heritage, May 2005.

With a diameter 22% smaller than the Roosevelt dime in use today, the silver three-cent piece (sometimes called a trime) ranks as the smallest U.S. coin. In its initial incarnation (Variety 1, sometimes called Type I), the metallic composition was, as noted above, 75% silver and 25% copper—an alloy known as high-grade billon—and there were no lines bordering the six-pointed star on the obverse.

In 1851, the government lowered (!) the price of postal rates by 40%—from five cents to three cents—for a 1/2-ounce prepaid letter. The large copper cents and half cents current at the time were not popular with the public, so a new three-cent coin was a logical solution.

Lesson 25: Add interest to your collection by including some mintmarked coins. The 1851-O is a perfect example and a wonderful coin to own. It was made at the storied New Orleans Mint and was produced in the first year of issuance of the silver three-cent piece. Its mintage was modest (720,000 pieces), and it is the only mintmarked coin in the 23-year lifespan of the silver trime. I bought a PCGS MS-65 1851-O from Legend Numismatics in late 2000 for $1,975 and sold it four-and-a-half years later for $2,800, a gain of 44%. The sad thing is that I sold it to "upgrade" to this MS-66 example of a much more common date. As you can see, I didn't do very well the second time around.

Financials: Silver trime, Variety 1, 1851

Cost	Sale Price	Gain/Loss	Holding Period
$1,610	$1,380	-14%	2.5 years

THREE-CENT PIECE—SILVER TRIME, VARIETY 2 (1854–1858)

Lot 1026.
1854. MS-64.
PCGS #003670.

Auction description: Frosty and lustrous with rich and varied golden hues on both sides. A nicely struck example of Type II silver three-cent coinage.

From the Waccabuc Collection. Earlier from Kingswood Galleries' June 2003 Sale, Lot 107.

The Variety 2 silver three-cent piece, minted from 1854 through 1858, differs from its predecessor in several ways. It weighs less (0.75 grams vs. 0.80 grams). It is made of the standard silver alloy (90% silver and 10% copper) rather than the high-grade billon used for the preceding type. There are three lines bordering the six-pointed star on the obverse. And, some superfluous decorations (an olive sprig and a bundle of three arrows) were added to clutter up the tiny fields on the reverse.

This is a coin I bought on impulse to fill an empty hole in my type set. I wanted it because it was the first year of issue for the Variety 2 trime, and at the time I was trying to complete my set with first-year-of-issue coins. I bought it based mostly on a written description in an auction catalog—I certainly hadn't seen the coin in person, and I don't think there was much of a photo in the catalog or on the Internet.

The auction house—Kingswood Galleries—was a division of Bowers and Merena. It conducted mail-bid and Internet auctions, without the overhead of fancy color catalogs or live bidding sessions. Kingswood exists today only as part of numismatic lore. The Stack's cataloger did his best to put lipstick on this pig, but the truth is the coin was dull, mottled, not particularly attractive, and unexceptional in every way. For the avoidance of doubt: this purchase was a complete mistake.

Lesson 26: Impulse bids are not your friend. Do your homework, make sure you know what you want to buy, and wait for the right piece before spending your money. Except for a few great rarities, most dates and mintmarks of all denominations appear at auctions or in dealers' inventories with some regularity.

Financials: Silver trime, Variety 2, 1854

Cost	Sale Price	Gain/Loss	Holding Period
$1,859	$1,035	-44%	4.5 years

THREE-CENT PIECE—SILVER TRIME, VARIETY 3 (1859–1873)

Lot 1027.

1859. MS-65.

PCGS #003677.

Auction description: A lustrous, richly toned Gem from the first year of Type III coinage in the silver three-cent series. Deep gold, electric blue, and pale slate iridescence grace both sides of this lustrous Gem.

From the Waccabuc Collection. Earlier from Heritage's Long Beach Sale, February 2003, Lot 5529.

In 1859 the design of the silver three-cent piece was changed yet again. The Variety 3 version has two lines, rather than three, bordering the six-pointed star on the reverse, narrower lettering (characteristic of Anthony Paquet, who assisted the designer, James B. Longacre), and tiny numerals in the date.

From 1863 through the end of the series in 1873, mintage levels were small, never exceeding 25,000 in any year, and not even reaching 10,000 in eight of these eleven years. Further, 74,000 trimes were melted by the Mint after the denomination was abolished on February 13, 1873. The result is that circulation strikes from 1863 onward are all very scarce.

Lesson 27: Be very cautious when buying darkly toned coins—their appeal to other collectors may be quite limited when it comes time to sell. My 1859 trime was actually quite attractive when viewed under a very bright light, but under normal lighting, it was just plain dark. The Stack's description gives some hints that should serve as red flags: "richly toned" and "deep gold." These attributes aren't always bad, but be sure to take a close look at the coin to be sure you like it. If you come across a coin described as having ebony or charcoal toning, you'd be well advised to move on to something else.

Financials: Silver trime, Variety 3, 1859

Cost	Sale Price	Gain/Loss	Holding Period
$1,035	$748	-28%	4.8 years

Nickels

Two golfing buddies who had not played together for some time met on the course one day for a round of golf. Bob asked his friend, "Hey, Mel, how's your game going?" Mel replied, "My game is so bad right now I had to have my ball retriever re-gripped."

O ne of the many joys of coin collecting is that you can be away from the hobby for weeks, months, or even years and still come back to it without the frustrations faced by golfers who don't practice and play regularly. A number of today's serious numismatists collected Buffalo or Jefferson nickels when they were young by searching through coins found in circulation. They may have put those early collections aside in their college and early working years, but later returned to numismatics with enthusiasm and a heightened appreciation for history, artistic merit, rarity, and quality. *Frustration*, unlike in golf, is not a word often associated with coin collecting.

Five-cent pieces have been a feature of American coins since 1792. For the first seven decades of their issuance, they were made of silver and were called *half dimes* (or, in the earliest days, *half dismes*). After the Civil War, five-cent pieces made of a nickel alloy were introduced, and they have been a familiar sight in change ever since. In numismatics it is traditional, in reference books and auction catalogs, to consider the base-metal nickels first before moving on to the precious-metal half dimes, even though the date sequence of mintage would suggest otherwise. Following that practice, the four major designs of nickels made since 1866 (Shield, Liberty Head, Buffalo, and Jefferson) are discussed in this chapter, while the older half dimes are addressed in chapter 8.

NICKEL FIVE-CENT PIECE—SHIELD, RAYS BETWEEN STARS (1866–1867)

Lot 1028.
1866, Rays. Proof-66.
PCGS #003817.

Auction description: Gem Proof 1866 Shield Nickel. A sparkling cameo Gem from the first year of the denomination in copper-nickel; the cameo contrast is not noted on the PCGS holder. Sparkling mirror fields and frosted motifs display pale rose, champagne, and faint blue iridescence. Centering dot on both sides, reverse rays point to C, N, S in CENTS on reverse. From a Proof production of the date of somewhat more than 200 pieces, the present Gem survivor is boldly struck. No post-striking marks are present and we note some reverse planchet flaws—tiny and as struck. An exceptional Gem, a coin exceeded in quality in the eyes of PCGS by just a solitary specimen. PCGS Population: 44; 1 finer within the designation (Proof-67).

From the Waccabuc Collection. Acquired from Superior, July 2000.

The shield design is "the ugliest of all known coins." At least that was the opinion of some critics when this coin made its appearance just after the end of the Civil War. It served a good purpose (like the three-cent nickel coin, to replace the hated five-cent paper currency), but was difficult to strike because of the hardness of the metal. Nevertheless, the "nickel" (actually 75 percent copper and 25 percent nickel) was soon well-accepted by the public and continues to be minted today in the same metallic composition.

This particular variety, with 13 rays positioned between the 13 stars on the reverse, proved to be particularly hard to strike and was abandoned early in 1867. Circulation strikes of 1866 (14.7 million minted) and 1867 (2.0 million) are easy enough to find in all conditions, though die cracks are very common on these. Proofs of 1866 (with a mintage of probably more than 200 and possibly as many as 600) are somewhat scarce and expensive. Proofs of 1867, of which only an estimated 55 to 80 were produced, are genuinely rare.

Lesson 28: As noted by the Stack's cataloger, the cameo contrast on my 1866 Rays nickel was not noted on the PCGS holder. An interesting thing to keep your eyes open for is a coin that has such contrast but is not designated as "Cameo" on the coin holder. The grading services did not recognize cameo appearance as a distinct attribute until recent years and have not been entirely consistent in their application of this terminology across all denominations. Finding an unattributed cameo and getting it re-holdered with its correct designation is a satisfying way of upgrading your collection.

Financials: Nickel five-cent piece, Shield, Rays Between Stars, 1866

Cost	Sale Price	Gain/Loss	Holding Period
$4,900	$6,900	+41%	7.3 years

NICKEL FIVE-CENT PIECE—SHIELD, WITHOUT RAYS (1867–1883)

Lot 1029.
1869, Doubled Die Obverse. MS-66.
PCGS #003796.

Auction description: Impressive Gem 1869 Shield Nickel. Tied for Finest Graded by PCGS. Doubled Die Obverse Variety. A satiny pale golden Gem with intense cartwheel luster and some deeper toning. The strike is incredible for the design type, with bold, crisp features in even the finest areas of detail. Deservedly at the top of the PCGS Population Report for the date. PCGS Population: 10; none finer. The doubled-die obverse feature is not noted on the PCGS label.

FS5¢-004; Fletcher-413 for similar variety. Here the obverse doubling is much stronger than illustrated in the Fletcher or Fivaz-Stanton references; this may simply be a very early die state, though here the doubling at the annulet, surrounding leaves, cross, and IN GOD WE TRUST is bold and unmistakable.

From the Waccabuc Collection. Earlier from ANR's sale of the Worthington Collection, May 2005, Lot 66.

As noted above, the rays between the stars on the reverse of the 1866–1867 Shield nickel contributed to the striking difficulties faced by the Mint. After producing two million of the original version in 1867, the Mint prepared new dies without the rays, and this design was continued through 1883.

Almost 29 million Without Rays nickels were issued in both 1867 and 1868, and these are the dates most commonly found in type sets. For six years, the Without Rays nickel in my collection was a perfectly nice 1867 in PCGS MS-65. I sold it in 2007 for about the same price I bought it for (a little more than $800). Its place in the Waccabuc Collection was taken by the much more interesting 1869 doubled die. As noted by the Stack's cataloger, the doubling is quite pronounced—though not as evident as seen on the more famous 1955 doubled-die cent. The excellent strike also made this a special coin in the context of this series.

Lesson 29: Although there's nothing wrong, per se, with including the obvious common dates in your type-set collection, you will probably get more enjoyment out of waiting to find something a bit unusual. And while you may well have to pay more for a piece that is, in some way, out of the ordinary, you are far more likely to realize a gain when the time comes to sell it. I was pleased with the price I got on selling this coin, and I suspect the new owner will also do well if he holds it for a few years or more.

Financials: Nickel five-cent piece, Shield, Without Rays, 1869, DDO

Cost	Sale Price	Gain/Loss	Holding Period
$3,220	$4,140	+29%	2.5 years

NICKEL FIVE-CENT PIECE—LIBERTY HEAD, WITHOUT CENTS (1883)

Lot 1030.
1883, No CENTS. Proof-66 CAM.
PCGS #083878.

With the exception of a few Morgan silver dollars, the 1883 Without CENTS Liberty Head nickel is the most common 19th-century coin in Mint State condition. Almost 12,000 Uncirculated examples have been encapsulated by the two leading grading services. On the surface, this seems curious, as the mintage of about 5.5 million was lower than all but four other date-mintmark varieties in the 30-year regular-issue span of this series (1883 to 1912).

The reason all these pristine coins exist today is that they were extensively hoarded at the time of issue, on the erroneous assumption that the Treasury Department was about to recall the 1883 nickels because they lacked the word CENTS and were being gold-plated and exchanged as $5 coins rather than five-cent coins. The recall never happened, and today it is extremely easy to find a nice Without CENTS nickel for a type set.

Shortly after the first release of the Without CENTS nickels, some unscrupulous swindlers figured out that by gold-plating the coins (and sometimes adding reeding—the grooved edges seen on most precious-metal coins), these nickels could be passed off as $5 gold pieces. The difference in diameters was minor (21.2 mm for the nickels vs. 21.6 mm for genuine half eagles), and the ruse was both effective and profitable. The design was changed promptly, but thousands of so-called racketeer nickels were made. I had a circulated example, with the gold plating partially worn off but without reeding, in my collection in the 1960s.

Lesson 30: Grading opinions are just that—opinions. *Caveat emptor.* The Stack's description of my Proof 1883 Without CENTS nickel made me smile twice. One cause was the nice compliment about my "exceptional eye" for type coins. The other reason has to do with the provenance of this coin. As noted, it is the Eliasberg specimen, which was sold as lot 771 in Bowers and Merena's May 1996 auction. (By the way, the next two lots in that auction were made up of 80 [!] Mint State examples of the Without CENTS nickel.) The grade opinion given in that catalog for lot 771 was Proof-67, and some unhappy bidder paid a whopping $6,380 to become the owner. I bought the coin four years later, in February 2000, at a Superior auction. By then the coin was housed in a plastic holder, with a grading opinion from PCGS of Proof-66 CAM. The price was $2,243. At this level, it became a reasonable, if unspectacular, investment.

Financials: Nickel five-cent piece, Liberty Head, Without CENTS, 1883

Cost	Sale Price	Gain/Loss	Holding Period
$2,243	$2,990	+33%	7.8 years

NICKEL FIVE-CENT PIECE—LIBERTY HEAD, WITH CENTS (1883–1912)

Lot 1031.
1900. Proof-66.
PCGS #003898.

As noted earlier, the With CENTS Liberty Head nickel was minted in large quantities for 30 years through 1912. The low-mintage dates of 1885 and especially (in my view) 1912-S are worthwhile choices for a type set. The clandestine issue of 1913, of which only five examples exist, would make your type set truly special, but you'll need to bid well into seven figures to secure this great rarity the next time one comes up for auction . . . someone paid more than $3.7 million for the Farouk–"Hawaii 5-0" example in January 2010. I chose to include a coin dated 1900 in my collection because, like several other century-spanning series, this coin can be used in both the PCGS complete type set and the 20th-century type set.

Lesson 31: There's nothing wrong with having a collection within a collection. My "complete" type set incorporated a partial date set of 1900-dated coins, including a 1900 Indian Head cent, a 1900 Liberty Head nickel, a 1900-O Barber quarter, a 1900-O Morgan dollar, and a 1900 eagle. I may have been the only person who noticed, but this is all part of the joy of collecting.

Financials: Nickel five-cent piece, Liberty Head, With CENTS, 1900

Cost	Sale Price	Gain/Loss	Holding Period
$633	$863	+36%	3.8 years

NICKEL FIVE-CENT PIECE—BUFFALO, FIVE CENTS ON RAISED GROUND (1913)

Lot 1032.
1913. MS-67.
PCGS #003915.

Auction description: An exquisite Gem with intense cartwheel luster, a satiny champagne glow, a bold strike, and truly extraordinary eye appeal. Matte-like in appearance and of Gem quality.

From the Waccabuc Collection. Earlier from Heritage's Long Beach Sale, February 2003, Lot 5851.

The Buffalo (or Indian Head) nickel was designed by James Earle Fraser and was produced from 1913 through 1938. The design was highly acclaimed, and this series remains popular and is widely collected today.

The first type, imaginatively called Variety 1, had an area of raised ground for the bison to stand on. As kids, my friends and I used to imagine that Black Diamond, the Central Park Zoo bison after which the bison on the nickel was modeled, had stamped down the mound, creating the "flat ground" Variety 2. The real story is less fantastic but makes more sense. Soon after the Variety 1 nickels were issued, Mint officials suspected, correctly as it turned out, that the denomination FIVE CENTS appearing on the mound would wear down too quickly, so they flattened the mound and placed the denomination immediately below.

As with most other first-year-of-issue coins, many Variety 1 (and Variety 2) nickels were saved. PCGS and NGC have together graded almost 700 1913 Variety 1 nickels as MS-67. I clearly paid too much for mine, but at least I made the under-bidder happy by beating him with my even-sillier bid.

Lesson 32: One major drawback of auctions is that you can become caught up in the spirit of bidding and make ill-advised purchases. This is an entirely avoidable mistake when you're trying to acquire a "common" rare coin such as the 1913 Variety 1 Buffalo nickel. I would have been far better off buying a different example of this coin from a reputable dealer or waiting for another example to appear at auction.

Financials: Nickel five-cent piece, Buffalo, FIVE CENTS on Raised Ground, 1913

Cost	Sale Price	Gain/Loss	Holding Period
$1,610	$978	-39%	4.8 years

NICKEL FIVE-CENT PIECE—BUFFALO, FIVE CENTS IN RECESS (1913–1938)

Lot 1033.

1937-S. MS-67.

PCGS #003983.

Auction description: Tied for finest certified by PCGS. A satiny Gem with splendid eye appeal, intense cartwheel luster, and faint golden toning highlights. Nicely struck for the date, with essentially full design details on both sides. PCGS Population: 79; none finer.

From the Waccabuc Collection. Earlier from Heritage's F.U.N. Convention Sale, January 2007, Lot 2374.

The Variety 2 Buffalo nickel, minted from mid-1913 through 1938, is readily available in grades up through MS-66, and a few thousand pieces are available in MS-67 or better. While there are a number of challenges to completing a date-and-mintmark set, particularly if you are seeking high-grade examples with strong strikes, finding a single example for a type set is a trivial exercise. The most affordable high-grade coins are those minted in the 1930s. You can add some pizzazz to your set by obtaining a colorfully toned Proof or the 1918-D with the 8 engraved over a 7 (created when the Mint, as a wartime economy measure, re-used a 1917 die after the year ended), or the 1937-D three-legged variety (created when an over-enthusiastic Mint employee re-ground a working die to remove clash marks and ended up removing the bison's left foreleg). I didn't follow this advice but probably should have.

Lesson 33: Having some "pop top" coins (i.e., the highest-rated coins in a grading service's population report) in your collection is usually a good thing. However, when there are 78 other "pop top" coins just as nice as the one you have (as was the case with my 1937-S Buffalo nickel), then the likelihood that you will see price appreciation over time is greatly diminished.

Financials: Nickel five-cent piece, Buffalo, FIVE CENTS in Recess, 1937-S

Cost	Sale Price	Gain/Loss	Holding Period
$1,380	$1,150	-17%	0.8 years

NICKEL FIVE-CENT PIECE—JEFFERSON (1938–PRESENT)

Lot 1034.
1938-S, MS-66; 1942-S, MS-66; 1964, Proof-69 DCAM.

Auction description: Trio of PCGS-certified Jefferson nickels: * 1938-S MS-66. Faint lilac and gold iridescence on highly lustrous surfaces * 1942-S MS-66. Intensely brilliant cart-wheel luster, heavy die breaks on both sides * 1964 Proof-69 DCAM. Heavily frosted motifs and richly mirrored fields. (Total: 3 pieces)
From the Waccabuc Collection.

According to Flip Wilson, "The devil made me do it." In my case, it was PCGS's set registry that made me buy these three common Jefferson nickels. These were the only Waccabuc Collection coins that did not sell in the November 2007 auction. I still own them as of this writing, and I will accept the first offer of $200 or more that comes my way, or you can host me for a round of golf at your expensive private club.

Although most Jefferson nickels are very common, there are a number of date-and-mintmark combinations that are notorious for weakly struck details. Those that are well struck, in the opinion of the major grading services, are awarded the designation of FS, which stands for Full Steps. This means that the stairs on the depiction of Monticello on the reverse are well defined. (NGC goes further and distinguishes between five full steps and six full steps.)

Collectors of "Full Steps" nickels will pay up for rare examples. The extremely common 1962 Jefferson nickel is a case in point. Despite a mintage of almost 100 million pieces, there's only one coin (currently) graded PCGS MS-67+ FS. Someone paid $21,150 for this coin at an August 2013 auction.

Lesson 34: If you're building a collection of rare coins, try to avoid the temptation of buying the common, late-date issues. If you feel you can leave these out of your collection entirely, then that's probably best. If you demand completeness, then put off these purchases until you've tracked down the hard stuff first. No one looking at my nice collection of early American coins ever spent more than a moment glancing at my Jefferson nickels, except for the one featured next.

Financials: Nickel five-cent piece, Jefferson, 1938-S, 1942-S, 1964

Cost	Sale Price	Gain/Loss	Holding Period
$200	Did not sell	n/a	n/a

FIVE-CENT PIECE—JEFFERSON, WARTIME SILVER ALLOY (1942–1945)

Lot 1035.
1943-P. MS-67 FS.
PCGS #084018.

Auction description: Spectacular rainbow toning in deep crimson, electric blue, fiery gold, and rich peach engages both sides of this incredibly lustrous Gem Jefferson "nickel" from the war years. If you appreciate vividly toned 20th-century coins, you owe it to yourself to examine this coin carefully then place a forceful bid. PCGS Population: 31; 1 finer within the designation (MS-68 FS).

From the Waccabuc Collection. Acquired from Heritage, January 2006.

The Jefferson nickel, designed by Felix Schlag, has been in production since 1938. Except for the war years, the metallic composition has been 75% copper and 25% nickel. From October 1942 through the end of 1945, to free up nickel for use in the war effort, the composition was changed to 56% copper, 35% silver, and 9% manganese. These metals oxidize at different rates and turn different colors, and very occasionally the results are truly spectacular. By the way, I don't think there's any way of knowing whether the toning on this coin occurred naturally or was induced by artificial methods. Whatever the case, when I saw it, I wanted to own it, and I would bid strongly if something like it appeared at auction in the future. The right price for this coin without the toning is about $500.

Lesson 35: Include at least one stunningly toned coin in your collection. Collecting coins with "rainbow toning" is a sub-specialty. In general, silver coins come with the liveliest toning, though you will sometimes see copper Proofs with glorious deep blue and pink hues. The early silver commemoratives—from 1892 through 1954—are sometimes collected only with vivid toning, often caused by the original Mint packaging. Morgan dollars that were stored in bank vaults for decades in canvas bags also sometimes acquired brilliant colors on the side that came in contact with the canvas.

Financials: Nickel five-cent piece, Jefferson, Wartime Silver Alloy, 1943-P

Cost	Sale Price	Gain/Loss	Holding Period
$3,565	$3,220	-10%	1.8 years

Half Dimes

A husband and wife were out golfing together one day when they came upon a tough par-4 hole. The husband hooked his drive deep into the woods and proclaimed that he would have to chip out.

Then the wife said, "Maybe not, dear! Do you see that barn over there? If I open the doors on both sides, I do believe you could hit it right through and reach the green."

So the husband agreed to give it a try, but when he hit the ball it went straight through the first set of doors of the barn, hit a crossbeam, ricocheted back and hit his wife square in the head, killing her stone dead.

Well, about a year later the man was golfing with a friend. He found himself on the same hole, with the same results: a hook deep into the woods. He was all set to chip out when his friend ran up to him and said, "Wait! Do you see that barn over there? If I open the doors on both sides, I think you can still reach the green."

"No way," replied the man, "I tried that last year and got a 7."

A recurring theme in golf and in numismatics is to learn from your mistakes and those made by others. In golf, you now know not to try to hit a ball through a barn. With half dimes, you need to recognize that, with the exception of a few great rarities (most notably the unique 1870-S), half dimes have never captured the imagination of investment professionals, probably in part because of their unimpressive size. Therefore, prices are generally modest, on a relative scale, and stable over long periods of time. Genuinely scarce coins are available and within reach for many collectors, but because half dimes are not as widely collected as some other series, you should not count on great price appreciation.

Half dimes were made from 1792 through 1873. The iconic and elusive 1792 issue is considered by many to be the first regular-issue coin made by the United States. The Flowing Hair design followed, but as quoted by Walter Breen, a contemporary letter-writer may have reflected public opinion when he wrote that the design had "an unmeaning fool's head on one side, and something that resembles a turkey cock on the other. Oh, shame, shame, shame!" The Draped Bust design (with small and then large eagles) was used from 1796 through 1805, after which there was a long hiatus until 1829 when the Capped Bust design was adopted. Finally, the Liberty Seated design, with several varieties over the years, was employed from 1837 through 1873. These are all discussed in more detail below.

HALF DIME—FLOWING HAIR (1794–1795)

Lot 1036.
1794. MS-63.
LM-4, V-4. Rarity-4. PCGS #004250.

Auction description: Choice Uncirculated 1794 Half Dime. First Flowing Hair Issue. Lustrous golden gray with deepening gold on both sides, especially toward the respective rims. Nicely struck from heavily clashed dies with evidence of such heaviest on the obverse. Double obverse centering dot with curious raised circle around, reverse centering dot on eagle's sinister wing. Choice for the grade with pleasing surfaces and a well-cherished place in numismatics. The present piece would make a superb cornerstone in your U.S. type set.

From the Waccabuc Collection. Earlier from ANR's sale of the Frog Run Farm Collection, November 2004, Lot 470.

Under the Authorizing Act of April 2, 1792, 1,500 (or possibly 2,000) silver half dismes were produced in 1792. The word *disme*, an early spelling of *dime*, was pronounced either "deem" (my preference) or "dime," depending on whom you ask. All agree it is not pronounced "diz-may" or "diz-mee." The designer was probably either William Russell Birch or Robert Birch. The coins were minted in Philadelphia, but not at the Mint, which had yet to be built. Although most of the 200 to 300 surviving specimens show extensive evidence of circulation, the coins were not released through normal commercial channels but rather were delivered by Thomas Jefferson to George Washington, who is reported to have given them out as souvenirs.

The *Red Book* lists this coin in its section on Contract Issues and Patterns, but PCGS's set registry includes the 1792 half disme as part of the regular federal series. The finest known example (the Floyd Starr specimen) sold for more than $1.3 million in a Heritage auction in April 2006. If you can afford one, you should definitely add this storied coin to your collection. I bid on several well-circulated examples over the years but was always unsuccessful. More than two years after I sold the Waccabuc Collection, I finally acquired a 1792 half disme[8]. It resides comfortably somewhere between my small collections of colonial coins and patterns.

Half dimes of the Flowing Hair type, the first half dimes that were definitively issued by the U.S. Mint, were designed by Robert Scot and produced with only two dates, 1794 and 1795. (The old-style spelling *disme* did not survive beyond 1792.) Although the dies for 1794 were manufactured in that year, all of the 1794 and 1795 half dimes were struck in 1795. Today, examples of both years are quite elusive, with the 1794 being somewhat scarcer. The vast majority of existing pieces are quite worn, typically Very Good to Very Fine or so.

The obverse of my 1794 half dime is interesting to study under magnification. At the center, immediately below Miss Liberty's earlobe, are two tiny centering dots, together with some raised scribe lines, used by the engraver to position the separately added design elements (the stars, letters, and date). These dots and scribe lines give Miss Liberty the appearance of wearing a fancy earring. The field, particularly the left obverse, shows evidence of clash marks, which are also seen on the reverse. Several of the stars are double punched, some dramatically so. The cataloger for American Numismatic Rarities, from whose November 2004 auction I obtained this piece, opined, "Apparently the engraver had an unsteady hand. Perhaps he had too much rum, a drink that was frequently brought into the mint and mentioned in correspondence."

Lesson 36: Buy a 1792 half disme if you can possibly afford one. It is a wonderful coin to read about, study, and own, and its immense popularity means that it will likely retain its value over time. Similarly, though not to the same extent, the 1794 half dime is a worthwhile artifact of the early days of the U.S. Mint and deserves a place in any collection of rare U.S. coins. You will have opportunities—a few examples of both dates appear in auctions each year. When you spot a nice one, stretch for it.

Financials: Half dime, Flowing Hair, 1794

Cost	Sale Price	Gain/Loss	Holding Period
$25,300	$27,600	+9%	3.0 years

HALF DIME—DRAPED BUST, SMALL EAGLE REVERSE (1796–1797)

Lot 1037.
1796. EF-45.
LM-1, V-1. Rarity-3. PCGS #004254.

Auction description: Choice EF 1796 Half Dime. Bright centers yield to deep gold, crimson, and violet toning at the rims. A few scattered marks present, the most obvious of these in the obverse field before Liberty's portrait. We note the strike is bold and just a brief stint in circulation has diminished some of the highest details. From the first year of the Draped Bust, Small Eagle coinage in the denomination.

From the Waccabuc Collection. Earlier from Heritage's A.N.A. Convention Sale, July 2005, Lot 5754.

Like the preceding Flowing Hair design, the Draped Bust, Small Eagle half dime was produced with only two dates to choose between—in this case, 1796 and 1797. Both are scarce, with the 1796 being slightly more so. Despite the small mintages in these two years, there are several interesting varieties to choose among. For the 1796, you have an overdate (1796, 6 Over 5) and the curious LIKERTY variety—not a misspelling, but just a broken B that resembles a K. For the 1797, there were first 15 stars on the obverse, then 16 (to honor the recently admitted state of Tennessee), and finally 13 when someone figured out that there would soon be no room on our coins for anything except stars as more states joined the Union.

The cataloger describes the central areas of this coin as "bright." What he did not say, however, was that the bright centers were original. In my opinion, this coin was probably, at one time, very dark. Someone almost certainly dipped it at some point to brighten its appearance. Within reason, the major grading services will accept this type of enhancement.

 Lesson 37: This design, along with several others in the U.S. series, was produced for only a short period and in limited quantities. Keep your eyes open for these scarce designs and be ready to pounce when you find one with nice eye appeal. You'll enjoy owning it and will likely do well financially: rarity doesn't go out of style.

Financials: Half dime, Draped Bust, Small Eagle, 1796

Cost	Sale Price	Gain/Loss	Holding Period
$6,325	$8,740	+38%	2.3 years

HALF DIME—DRAPED BUST, HERALDIC EAGLE REVERSE (1800–1805)

Lot 1038.
1800, LIBEKTY. MS-62.
LM-3, V-2. Rarity-4. PCGS #004265.

Auction description: Uncirculated 1800 Half Dime. LIBEKTY Variety. Among 10 Finest Certified by PCGS. Lustrous deep golden gray surfaces display a wealth of rose, electric blue, and lilac highlights. The strike is crisp and clear, with essentially no serious weakness at any particular point. The popular variety with a broken R in LIBERTY, lending the appearance of a K instead, hence its famous sobriquet. An altogether pleasing example of the date that will see strong bidding activity. PCGS Population: 2; 8 finer within the designated variety (MS-66 finest).

From the Waccabuc Collection. Acquired from Legend Numismatics, September 2004.

The Draped Bust, Large (or Heraldic) Eagle half dime, designed by Robert Scot, was minted in five years from 1800 through 1805, with a break in production in 1804. Fewer than 125,000 coins of this design were produced, so all dates are scarce today. In 1802, mintage was a puny 3,060 pieces, making this date a classic rarity. Only about 15 examples reside in major grading-service holders, and none of these grade better than AU-50. On the rare occasions when one comes up for auction, you should not be surprised to see a six-figure price. Counterfeit examples of the 1802 half dime exist, and both the Smithsonian and the American Numismatic Association have one of these in their institutional collections. Of the other four dates, the 1800 is clearly the best struck and the most readily available, while the remaining three dates are all about equally scarce.

In September 2004 I spotted an Uncirculated 1800 half dime in the online inventory of Legend Numismatics. It was listed as "on hold," but I knew from prior experience that the coin might still be available. I called Laura Sperber. She told me that her client had just rejected the coin, apparently because he "didn't appreciate its original look." While it is true that the coin did not possess "blast white" surfaces, to my eye it looked just the way a two-century-old coin should look. I snapped it up and smiled contentedly when it sold for a big premium just over three years later.

Lesson 38: Bright and "shiny" silver coins from the early years of the 19th century shouldn't exist; those that do have almost certainly been cleaned. If the cleaning is too obvious, the grading services will note that fact and refuse to assign a grade. Stick to coins with original toning that don't look like they've been tampered with. One caveat, however: you'll sometimes see dealers and catalogers describe a very dark coin as having an "original" appearance. While this may be true, you should avoid buying such coins. They're usually not attractive to look at, the toning will often obscure other problems like hairlines or scratches, and they are harder to sell. Remember: eye appeal never goes out of style.

Financials: Half dime, Draped Bust, Heraldic Eagle, 1800, LIBEKTY

Cost	Sale Price	Gain/Loss	Holding Period
$10,000	$18,400	+84%	3.2 years

HALF DIME—CAPPED BUST (1829–1837)

Lot 1039.
1831. MS-66.
LM-6, V-1. Rarity-1. PCGS #004278.

Auction description: Gem Mint State 1831 Half Dime. An exceptional gem example of the date, richly toned in deep lilac and gray with varied blue highlights. Frosty and lustrous as well, with a bold strike that shows all of the tiniest design elements to their finest effect. An exceptional Capped Bust half dime, a coin carefully hand-selected to meet the stringent requirements of our consignor, a collector who understands that grades are far more than just surface quality—eye appeal, strike, and many other aspects beyond just the assigned grade are needed for a coin to be a true Gem.

From the Waccabuc Collection. Earlier from Heritage's Dallas Sale, December 2005, Lot 372.

I can't remember if I thanked Stack's for writing this particular coin description. If not, let me do so now: Thank you, Stack's. It's always nice to receive a compliment. Whether it helped to sell this coin, no one will ever know. But there's no disputing that this was an attractive and high-quality coin.

When the Draped Bust half dime was discontinued after 1805, the denomination was not produced by the U.S. Mint for the next 24 years. I've never read a logical explanation for this. Eventually, perhaps, people just got fed up with carrying around large quantities of heavy one-cent coins to make change or pay for items costing less than a dime, and so the half dime was reintroduced in 1829. It was minted in every year thereafter through 1873, when the denomination was discontinued forever. (Recall that production of the five-cent nickel commenced in 1866, so for eight years there were two different five-cent coins in circulation.)

John Reich, the skilled "Second Engraver" (working under Chief Engraver Robert Scot), was employed by the U.S. Mint for a decade beginning in 1807. During that period he redesigned most of the coins then in circulation, beginning with the half dollar and the half eagle. It is often speculated that his Capped Bust and Capped Head designs were based on modeling he did of his "fat German mistress," but this story is almost certainly apocryphal.

In 1829, a dozen years after Reich left the Mint, Chief Engraver William Kneass (Robert Scot's successor) adapted Reich's Capped Bust design for the new half dime. This design was produced at the Philadelphia Mint for nine years. Mintages were sizeable in each year, and a complete date set in Uncirculated condition is achievable at a reasonable cost, though certain varieties are scarce or rare.

Lesson 39: Unlike earlier designs of this denomination, Capped Bust half dimes usually come well struck, so this is not a useful differentiating factor when deciding to buy one of these coins. Instead, you should hold out for one that has excellent eye appeal at whatever grade level you are seeking. There are enough available that you can wait for one that meets your standards.

Financials: Half dime, Capped Bust, 1831

Cost	Sale Price	Gain/Loss	Holding Period
$4,300	$5,750	+34%	1.9 years

HALF DIME—LIBERTY SEATED, NO STARS ON OBVERSE (1837–1838)

Lot 1040.
1837, No Stars, Large Date. MS-65.
PCGS #004311.

Auction description: Gem Uncirculated 1837 No Stars Half Dime. Large Date, Triple-Punched. A frosty deep golden gray specimen with expansive underlying luster that supports a wealth of varied slate, peach, and golden highlights. Sharply struck in all places. Triple-punched date numerals; this die was also used to prepare the rare Proofs of the date. An exciting Gem from the first year of Christian Gobrecht's Liberty Seated design motif issued for general circulation.

From the Waccabuc Collection. Earlier from Teletrade's August 1999 Sale, Lot 1191.

The No Stars on Obverse Liberty Seated half dime was minted in only two years—1837 (in Philadelphia) and 1838 (in New Orleans). With only 70,000 of the 1838-O having been minted, and with most of these having gone right into circulation, most type collectors opt for an example dated 1837. A reasonable number of these from the original mintage of more than 1.4 million pieces were saved as first-year-of-issue curiosities, and therefore nice examples are regularly available at auctions; the two leading grading services have certified more than 300 pieces at grades of MS-65 or better. Most are well struck.

The No Stars half dimes represent a short "sub-series" within the grander series of Liberty Seated half dimes, which were minted through 1873. They are also, to my eye, the most attractive. In later years, as detailed below, obverse stars were punched into the periphery, then drapery was added to Liberty's elbow, then arrowheads were added at the date (for three years), and finally the stars were replaced with UNITED STATES OF AMERICA, which had appeared on the reverse in earlier years. All these improvements just served to clutter the original elegant design.

The Large Date and Small Date varieties of the 1837 half dime are virtually indistinguishably different in size. The real difference lies in the shape of the top of the 1 in the date. Those called Large Date have a curled (or curved) top, while the much scarcer Small Date coins have a flat top. Walter Breen and others have argued that the Large Date and Small Date monikers are misleading and have urged that they be dropped, but they live on.

Lesson 40: As noted, the 1837 No Stars half dime is relatively common, including in high grades. Therefore, you should not expect to achieve much financial appreciation, even over a period of years. (My 5.7% annual compounded return over eight-plus years is a better-than-average result.) Your best choices are to take great care not to overpay for a nice example of the 1837 if you need one for a type collection or to spend more for a reasonable example of the more exotic and far rarer 1838-O.

Financials: Half dime, Liberty Seated, No Stars on Obverse, 1837, Large Date

Cost	Sale Price	Gain/Loss	Holding Period
$2,315	$3,680	+59%	8.3 years

HALF DIME—LIBERTY SEATED, STARS ON OBVERSE, NO DRAPERY (1838–1840)

Lot 1041.
1838, Stars on Obverse, No Drapery. MS-66.
PCGS #004317.

Auction description: Gorgeous Gem Uncirculated 1838 Half Dime. No Drapery. An exceptional example of the date and grade combination, a highly lustrous Gem with a rich array of varied golden hues. The fields are faintly prooflike and the strike is bold, making for a strong, exciting contrast. Fewer than a half dozen examples of this date have been certified finer than the presently offered Gem, making this sharply struck beauty all the more enticing. PCGS Population: 18; 5 finer within the designation (MS-68 finest).

From the Waccabuc Collection. Acquired from Larry Whitlow, September 2002.

To begin the cluttering of the design of this tiny coin, 13 stars were added to the obverse of the Liberty Seated half dime in 1838, remaining there through 1859. For only three years, however, through 1840, did Miss Liberty appear without drapery hanging from her left (right-facing) elbow. This sub-type was minted in reasonably large quantities in all three years at Philadelphia and, in 1839 and 1840, at the New Orleans Mint. The coins dated 1840 from both mints are modestly scarcer.

I bought this coin from Larry Whitlow, Ltd., of Oakbrook Terrace, Illinois. I always enjoyed chatting with one or another of the small staff when I called to ask about an item I'd seen on their Web site. The coins were always nice, the service was excellent, and the people were knowledgeable. I didn't make much money on this particular purchase, but I still have good memories of the overall experience.

Lesson 41: Remember to enjoy the process of building your collection. Smell the flowers along the way. You won't always make huge amounts of money, but that's not the only objective. If you're not enjoying yourself, move on to something else.

Financials: Half dime, Stars on Obverse, 1838, No Drapery

Cost	Sale Price	Gain/Loss	Holding Period
$2,900	$3,220	+11%	5.2 years

HALF DIME—LIBERTY SEATED, ARROWS AT DATE (1853–1855)

Lot 1042.
1853. MS-64.
PCGS #004356.

Auction description: A frosty, sparkling example of this ever-popular issue, a sharp half dime with a brisk array of orange, gold, and sky blue on both sides. Nicely struck.

From the Waccabuc Collection. Earlier from Kingswood Galleries' October 2002 sale, Lot 341.

With so much gold coming out of California in the late 1840s and early 1850s, the price of silver rose in comparison to the price of gold. By 1850, many silver coins disappeared from circulation. Some were hoarded, but many were melted and then exchanged for a higher dollar value of gold coins.

To solve this problem, the Mint reduced the weight and added small arrows to either side of the date on half dimes (and also dimes, quarters, and half dollars) beginning in 1853. The practice was continued on the half dimes through 1855. Coins of this type were produced in both Philadelphia and New Orleans in each of these three years.

Lesson 42: The total production of Arrows at Date half dimes was a bit greater than 25 million pieces. More than half of these were made in Philadelphia in 1853. This is a very common coin and not particularly exciting to own. I owned one and speak from experience. Its price performance over the years has been singularly unimpressive. Instead, you should try to find a well-struck 1855-O to represent this design. It's about 20 times as rare as the 1853—both in terms of the number minted and in the number entombed in grading-service holders. Yet its price is only two to four times that of the 1853 in choice to gem Mint State grades. I wish I'd followed my own advice.

Financials: Half dime, Liberty Seated, Arrows at Date, 1853

Cost	Sale Price	Gain/Loss	Holding Period
$518	$552	+7%	5.1 years

HALF DIME—LIBERTY SEATED, STARS ON OBVERSE, WITH DRAPERY (1840–1859)

Lot 1043.
1857. MS-66.
PCGS #004365.

Auction description: An exceptionally lustrous Gem with an incredible array of vibrant violet, sea green, and electric blue on both sides. Nicely struck from moderately clashed dies, though we note some weakness in the peripheral dentils as virtually always seen for the date. Just three examples of this popular half dime issue have been certified finer by PCGS. PCGS Population: 16; 3 within the designation (all MS-67).

From the Waccabuc Collection. Acquired from Larry Whitlow, January 2004.

The With Drapery half dimes were made from 1840 through 1859, except for the three years when the With Arrows type was produced (see preceding entry). The added drapery appears behind and to the right of Miss Liberty's left (right-facing) elbow. Less well known is that the designer, Robert Ball Hughes, made several other design changes, including adding some pounds to Liberty's figure, raising the neckline of her dress (some considered the earlier version immodest), and having her hold the shield in an upright position rather than tipped to the left. The coins from 1856 through 1859 are about 7% lighter than the early dates, but few collectors bother to collect both types as the designs are identical.

Most date-and-mintmark combinations can be obtained with little difficulty. The one major exception is the 1846, of which only 27,000 were produced. Roughly 100 examples of this date now reside in PCGS and NGC holders, almost all of them in circulated grades. These appear infrequently at auction and, when they do, are recognized by specialists as significant rarities.

Lesson 43: Liberty Seated half dimes are, in general, common, and very few collectors try to assemble a complete set by date and mintmark. With high supply and modest demand, prices are steady and reasonable. I "paid up" for a particularly nice-looking example, but in this case I was not rewarded with a profit because there are just too many decent coins out there and not enough collectors to drive up the price. This was a very nice coin but a lousy investment.

Financials: Half dime, Liberty Seated, With Drapery, 1857

Cost	Sale Price	Gain/Loss	Holding Period
$2,350	$1,725	-27%	3.8 years

HALF DIME—LIBERTY SEATED, LEGEND ON OBVERSE (1860–1873)

Lot 1044.
1860. MS-67.
PCGS #004377.

Auction description: An exceptionally lustrous Gem, frosty and sharply struck, with intense peach, rose, and fiery orange highlights on both sides. A splash of electric blue can be seen in the protected areas. Just two examples of the date have been certified finer than the present Gem by PCGS, a true testimony to the overall appeal of the presently offered beauty.

From the Waccabuc Collection. Earlier from Heritage's F.U.N. Convention Sale, January 2004, Lot 5567.

The final variety of the Liberty Seated half dime was produced from 1860 through 1873. In this version, the words UNITED STATES OF AMERICA were moved from the reverse to the obverse, and the obverse stars were eliminated. The extra space on the reverse was filled with a larger wreath.

The Liberty Seated With Legend series is home to one of the great rarities in all of American numismatics, namely the 1870-S, of which only one example is known in collectors' hands. (A second example may reside in the cornerstone of the second San Francisco Mint building, which was laid in 1870.) This "unique" coin is today housed in a PCGS holder with a grade of MS-64, though at the time of its discovery it was given a grade of AU-55. A little-known fact: Louis Eliasberg, the only person ever to have assembled a complete set of U.S. coins, did *not* own the 1870-S half dime. Mr. Eliasberg died in 1976, and the 1870-S half dime was only discovered (possibly in a dealer's junk box, though other stories exist) in 1978. This coin most recently changed hands for more than $1 million in 2009.

Lesson 44: As a type, these coins are quite common. However, several dates produced at the Philadelphia Mint in the mid-1860s are scarce (fewer than 15,000 pieces were made in each of the years 1865 to 1867). These make excellent targets for an advanced type collection and are not especially expensive relative to their more common brethren.

Financials: Half dime, Liberty Seated, Legend on Obverse, 1860

Cost	Sale Price	Gain/Loss	Holding Period
$2,701	$3,220	+19%	3.8 years

Dimes

An American named Bill was golfing at the Old Course in Saint Andrews, Scotland. He sliced his opening drive out of bounds onto the beach, so he teed another one up and smacked it right down the middle. Bill turned to his old Scottish caddy and told him that in America this second shot was called a "Mulligan" and asked if there was a name for it in Scotland.

The caddy replied, "Aye, laddie, here we call it a three."

I wish I'd been able to take a mulligan the first time I tried to buy a dime dated 1796, the first year of issue for this denomination. I bid $6,000 in an auction for an attractive Uncirculated example but lost to an earlier bid of the same amount submitted by mail. A few years later, I paid almost twice as much for a nice but clearly inferior example. Sadly, there are no such things as mulligans in real golf or in real numismatics.

The production of dimes by the U.S. Mint began in 1796—two years later than the earliest date on their tiny five-cent cousins—but their usefulness and popularity were such that they have been issued almost without interruption right up to the present day, except for a few years in the early decades of production. The elegant Draped Bust design (with small and large eagles) lasted through 1807. It was followed by the appealing Capped Bust design from 1809 through 1837 (with the Open Collar and Close Collar types, which are sometimes called Large Diameter and Small Diameter [or Wide Border and Modified Design]). The Liberty Seated design, which looks so regal on the dollars of 1836 and later but which, to me, seems terribly cramped on small-denomination coins, was produced from 1837 through 1891, with several varieties along the way. The Barber dimes (1892 to 1916) did not win any design awards when they first appeared but are more appreciated today. Mercury dimes (1916 to 1945), on the other hand, were lauded from the start and remain extremely popular with collectors now. The Roosevelt dime first appeared in 1946, not long after that president's death, and it remains in production today. All of these are discussed in more detail below.

DIME—DRAPED BUST, SMALL EAGLE REVERSE (1796–1797)

Lot 1045.
1796. AU-50.
JR-4. Rarity-4. PCGS #004461.

Auction description: Lovely AU 1796 Dime. A choice example for the date and grade, possibly lightly cleaned long ago, now long since retoned to a natural state. Somewhat reflective in the fields with pale gold and deep silver highlights in the protected areas. No serious marks present, though we note a few scattered tics. All told, we doubt you will ever see a finer example of the date and grade.

From the Waccabuc Collection. Earlier from ANR's sale of the Frog Run Farm Collection, November 2004, Lot 494.

The Philadelphia Mint finally got around to producing dimes (called "dismes" at the time) in 1796. Robert Scot's elegant Draped Bust design was used for the obverse, coupled with a small eagle on the reverse. This combination was used for just two years, 1796 and 1797.

Although the mintage figures for the two years are similar (about 22,000 and 25,000), coins dated 1797 are significantly scarcer—about four times so, per some sources. The certified populations suggest the disparity is even wider: there are close to 500 certification events for the 1796 (certainly including an unknown number of resubmissions) but only about 30 for the 1797. A stunningly beautiful 1796 dime graded NGC MS-67 sold for $253,000 in April 2009. Less than a year earlier, a slightly less beautiful 1797 dime in an NGC MS-65 holder sold for almost $150,000 more. I would judge the latter to be the better investment decision.

Lesson 45: The 64-word description written by the Stack's cataloger provides a good example of the balance that auction houses aspire to achieve. To satisfy the seller, the coin is praised: "a choice example for the date and grade . . . no serious marks present . . . we doubt you will ever see a finer example of the date and grade." To establish credibility and educate the buyer, however, the flaws are also disclosed: "possibly lightly cleaned long ago . . . a few scattered tics." If you see a catalog description (or other offering) that only lists the positives, be sure to take a very close look at the coin or ask an independent dealer for an opinion.

Financials: Dime, Draped Bust, Small Eagle Reverse, 1796

Cost	Sale Price	Gain/Loss	Holding Period
$11,500	$13,800	+20%	3.0 years

DIME—DRAPED BUST, HERALDIC EAGLE REVERSE (1798–1807)

Lot 1046.
1798, Large 8. AU-55.
JR-4. Rarity-3. PCGS #004467.

Auction description: Choice AU 1798 Dime. Large 8 Variety. Among Three Finest Seen by PCGS. Large 8 variety, though "Small 8" is noted on the PCGS holder. Medium silver gray with warm golden highlights on both sides. Strong luster remains, especially in the protected areas and beneath much of the warm golden toning. Scattered marks are present, especially under low magnification, but the unaided eye appeal is substantial. Overall, an exceptional example of this moderately scarce variety from the first year of Draped Bust, Heraldic Eagle coinage within the denomination. PCGS Population: 1; 2 finer within the designation (MS-65 finest). Holder incorrectly labeled "Small Date."

From the Waccabuc Collection. Earlier from ANR's sale of the Frog Run Farm Collection, November 2004, Lot 499.

The Draped Bust obverse was continued from the prior dime design through 1807, but the reverse was modified in 1798 when a heraldic eagle, modeled after the Great Seal of the United States, was adopted. No dimes were minted in 1799 and 1806. Most coins in this series were poorly struck. If you find one with full details, including the stars, snap it up. Like many other early American coins, there is no denomination indicated on this coin's obverse or reverse.

This design was produced in typically small quantities (8,000 to 34,000 per year) through 1804. Then in 1805, production jumped to 121,000, followed by a further increase to 165,000 in the last year of issue (1807). As expected, most type collections contain one of these two late dates (see next lot). I initially chose the first year of issue to represent the type, but an astute collector should consider the 1804. It's a magical date (because of its association with the storied 1804 silver dollar), and the reported mintage was a tiny 8,265 pieces. Most of these are in lower grades—a representative Very Fine example will set you back $20,000 to $30,000 or so. Probably the finest 1804 dime, graded NGC AU-58, was sold at auction for more than $630,000 in July 2008.

Lesson 46: The Stack's cataloger was correct to note that my coin was the "Large 8" variety, not the "Small 8" as described on the PCGS holder. Unfortunately for me, the "Small 8" variety is the rarer type. The prior cataloger in 2004 didn't comment on the size of the final digit in the date, and clearly PCGS made an error. But the mistake was really mine: I didn't take a close-enough look at the coin, and I didn't do your homework on varieties. Walter Breen's *Encyclopedia* was on my bookshelf, but I didn't open it. I might have bought this coin anyway because I liked its "look," but it would have been better if I'd known exactly what I was buying. So, do your homework—it is useful and fun.

Financials: Dime, Draped Bust, Heraldic Eagle Reverse, 1798, Large 8

Cost	Sale Price	Gain/Loss	Holding Period
$5,520	$5,750	+4%	3.0 years

DIME—DRAPED BUST, HERALDIC EAGLE REVERSE (1798–1807)

Lot 1047.
1805, 4 Berries. MS-63.
JR-2. Rarity-2. PCGS #004477.

Auction description: Choice Uncirculated 1805 Dime. 4 Berries Variety. Satiny pale lilac-gray with rich golden highlights, strong underlying luster, and exceptional eye appeal for the assigned grade. The strike is quite bold for the design type, with very little weakness even upon magnified scrutiny. The surfaces are essentially flawless, especially within the context of the grade, which adds to the overall aesthetic appeal. Some faint vertical planchet adjustment marks can be seen in the reverse clouds, though even these natural surface disturbances are barely evident under low magnification. Absolutely choice for the grade, and yet another testimony to the overall quality of the entire collection.

From the Waccabuc Collection. Earlier from Heritage's Long Beach Sale, February 2006, Lot 717.

As I got closer to completing my type collection, there arose fewer and fewer opportunities to acquire design types I did not already own. This can be frustrating. So, from time to time, I would buy a finer example of a coin type in order to upgrade the point value of my collection on the PCGS Set Registry. This is how I became the owner of an 1805 Draped Bust dime in 2006. As a type, it is no different from the coin seen in the immediately preceding entry.

The cataloger mentioned that "faint vertical planchet adjustment marks can be seen in the reverse clouds." This is accurate, but the much more visible diagonal adjustment marks on the obverse somehow escaped mention. These run from Miss Liberty's bodice through her hair and into the L in LIBERTY. See lesson 93 for a further discussion of adjustment marks.

Lesson 47: Upgrading one's coin collection is a common, and usually expensive, habit. Collectors will often buy the first example they find of a coin they need for their collection. Later, they will see a better example, and the desire to own it will overwhelm them. The result is two purchases and one sale—with the attendant buyer's and seller's fees to be paid. Though it's often hard to do, try to make your first purchase your best purchase.

Financials: Dime, Draped Bust, Heraldic Eagle Reverse, 1805, 4 Berries

Cost	Sale Price	Gain/Loss	Holding Period
$10,350	$9,775	-6%	1.8 years

DIME—CAPPED BUST, WIDE BORDER (1809–1828)

Lot 1048.
1824, 4 Over 2. MS-64.
JR-1. Rarity-3. PCGS #004502.

Auction description: Very Choice Uncirculated 1824/2 Dime. Strong mint luster cascades broadly beneath pale gold, lilac, and electric blue highlights. Overdate details plainly visible. Some central striking weakness, virtually a "given" for this particular date as well as other dime varieties of the immediate era. A truly choice coin that holds up well to careful scrutiny when a few tiny, essentially meaningless marks come to light. Among the top seven examples of the date certified thus far by PCGS. PCGS Population: 5; 2 finer (MS-66 finest).

From the Waccabuc Collection. Earlier from ANR's sale of the Prescott Collection, January 2006, Lot 254.

The Capped Bust, Large Diameter (alternately *Open Collar* or *Wide Border*) dimes, designed by John Reich, were produced from 1809 through 1828, though there were several years during this period when no dimes were minted. "Open collar" refers to the more primitive method of minting dimes used until 1828, when the "close collar" technique was introduced. An open collar held the coin blank loosely in position during the striking process, while a close collar constrained the coin blank to a uniform size and imparted reeding when the coin was struck. The manufacturing techniques are discussed in more detail in connection with the next lot.

Striking quality varied widely, so it's worthwhile to search for an example with strong details. There are no prohibitively rare dates in this series. However, dimes struck in 1822, with a reported mintage of just 100,000 pieces (many of which probably bore the date 1821), appear at auction only infrequently. An MS-64 example of this date (one of perhaps 12 certified Mint State 1822 dimes) sold in a Heritage auction for just less than $30,000 in July 2008.

Lesson 48: In series where striking quality varies, it pays to know what parts of a coin's design are most often subject to weak striking. In his many books on coins and investing, Dave Bowers consistently addresses this issue. For example, in his *Guide Book of United States Type Coins*, in the section on Capped Bust, Open Collar dimes, Dave notes that light striking may occur at "the center of the portrait and around the brooch, the star centers, and the dentils" as well as in "the area in and around the upper right of the shield." If you do a little homework, you'll be way ahead of most other collectors (and many dealers).

Financials: Dime, Capped Bust, Wide Border, 1824, 4 Over 2

Cost	Sale Price	Gain/Loss	Holding Period
$6,325	$8,050	+27%	1.8 years

DIME—CAPPED BUST, MODIFIED DESIGN (1828–1837)

Lot 1049.
1828. MS-62.
JR-1. Rarity-2. PCGS #004510.

Auction description: An undeniably prooflike example of the date, a coin with lightly dusted motifs and highly reflective fields, especially on the obverse. Pale shades of blended lilac and electric blue grace both sides, with hints of gold and violet. Nicely struck for the date with no serious weakness at any point. Choice for the grade.

From the Waccabuc Collection. Earlier from Goldbergs' February 2003 Sale, Lot 323.

The Capped Bust, Small Diameter (alternately *Close Collar* or *Modified Design*) dimes were minted in all years from 1828 through 1837. Striking quality was generally better than for the predecessors made with an open collar. Mintage figures were generous in most years, and a very attractive collection of all dates and most major varieties can be assembled for a reasonable cost.

Most people don't know what a close collar is. Walter Breen, in his massive *Complete Encyclopedia of U.S. and Colonial Coins*, provides a clear description, which I will quote here:

> Among the mechanical improvements [William] Kneass introduced was what mint people called a close collar. This is a heavy steel slug into which a hole is bored in the exact diameter of a finished coin. If intended for gold or silver coinage, its cylindrical wall is grooved to impart a reeded edge at the exact moment of striking; otherwise plain. A close collar fits just above the reverse die, forming the coining chamber confining each blank as it is stamped. After striking, one and the same continuous motion of the flywheel causes the upper die to retract, the lower die to rise through the collar (ejecting the newly minted coin), and feeder fingers to push the coin into a receiving bin. Then the lower die sinks again below the collar, the upper die begins to descend, another blank is released from the hopper and guided by the feeder fingers into the coining chamber, resting atop the lower die, whereupon the sequence repeats. This process enormously speeds up coinage, saving the time of separately reeding edges of blanks before striking (previously done by the Castaing machine), and imparting "a mathematical equality to diameters" (to quote Mint Director Samuel Moore, 1829); it is the basic method still in use. Earlier issues had been struck in an open collar, which positioned the blanks on the reverse die but did not confine them, as this would have flattened edge reeding or lettering.

Lesson 49: My 1828 coin was "Choice for the grade," according to the Stack's cataloger. Well, I should say so! This coin was in an NGC holder with a grade of MS-64 when I bought it. I generally buy coins only in PCGS holders, but I just loved the color of this particular coin. Then came the disaster. I sent it off to PCGS to be encapsulated in one of their holders. They judged the coin to be MS-62. And that's the reason I lost 40% on this investment. But I still love the look of this coin. Unless you're a nationally renowned grading expert, leave your coins in the holders they came in. There are far more horror stories out there than there are successes.

Financials: Dime, Capped Bust, Modified Design, 1828

Cost	Sale Price	Gain/Loss	Holding Period
$4,388	$2,645	-40%	4.8 years

DIME—LIBERTY SEATED, NO STARS ON OBVERSE (1837–1838)

Lot 1050.
1838-O, Repunched Mintmark. MS-64.
PCGS #004564.

Auction description: Choice Uncirculated 1838-O Dime. No Obverse Stars, Repunched Mintmark. Highly lustrous champagne gold surfaces with some deeper toning on both sides. The strike is bold and crisp, which serves to highlight Gobrecht's cameo-like design. The seateddimevarieties.com Web site offers the following concerning this date: "Typically available in grades VG through EF. A difficult date in AU or better with few Mint State examples known." Indeed, that Web site gives the date an overall Rarity-3 designation, though at Mint State grades the rarity increases substantially to Rarity-6. A truly exceptional representative example of the date and grade. PCGS Population: 9; 5 finer (MS-65 finest). Fortin-101. Rarity-3; Rarity-6 as Mint State.

From the Waccabuc Collection. Earlier from Teletrade's November 1998 Sale, Lot 1037.

The No Stars on Obverse "mini-Gobrecht" dimes were minted in Philadelphia in 1837 and in New Orleans in 1838. The cameo-like seated figure of Miss Liberty was modeled after the Gobrecht dollar, introduced in 1836.

The No Stars dimes, like their half-dime cousins, represent a short "sub-series" within the grander series of Liberty Seated dimes, which were minted through 1891. They are also, to my eye, the most attractive. In later years, as detailed below, obverse stars were punched into the periphery, then drapery was added to Liberty's elbow, then arrowheads were added at the date (for three years), then the stars were replaced with UNITED STATES OF AMERICA, which had appeared on the reverse in earlier years, and finally stars were added at the date again (for two more years). All these improvements just served to clutter the original elegant design.

Lesson 50: Although the mintage figures for the two dates in this series are not wildly disparate (682,500 for the 1837 issue made in Philadelphia and 406,034 for the 1838 issue made in New Orleans), their availability in Mint State condition differs to a huge extent. The two leading grading services have certified more than 300 1837 dimes in MS-63 condition or better. In contrast, there are only about 55 1838-O dimes in PCGS or NGC holders in the same grade range. You won't be paying six times as much for an Uncirculated 1838-O dime, so opt for one of these rather than the pedestrian 1837 issue.

Financials: Dime, Liberty Seated, No Stars, 1838-O, Repunched Mintmark

Cost	Sale Price	Gain/Loss	Holding Period
$7,012	$12,650	+80%	9.0 years

DIME—LIBERTY SEATED, STARS ON OBVERSE, NO DRAPERY (1838–1840)

Lot 1051.

1838, Partial Drapery. MS-63.

PCGS #004570.

Auction description: An exceptionally lovely example of the date, sharply struck and intensely lustrous with a rich array of varied gold and smoky gray toning highlights. The strike is superb, and the present beauty, while "just" MS-63, has all the earmarks and appeal of a much finer assigned grade. Only nine examples of this popular issue have been certified at MS-63 or finer by PCGS. PCGS Population: 3; 6 finer (MS-67 finest).

From the Waccabuc Collection. Earlier from ANR's Classics Sale, December 2003, Lot 612.

The second variety of the Liberty Seated dime, with 13 stars around the obverse and no drapery from Miss Liberty's elbow, was minted from 1838 through 1840. The mintage figures from both the Philadelphia and the New Orleans mints were generous, and therefore there are no rarities in this short series.

To represent this variety, I chose the curiously named Partial Drapery version of the 1838 dime. It sounded exotic, but I will admit I didn't know until I sat down to write this section how the Partial Drapery feature came into being—especially since the official "extra drapery from elbow" type wasn't introduced until two years later. The truth is that the Partial Drapery moniker is a misnomer. There is no extra drapery on the Partial Drapery 1838 dime, only some evidence of die clashing in the vicinity of the existing limited drapery at Liberty's elbow.

Lesson 51: A 6% loss after a holding period of almost four years on an "exceptionally lovely" coin (per the cataloger) with a low population figure (three in MS-63 and only six finer) was a very poor result. I blame my lack of research into the nature of the variety, which is not really a die variety at all. Do your research before buying the coin, not after. The new owner may have gotten a good deal, but the fact remains that this particular coin will unlikely ever be coveted by a wide circle of collectors.

Financials: Dime, Liberty Seated, Stars on Obverse, 1838, Partial Drapery

Cost	Sale Price	Gain/Loss	Holding Period
$2,070	$1,955	-6%	3.9 years

DIME—LIBERTY SEATED, ARROWS AT DATE (1853–1855)

Lot 1052.
1853. MS-65.
PCGS #004603.

Auction description: A sharp and satiny Gem with even golden highlights on intensely lustrous surfaces. All of the design elements are crisply presented, and the overall eye appeal and aesthetic quality is easily equal to the MS-65 grade level.

From the Waccabuc Collection. Acquired from Larry Whitlow, September 2002.

The third variety of Liberty Seated dime, with arrowheads to the left and right of the date, was minted from 1853 through 1855 at the Philadelphia Mint and in 1853 and 1854 at the New Orleans Mint. These new dimes contained

7 percent less silver than their predecessors, making their intrinsic value slightly less than 10¢. The arrowheads served to differentiate these coins from their heavier brethren.

As noted earlier, the discovery of gold in California in 1848 caused silver to become more valuable in relation to gold. As a result, it became profitable to melt silver coins, including dimes, and these largely disappeared from circulation by 1850.

Aristophanes in the fifth century B.C. and Nicolaus Copernicus in the early 1500s, and eventually Sir Thomas Gresham (who lent his name to what came to be known as Gresham's Law), noted that bad money drives out good. In effect, gold coins were the "bad money" (since they were worth less per unit of face value than silver coins) that drove out "good money" (silver coins) from circulation. People could, for example, melt $100 in face value of old silver coins and then exchange the bullion for more than $100 worth of gold coins. Similarly, the less-valuable dimes with arrows that made their appearance in 1853 (the bad money) reinforced the disappearance from circulation of any remaining early dimes (the good money). This same phenomenon was experienced by many of us firsthand when 90 percent silver coins were discontinued in the 1960s and replaced by base-metal clad coins. The silver coins quickly became very hard to find in circulation.

Lesson 52: Although type collectors have five date-and-mintmark combinations to choose among, most decide to buy the 1853 issue made in Philadelphia. The reason is not surprising: greater than half of the total production of arrowhead dimes was made in Philadelphia in that year—more than 12 million pieces. This is what I did, and it was a mistake. Although my coin was attractive, it is also very common. Spend a little more money and get one of the other dates. All are available if you have a little patience.

Financials: Dime, Liberty Seated, Arrows at Date, 1853

Cost	Sale Price	Gain/Loss	Holding Period
$2,275	$2,013	-12%	5.2 years

DIME—LIBERTY SEATED, STARS ON OBVERSE, WITH DRAPERY (1840–1860)

Lot 1053.
1857. PF-64.
PCGS #004746.

Auction description: Choice Proof 1857 Dime. A pleasing Proof example of this date, one of an untold number of Proofs of the date struck, with today's numismatic community in general agreement that the Proof mintage was modest at best for this date. Pleasing rose, violet, and lilac iridescence glows warmly on the well struck motifs and mirrored fields. The present specimen is among the dozen finest Proofs of the date certified thus far by PCGS, and was a highlight of ANR's sale of the Jewell Collection in March 2005. PCGS Population: 8; 4 finer within the designation (Proof-67 finest).

From the Waccabuc Collection. Earlier from ANR's sale of the Richard C. Jewell Collection, March 2005, Lot 1605.

The fourth variety of Liberty Seated dime was minted from 1840 through 1853 and again, with a slightly reduced weight, from 1856 through 1860. It closely resembles the "stars on obverse" type produced from 1838 to 1840 except that some additional drapery was added to Miss Liberty's left arm, and the shield on which her right hand is resting was rotated into an upright position. There were also some other less obvious changes made.

Many numismatic texts describe the changes as "improvements" to the design. Numismatic scholar Walter Breen disagreed. In his *Encyclopedia*, he wrote: "[Robert Ball] Hughes's totally redrawn conception of Ms. Liberty (popularly known as 'With Drapery') fattened her arms, enlarged her head, flattened her bosom, replaced her décolleté by a high collar, chipped away much of her rock, moved her shield to an upright position, and replaced her thin Greek chiton by a much heavier fabric (of at least army-blanket thickness), with a peculiar bulla or heavy pendant (on half dimes and dimes only) on its lower edge, lest the garment ride up far enough to reveal her ankles. Over her elbow, in what must have been an extremely uncomfortable position for Hughes's model, if any, hangs a bulky cloak or himation, irregularly folded." So much for the so-called "improvements"!

More than 36 million "With Drapery, With Stars" dimes were produced. Finding a nice example will not be difficult. Look for one with attractive toning and a good strike (full stars, strong detail on the head of Liberty, distinct leaves and dentils). You might want to consider one of the six dates (1844; 1846; 1853, No Arrows; 1856-S; 1858-S; and 1859-S) that had mintages under 100,000 pieces to add some fundamental rarity to your collection.

Lesson 53: The Philadelphia Mint began to strike coins in Proof format for the general public in 1858. Before that date, Proofs were made sporadically, often at the request of individual collectors. Records of how many were produced in the early years are incomplete or non-existent. I chose an attractive (but not especially well struck—check the stars on the right side of the coin) Proof dated 1857 to represent the With Drapery dime. Depending on which source you consult, this coin is either rare or extremely rare. However, early Proofs are not widely collected, so the prices are often not as extreme as you might otherwise expect. Keep your eyes open for opportunities to acquire genuinely rare coins at reasonable prices. They add interest to your collection, and they may yield a nice profit in the future.

Financials: Dime, Liberty Seated, Stars on Obverse, With Drapery, 1857

Cost	Sale Price	Gain/Loss	Holding Period
$3,680	$4,255	+16%	2.7 years

DIME—LIBERTY SEATED, ARROWS AT DATE (1873–1874)

Lot 1054.
1873. Proof-65.
PCGS #004769.

Auction description: Gem Proof 1873 Arrows Dime. Richly Toned. Frosty motifs and mirrored fields display a rich and vibrant array of deep rose, pale violet, peach, and electric blue. The motifs are frosty and the fields are reflective with cameo contrast in abundance, though such is not noted on the PCGS holder. From a Proof mintage for the date of 800 pieces; of those Proofs seen thus far by PCGS, only a half dozen examples have received a finer grade. Sharply struck and aesthetically appealing. PCGS Population: 16; 6 finer within the designation (all Proof-66).

From the Waccabuc Collection. Earlier from Heritage's Long Beach Sale, September 2003, Lot 6426.

As in the early 1850s, arrowheads were added to both sides of the date on some dimes in 1873 and all dimes in 1874. Unlike the situation in the 1850s, however, there was virtually no measureable change in the weight of the coins produced before and after the design modification. The change was just in the way the coins were weighed—in grams (the metric system) rather than in grains.

Specifically, the standard weight changed from 38.4 grains to 2.50 grams—an increase in weight of 0.4 percent which was within the tolerance of the old standard. Since there was no monetary advantage in saving or melting earlier dates, this did not happen in the marketplace—but it did at the Mint, where perfectly acceptable dimes of the earlier type were melted down, providing just another example of government profligacy.

The With Arrows dimes of 1873 and 1874 were produced in large quantities at the Philadelphia Mint, in modest quantities at the San Francisco Mint, and in tiny quantities in Carson City. Most coins of this type were well struck.

Lesson 54: With lots of nice coins of this type to choose among, don't settle for an average or inferior example. I opted for a Proof with gorgeous toning and an excellent strike. I was happy with my purchase and always enjoyed looking at this little gem.

Financials: Dime, Liberty Seated, Arrows at Date, 1873

Cost	Sale Price	Gain/Loss	Holding Period
$6,750	$8,050	+19%	4.2 years

DIME—LIBERTY SEATED, LEGEND ON OBVERSE (1860–1891)

Lot 1055.
1879. MS-67.
PCGS #004687.

Auction description: Gem Uncirculated 1879 Dime. None Graded Finer by PCGS. A frosty Gem example of the date, one of only 14,000 pieces struck for intended circulation. Frosty motifs and satiny fields form a pleasing cameo contrast, as might be expected from an early strike from the dies used to produce this popular low-mintage scarcity. Largely brilliant with just a hint of warm champagne on both sides. PCGS Population: 21; none finer.

From the Waccabuc Collection. Earlier from Heritage's Long Beach Sale, January 2004, Lot 5603.

The final variety of the exhausting Liberty Seated dime series made its appearance in 1860 and continued through the end of the series in 1891. The stars on the obverse were eliminated. The legend UNITED STATES OF AMERICA was moved from the reverse to the obverse, where the stars used to be. And to fill the extra space created on the reverse resulting from the removal of the legend, the wreath grew in size and complexity. Supposedly the changes were designed to improve striking quality and extend die life, but there's scant evidence that these objectives were realized.

The Legend on Obverse dime sub-series contains one of the classic rarities in U.S. numismatics—the 1873-CC No Arrows dime. Although 12,400 are reported to have been minted, there is only one known survivor, an example originally graded MS-64 by PCGS and, later, MS-65 by NGC. Although the facts are not entirely clear, it seems likely that, except for a few assay coins, all of these dimes were melted before any were released into circulation. One of the assay coins found its way into the Mint Collection and then, in 1909, it was acquired by two private coin dealers as a small part of a much larger trade of coins and patterns. After being owned by a number of prominent collectors, this coin was acquired in November 1950 by Louis Eliasberg Sr. It was the final piece he needed to complete his set of all U.S. coins. Since then, this coin sold for $550,000 in 1996, $632,500 in 1999, $891,250 in 2004, and $1,840,000 in 2012.

Lesson 55: With dozens of common dates to choose among, this is an easy "hole" to fill in your collection, in either Proof or circulation-strike format. *Select*, don't settle. I was attracted by the low mintage (14,000) of the 1879 issue. But even at the lofty grade of MS-67, there were at least a score of equally nice PCGS coins of this date available to collectors. And the virtual absence of toning strongly suggests that this coin was dipped. Thus, my financial results were unimpressive.

Financials: Dime, Liberty Seated, Legend on Obverse, 1879

Cost	Sale Price	Gain/Loss	Holding Period
$3,795	$3,450	-9%	3.8 years

DIME—BARBER (1892–1916)

Lot 1056.

1911. MS-67.

PCGS #004857.

Auction description: Exceptional Gem 1911 Barber Dime. A frosty Gem with intense cartwheel luster that supports a wealth of deep and vibrant rainbow hues at the rims. Boldly struck with all of Barber's design elements crisply represented. PCGS Population: 12; 2 finer (both MS-68).

From the Waccabuc Collection. Earlier from Heritage's F.U.N. Convention Sale, January 2005, Lot 4061.

The Barber dime, which was produced from 1892 through 1916, was named after the designer of the obverse of this coin, Charles E. Barber, the Mint's chief engraver. In his *Encyclopedia*, Walter Breen has this to say about Barber's effort: "Barber must have been feeling unusually lazy. He left the reverse design as it had been since 1860, with minor simplifications. His obverse was a mirror image of the Morgan dollar head, with much of Miss Anna Willess Williams's back hair cropped off, the rest concealed . . . within a disproportionately large cap. A plain laurel (?) wreath replaced the assorted vegetation on the dollar."

Barber dimes were struck in large quantities in most years, so finding an example that fits your budget and sensibility will not pose a problem. I've seen different, highly experienced experts say either that most Barber dimes were well struck or that poor strikes were common (particularly on coins from the New Orleans Mint). In either event, it is worthwhile to get in the habit of checking the higher details of the hair on the obverse and the wreath on the reverse.

As with the immediately preceding dime series, there is one coin within the Barber dime series that stands head and shoulders above the rest. It is the 1894-S issue, which was produced to the extent of only 24 coins, all in Proof format. Long articles have been penned by serious researchers about why only 24 examples were minted, but the short answer is that no one really knows the reason. What is known is that these coins were not produced clandestinely (like the 1913 Liberty Head nickel rarity), that only nine can be traced today, and that most of us cannot even dream of owning one. Stack's sold a PCGS PF-65 example in October 2007 for more than $1.5 million.

Lesson 56: I got carried away by this coin's beautiful peripheral rainbow toning—it's attractive, but not special enough to go crazy over. Unfortunately, there must have been at least one other starry-eyed bidder in the auction room with me, and I was the sad sack who kept his hand up in the air the longest. I clearly overpaid for this coin. The sale price I achieved when I sold it was a good solid price, and as of this writing, you could probably buy this coin for slightly less than I received in 2007. In the case of a common coin and series like this one, know what the coin should bring and drop out of the bidding if the competition gets silly.

Financials: Dime, Barber, 1911

Cost	Sale Price	Gain/Loss	Holding Period
$6,325	$4,600	-27%	2.8 years

DIME—MERCURY (1916–1945)

Lot 1057.
1944-D. MS-68 FB.
PCGS #005053.

The Mercury (or, rarely, Winged Liberty Head) dime was produced from 1916 through 1945. The design, by sculptor Adolph A. Weinman, is magnificent, and the series is widely collected today. The figure of Miss Liberty in a winged cap on the obverse reminded some people of the Greek god Hermes or the Roman god Mercury. The latter name stuck. The design on the reverse depicts a Roman fasces, which is an executioner's axe bound within a bundle of rods. This warlike motif anticipated the United States's entry into World War I.

The Mercury dime series is one of the few where strike quality is universally considered as part of the grade. A well-struck coin, which means one with distinctly split bands at the center of the fasces ("Full Split Bands"), will always command a premium over one with mushy bands.

I bought this common coin because of its color and paid about twice the price guide. Clearly, the market for beautifully toned 1944-D gem dimes wasn't quite as strong when it came time to sell. Sadly, the financial result for this coin was very similar to my experience with the immediately preceding lot.

Lesson 57: Sometimes you hit a good shot, and it goes into the bunker. Sometimes you buy a great-looking coin, but you lose money when you sell it. I loved looking at this coin, but I did far better financially with an earlier purchase and sale of the scarce 1916-D issue.

Financials: Dime, Mercury, 1944-D

Cost	Sale Price	Gain/Loss	Holding Period
$2,185	$1,265	-42%	1.8 years

DIME—ROOSEVELT (1946–PRESENT)

Lot 1058.
1946-S, MS-67; 1960, Proof-70; 1965, MS-68.

Auction description: Trio of PCGS-certified Roosevelt dimes: * 1946-S MS-67. Faint golden tones * 1960 Proof-70. A sparkling brilliant Gem * 1965 MS-68 SMS. Highly reflective and fully lustrous. (Total: 3 pieces)
From the Waccabuc Collection.

I bought these three Roosevelt dimes because I needed them for inclusion in my 20th-century type set. The 1946-S is a first-year-of-issue coin. The 1960 was one of the very few coins in my collection grading Proof-70. The decidedly un-special 1965 came from a Special Mint Set (SMS). None of these qualifies as a rare coin, though all are in much finer condition than normally seen. I have to admit that I got very little excitement from acquiring these coins, and I felt absolutely no seller's remorse when the hammer came down on this lot. Adding insult to injury, they also turned out to be lousy investments.

There is one very special Roosevelt dime. In 1975, more than 2.8 million Proof dimes were minted in San Francisco. All were supposed to have an S mintmark, but at least two did not. The first of these was discovered in 1977 and the second in 1984. Others might exist, but after almost three decades of searching, no one has found another. One of the two extant examples is housed in a PCGS holder with a grade of PF-68. It was sold at a Stack's Bowers Galleries auction in August 2011 for a whopping $349,600!

Lesson 58: Repeating lesson 22, don't spend a lot of time or money on items you don't care about. Yes, completing the collection of modern issues was somewhat satisfying, but I rarely looked at these coins or showed them to others. This is not to say that collecting modern coins isn't worthwhile. It can be interesting, educational, and fun. But for the most part they're not rare coins, and seeking an imperceptibly finer example of a common modern coin wasn't something that gave me much of a thrill.

Financials: Dime, Roosevelt, 1946-S, 1960, 1965

Cost	Sale Price	Gain/Loss	Holding Period
$573	$253	-56%	Various

Twenty-Cent
Pieces

No matter how badly you play golf, it is always possible to get worse.

In the annals of American coinage, things got worse in 1875: the unwanted and unneeded 20-cent piece was introduced to an unsuspecting public. As is still often the case, the culprits were money and politics.

The Fourth Coinage Act, also known as the Mint Act of 1873, effectively placed the United States on the gold standard and resulted in the discontinuance of production of silver three-cent pieces, half dimes, and silver dollars. Most of the silver mined in the United States came from Nevada, and the miners were not pleased with this development. Heeding the pleas of his constituents, Senator John Percival Jones, the junior senator from Nevada and an owner of the Crown Point silver mine (part of the famous Comstock Lode), introduced legislation in early 1874 to authorize coinage of silver 20-cent pieces. Little more than a year later, President U.S. Grant signed the bill into law, and production began shortly thereafter.

Immediately after the coins were released into circulation, confusion reigned. The diameter of the 20-cent pieces differed only slightly from that of the popular quarter dollar: 22 mm vs. 24.3 mm. The Liberty Seated obverse design on the new coins was virtually indistinguishable from that used on the quarter. The reverses of both the 20-cent coin and the quarter used a spread-eagle design, though the former had the eagle's head facing to the right (as on the trade dollar), while the latter used a left-facing eagle with a shield on its breast. The 20-cent piece did have a plain edge that clearly differed from the quarter's reeded edge, but that was not enough to stop both consumers and merchants from making mistakes. Production dropped precipitously from more than 1.3 million pieces in 1875 to fewer than 26,000 in 1876 to less than 1,000 (all Proofs for collectors) in total for 1877 and 1878, after which no more were ever produced.

Slightly more than 1,350,000 20-cent pieces were minted at Philadelphia, San Francisco, and Carson City in the four years of this denomination's existence. Fully 85 percent of these were produced by the San Francisco Mint in the first year of production (1875). Nicely struck, attractive examples are available at reasonable prices in all grades up through MS-65.

TWENTY-CENT PIECE—LIBERTY SEATED (1875–1878)

Lot 1059.
1875-CC. MS-64.
PCGS #005297.

Auction description: Choice Uncirculated 1875-CC 20¢. Frosty, lustrous surfaces richly imbued with warm rose and champagne iridescence. One of 133,290 specimens of the date produced in this, the only collectible year of Carson City coinage within the denomination; the only other year of issue from that mint was 1876, and the 1876-CC 20¢ is one of the great rarities in all U.S. numismatics. Nicely struck and exceptional for the grade.

From the Waccabuc Collection. Earlier from Kingswood Galleries' March 2001 Sale, Lot 181.

Despite the short length of this series (four years and seven date-mintmark varieties), almost no one tries to assemble a complete collection of 20-cent pieces. The problem is the 1876-CC, which, as noted by the Stack's cataloger, is a famous rarity. 10,000 were struck, but most had not been released into circulation (since no one wanted them) when Mint director Henry R. Linderman authorized the melting of Carson City's stock of 20-cent pieces in March of 1877. Fewer than 20 pieces are believed to exist today, and on the rare occasion when one appears at auction, big-money bidders appear. In May 2009, an example graded MS-66 by PCGS sold for $460,000 at a Heritage auction.

Lesson 59: Although hated in its time, the 20-cent piece is a wonderful coin to own today. Most people building type collections opt for the relatively common 1875-S, but I much prefer the 1875-CC. It's nine times as rare (in terms of the number minted), but generally only three or four times as expensive in mid-range Uncirculated grades. If you can't find a '75-CC you like (and they usually do come weakly struck), consider buying a Proof from 1877 (with a mintage of just 350) or 1878 (mintage of 600).

Financials: Twenty-cent piece, Liberty Seated, 1875-CC

Cost	Sale Price	Gain/Loss	Holding Period
$2,227	$7,475	+236%	6.7 years

CHAPTER
11

Quarters

*A "gimme" is defined as an agreement between two golfers,
neither of whom can putt very well.*

There's no numismatic equivalent of the "gimme" that's so common in friendly games of golf. This is a good thing. The collector must earn his treasures—either through assiduous searching for special coins in circulation or by buying coins at auctions or from dealers or other collectors. The non-financial rewards are substantial—the thrill of the hunt, the acquisition of knowledge, and the satisfaction that comes with success.

The quarter dollar denomination offers many opportunities for beginning and advanced collectors alike. Although authorized by the Mint Act of 1792, the quarter was actually produced in only a single year (1796) between 1792 and 1803, and then to the extent of only 6,146 pieces. That Small Eagle type was replaced in 1804 by the Large or Heraldic Eagle type, but this variety was also short-lived, with just a four-year life (1804 to 1807). The Capped Bust type was produced in two varieties (large and small diameter) in most years from 1815 through 1838. The Liberty Seated type had a protracted run from 1838 through 1891, with several sub-varieties as detailed below. The Barber (or Liberty Head) quarter was produced for a quarter century from 1892 through 1916. Its replacement was the exceptionally handsome Standing Liberty type that, sadly, was produced for a span of only 15 years (1916 to 1930). To commemorate the 200th anniversary of George Washington's birth, the Washington quarter was introduced in 1932. It is still being made today, though in recent years there have been a wide variety of reverse designs. All of these types are discussed in greater detail in the sections that follow.

QUARTER—DRAPED BUST, SMALL EAGLE REVERSE (1796)

Lot 1060.
1796. VF-30.
Browning-2. Rarity-3. PCGS #005310.

Auction description: Important 1796 Quarter Dollar Rarity. Solid Collector Grade. Medium lilac-gray with some deeper highlights in the protected areas. Visually enchanting to the unaided eye, though low magnification reveals some scattered marks, including a reverse rim nick at 3:00 in the dentils. A one-year-only type coinage, struck in just 1796 with Draped Bust and Small Eagle design elements; the next year of coin in the denomination, 1804, combined a Heraldic Eagle with the Draped Bust style. Technically Rarity-3, though much more rare than that number overall especially when you consider the demand placed on the surviving specimens of this popular rarity.

From the Waccabuc Collection. Earlier from the William Walser Collection; Bowers and Merena's Rarities Sale, July 2002, Lot 172.

By 2002, when I bought this Draped Bust, Small Eagle, 25-cent piece, I had gained enough confidence to bid aggressively when I found a coin that had all the attributes I was looking for. This 1796 quarter was one of those. It is the nation's first quarter dollar, a first-year-of-issue, one-year type that was minted, as mentioned, only to the extent of 6,146 pieces. This particular coin had nice, even color and looked just the way an old circulated coin should look—visually enchanting, as the cataloger called it. If you buy a good-looking, genuinely rare coin and hold it for more than five years, you should make some money. I paid 15 percent more than the "retail" *Red Book* value and did not regret it.

I attended the auction in person in New York City and beat out a determined New Jersey dealer who was bidding against me. At a break in the proceedings, the dealer came up to me and introduced herself. Her name was Laura Sperber, a principal in the Lincroft, New Jersey, firm of Legend Numismatics. She complimented me on my good taste in coins. This was an excellent sales pitch. Over the years, I did several deals with Legend, all to my complete satisfaction.

The finest 1796 quarter, and the only quarter of any date to surpass the $1 million barrier, changed hands at Heritage's November 15–16, 2013, auction held in New York City. The full 500-page catalog of that auction was dedicated to the sale of Part II of the Eric P. Newman Collection. Newman acquired many of his coins, including his stunning 1796 quarter, from the estate of Edward Howard Robinson Green, also known as Ned or "Colonel" Green. (That last moniker came from Green's appointment as a colonel on the staff of the governor of the State of Texas in 1910.) E.H.R. Green, a prominent numismatist and philatelist, was the free-spending son of the famous financier and miser, Hetty Green, the "Witch of Wall Street."

The Newman-Green quarter is graded NGC MS-67+*. The cataloger stated that he felt it was "the most beautiful American silver coin that exists today." Mr. Newman bought the coin for $100 in the late 1930s or early 1940s. In the late 2013 sale, it realized $1,527,500.

1796 is one of numismatics' magical years, along with 1792, 1793, 1804, and a few others. It was the first year in which dimes, quarters, and quarter eagles were produced (all in modest quantities), and many of the varieties of these and the other 1796 denominations are scarce or rare. One collector, John Whitney Walter, known as "Mr. 1796," had a goal of assembling a collection of all known varieties of U.S. coins dated 1796, from the half cent through the eagle. When that classic collection was sold by Stack's in May 1999, it was missing only a single variety of the beautiful No Stars quarter eagle (specifically, Breen-3, Hilt-2A). The auction was a sensation and a great success.

Lesson 60: If you choose to pursue a specialty collection, such as the one built by John Whitney Walter, and your chosen goal is not listed among the choices recognized by the PCGS or NGC set registry systems, do not despair. These leading grading services have often added new categories to their registry programs to accommodate collectors. If you build it, they will come....

Financials: Quarter, Draped Bust, Small Eagle Reverse, 1796

Cost	Sale Price	Gain/Loss	Holding Period
$13,800	$32,200	+133%	5.3 years

QUARTER—DRAPED BUST, HERALDIC EAGLE REVERSE (1804–1807)

Lot 1061.
1806. MS-62.
Browning-5. Rarity-4. PCGS #005314.

Auction description: Uncirculated 1806 Quarter Dollar. Medium steel gray surfaces with an expansive array of bright sea green, peach, gold, violet, and crimson iridescence on both sides. The underlying luster is at once supportive and frosty, and the aesthetic appeal is substantial for the assigned grade. No serious marks present, though low magnification reveals some central striking weakness and a few scattered tics. Heavy concentric circular lathe marks in Liberty's tresses at and around her neck, a distinct relic of the die making processes, and a worthwhile insight into early mint coinage practices.

From the Waccabuc Collection. Earlier from Bowers and Merena's Rarities Sale, July 1997, Lot 145.

I wrote earlier that my favorite grade for early U.S. coins is AU-58. The detail is all there, there's usually a good amount of luster, marks are minimal, and the price is better than for Mint State alternatives. The coin that most vividly taught me this rule was this beautiful Draped Bust, Heraldic Eagle, 1806 quarter.

I was at a coin viewing in a New York hotel prior to a mid-summer auction in 1997. I had finished looking at the patterns and trade dollars that I was focusing on at the time. I decided to flip through some of the other boxes to see if anything caught my eye. When I got to this coin, it jumped out of the pile, grabbed me by the shoulders, and said, "Buy me!" It had terrific color, it was shimmering with luster, and it was graded AU-58! I was thrilled to get it for only $3,300 at the live auction session the next evening—I was prepared to go much higher. A few months later, after joining the PCGS Collectors Club, which gave me grading submission privileges, I cracked the coin out of its holder and sent it in to see if I could get a higher grade. The coin came back as MS-61. A couple of years later, I cracked it out again, and when the coin came back from PCGS, its new grade was MS-62. Even at this level, as noted by the Stack's cataloger, "the aesthetic appeal is substantial for the assigned grade." Clearly, the new owner agreed with this assessment.

The "central striking weakness" noted by the cataloger is most evident on Miss Liberty's hair curls below her ear and on the eagle's head and chest and the scroll hanging from its beak. Such striking weakness is seen frequently on early U.S. coins and often will not negatively impact the price.

Lesson 61: When you see a coin in person that shouts, "Buy me!" you should take that advice very seriously. It's exceedingly unlikely you'll regret these types of purchases.

Financials: Quarter, Draped Bust, Heraldic Eagle Reverse, 1806

Cost	Sale Price	Gain/Loss	Holding Period
$3,300	$25,300	+667%	10.3 years

QUARTER—CAPPED BUST, LARGE DIAMETER (1815–1828)

Lot 1062.
1818, 8 Over 5. MS-64.
Browning-1. Rarity-2. PCGS #005323.

Auction description: Very Choice Uncirculated 1818/5 Quarter. A highly lustrous specimen with intense neon blue, rose, peach, and electric green on both sides. Satiny with good overall eye appeal, with just a touch of striking lightness present, the overall appearance is much more bold than typically seen for the date. Surface disturbances are at an absolute minimum, making for an exceptional selection for your growing U.S. type collection.

From the Waccabuc Collection. Earlier from Bowers and Merena's sale of the Hayward Collection, September 1997, Lot 665.

The Capped Bust, Large Diameter, quarter, designed by John Reich, was minted from 1815 through 1828, though no coins dated 1816, 1817, or 1826 were produced. According to Walter Breen, the "sporadic mintages of this denomination reflect public preference for Spanish and Mexican two-real coins, which were legal tender at par though lighter in weight; heavier federal quarters tended to be hoarded, finally many being melted in 1853." A fire at the Philadelphia Mint in January 1816 that ruined certain key equipment also interrupted production.

The highest mintage date is 1818, with slightly more than 360,000 having been made. Many of the dates have striking anomalies, including overdates, small and large digits, and even denomination corrections (where "25" was punched over an incorrect "50"—as happened with a die used in 1822 and again later in 1828). The 1822, 3 Over 2, is a significant rarity (fewer than three dozen are thought to survive), but the real key to the series is the 1827. 4,000 were reported to have been minted, but only 9 originals and perhaps 20 restrikes are known today. One of these would be a real highlight in any collection.

Lesson 62: All dates in this series are somewhat scarce in Mint State condition. Nevertheless, this series is not as avidly collected as Capped Bust half dollars or Morgan dollars or many others. Therefore, you should, with patience, be able to find a well-struck and attractive example for a reasonable price. And if you can find an 1827 (and can afford it), you should stretch for this classic rarity since even it seems to have flown a bit under the radar. A Proof-66 restrike was sold in a Heritage auction in 2009 for $69,000, which seems like a bargain for such a beautiful and rare coin.

Financials: Quarter, Capped Bust, Large Diameter, 1818, 8 Over 5

Cost	Sale Price	Gain/Loss	Holding Period
$5,060	$13,800	+173%	10.2 years

QUARTER—CAPPED BUST, REDUCED DIAMETER (1831–1838)

Lot 1063.
1831, Small Letters. MS-64.
Browning-4. Rarity-1. PCGS #005348.

Auction description: Very Choice Mint State 1831 Quarter. Impressive supportive cartwheel luster spins broadly across pale golden surface. The eye appeal is substantial for the grade, with a minimum of surface disturbances present, and the strike is bolder than typically seen for the date. Easily worthy of the assigned grade.

From the Waccabuc Collection. Acquired from John B. Hamrick, December 2002.

The Capped Bust, Reduced Diameter, quarter was minted in each year from 1831 through 1838. It differed from the preceding design only slightly. The most significant change was the reduction in its diameter, from 27 to 24.3 millimeters. The weight and metallic composition remained the same as its predecessor. The motto E PLURIBUS UNUM was removed from the reverse, and the sharpened letters, stars, numerals, and devices gave the piece a more cameo-like appearance, according to Q. David Bowers.

Although the reported mintages of individual dates varied widely (from 156,000 in 1833 to 1,952,000 in 1835), market prices do not reflect this. I opted for a first-year-of-issue example, as I did for many other coins in my collection, but the "rarer" 1833 would also be a good choice. The more important considerations, however, are strike and eye appeal.

Lesson 63: As with most early American coins, the striking quality of this variety of quarter varies widely. You may not be rewarded for owning a well-struck coin—there are no guarantees in this hobby. But by being choosy, you are likely to avoid disappointment when it comes time to sell, since discerning buyers will pass on weakly struck coins in favor of those with better definition.

Financials: Quarter, Capped Bust, Reduced Diameter, 1831, Small Letters

Cost	Sale Price	Gain/Loss	Holding Period
$3,820	$6,670	+75%	4.9 years

QUARTER—LIBERTY SEATED, NO MOTTO ABOVE EAGLE, NO DRAPERY (1838–1840)

Lot 1064.
1838. MS-63.
Browning-4. Rarity-1. PCGS #005391.

Auction description: Choice Uncirculated 1838 Liberty Seated 25¢. Vivid Rainbow Toning. First Year of Design Type. A sharp and lustrous example from the first year of Liberty Seated quarter coinage, here with an expansive array of vivid sea green, electric blue, crimson, and peach toning highlights. The strike is sharp and appealing, with just a hint of weakness in certain star radials on the obverse; all other design elements are crisply represented. Far finer aesthetically than the assigned grade indicates, and a coin that holds up well to careful magnified scrutiny. Superb within the parameters of the assigned grade.

From the Waccabuc Collection. Earlier from Heritage's Baltimore Sale, July 2003, Lot 6921.

Created by Christian Gobrecht, the Liberty Seated obverse design marked a sharp departure from the depictions of a bust of Miss Liberty seen up until this time on American quarters. The basic design, which would survive for more than half a century, shows Liberty seated on a rock holding a staff in her left hand. Atop the staff is a liberty cap. Her right hand supports a shield inscribed with the word LIBERTY. On the reverse, the eagle is a little stockier than on the preceding design, and the denomination is expressed as "QUAR. DOL." rather than "25 C."

For my taste, this design, with its abundance of detail, works well on the larger-denomination coins (the half dollar and, especially, the silver dollar). Here, on the quarter, it seems somewhat cramped to the naked eye, and on the dime and half dime it is virtually indiscernible. Of course, that's just my opinion.

For purposes of the PCGS set registry, there are six recognized varieties of the Liberty Seated quarter. The first is the No Drapery type, which was minted for only two years (1838 and 1839) in Philadelphia and one year (1840) in New Orleans. On this variety, there is no motto (IN GOD WE TRUST was not added to the reverse until 1866), and there is no drapery hanging from Liberty's left elbow.

The mintage totals for the three years of this first variety are all close to the same, and the market prices for these coins reflect this reality. I found a nice-looking, well-struck example of the first year of issue, but the 1840 issue from the New Orleans Mint, particularly if paired with its scarcer (43,000 mintage) but not more expensive With Drapery cousin of the same year and from the same mint, could represent an appealing choice.

Lesson 64: The catalog description of this coin stated that it was "far finer aesthetically than the assigned grade indicates, and a coin that holds up well to careful magnified scrutiny. Superb within the parameters of the assigned grade." The buyer of this coin probably agreed with this assessment and, accordingly, was willing to pay more than MS-63 "money" to get it. (I certainly felt it was better than the typical MS-63 coin when I bought it, though I never tried to get it re-graded.) You will sometimes need to ignore the standard price guides to get the coins you really want.

Financials: Quarter, Liberty Seated, No Motto, No Drapery, 1838

Cost	Sale Price	Gain/Loss	Holding Period
$4,600	$9,200	+100%	4.3 years

QUARTER—LIBERTY SEATED, NO MOTTO ABOVE EAGLE, WITH DRAPERY (1840–1865)

Lot 1065.
1840. MS-64.
PCGS #005397.

Auction description: Delightful Uncirculated 1840 Quarter. With Drapery Style. Among Four Finest Seen by PCGS. A highly lustrous specimen with reflective fields and frosty motifs that form a modest yet distinct cameo contrast. Largely lustrous with splashes of pale rose and gold. Diagonal planchet lines, parallel to each other and probably from the strip drying process, noted on the obverse but not overly distracting. Sharply struck toward the end of the year when the drapery feature was added at Miss Liberty's elbow. PCGS Population: 2; 2 finer (both MS-65).

From the Waccabuc Collection. Earlier from Heritage's Portland Sale, March 2004, Lot 5635.

The second variety of Liberty Seated quarter has drapery tumbling from Liberty's left elbow. This design was in use from 1840 through 1865, except for the years 1853 to 1855, when the third and fourth varieties were employed (see below).

With many date-and-mintmark combinations to choose among, you will be able to find an example that fits your collection in terms of condition and budget. As a general statement, the issues from the New Orleans Mint (especially 1849-O, 1851-O, and 1852-O) and the San Francisco Mint (all dates) are more expensive than those from the Philadelphia Mint. Don't rush to buy a coin of this type: wait for one with great eye appeal.

Lesson 65: The example I chose to represent the Liberty Seated With Drapery quarter in my type collection was, again, from the first year of issue. More importantly, I snared a coin that was among the four most highly graded by PCGS. When it came time to sell, this near "pop-top" coin (i.e., close to the top of the PGCS grading population report for this year) proved to be very desirable to at least two determined bidders. Population reports for 18th- and 19th-century coins are not likely to change significantly over time since most "old" coins have by now been professionally graded at least once. (A number of 20th-century issues, on the other hand, are not yet in plastic tombs, and population counts for these coins can and do change.) You will often be well rewarded for owning a classic American coin that's among the finest graded of its year or type. The "diagonal planchet lines" or striations mentioned by the cataloger are not as distracting as adjustment marks and did not seem to affect the desirability of this coin to its new owner.

Financials: Quarter, Liberty Seated, No Motto, With Drapery, 1840

Cost	Sale Price	Gain/Loss	Holding Period
$5,653	$16,100	+185%	3.7 years

QUARTER—LIBERTY SEATED, ARROWS AT DATE, RAYS AROUND EAGLE (1853)

Lot 1066.
1853. MS-64.
PCGS #005426.

Auction description: Lustrous Choice Uncirculated 1853 Quarter. Arrows and Rays Style. A frosty and highly lustrous example of this popular one-year-only design type; arrows remained at the date in 1854 and 1855, but 1853 was the only date of the design type to exhibit reverse rays around the central eagle. Mostly deep champagne on the obverse with some electric blue at the top; the reverse is a study in concentric circles of electric blue, crimson, and bright peach inward toward the pale golden center. Sharply struck.

From the Waccabuc Collection. Earlier from ANR's sale of the Frog Run Farm Collection, November 2004, Lot 1155.

The third variety of the Liberty Seated quarter, known as the Arrows and Rays type, was issued only in 1853. It was produced at both the Philadelphia Mint (just over 15.2 million pieces) and the New Orleans Mint (a little more than 1.3 million pieces).

With the discovery of vast quantities of gold in California in the late 1840s and early 1850s, the value of silver rose relative to the value of gold. This meant that silver coins were hoarded or melted for their precious-metal content. To combat this, the Act of February 21, 1853, provided for a reduction in weight of most silver coins. In the case of the quarter, the weight was reduced from 6.68 grams to 6.22 grams, with no change in fineness (90%) or diameter. To signify the change in weight, arrowheads were added on either side of the date on the obverse, and a circle of rays was attractively arranged around the eagle on the reverse.

As a single-year issue, there is considerable demand from collectors for an example of this type. Fortunately, the emission from the Philadelphia Mint was very large, and today it is not difficult to find an Arrows and Rays quarter in almost any grade desired up through MS-64. Gem and superb gem pieces (MS-65 through MS-67) are extremely elusive and expensive. If you want to include something a little different in your collection, you should give serious consideration to the 1853-O quarter or the 1854, 4 Over 3, overdate. Both are seen only rarely at auction, and their prices reflect this rarity.

Lesson 66: There are a couple of hundred certified MS-64 examples of the 1853 Arrows and Rays quarter in existence. I sold a particularly attractive one in late 2007 for almost $6,000, a modest gain over my cost. As I write this, I am aware of at least six comparably graded coins in PCGS or NGC holders that realized prices at auction of between $2,700 and $3,600 within the prior 12 months. Perhaps they weren't as appealing as the one I sold, but nevertheless, remember to be careful with common "rarities." Their potential for appreciation may be limited.

Financials: Quarter, Liberty Seated, Arrows at Date, Rays Around Eagle, 1853

Cost	Sale Price	Gain/Loss	Holding Period
$5,060	$5,980	+18%	3.0 years

QUARTER—LIBERTY SEATED, ARROWS AT DATE, NO RAYS (1854–1855)

Lot 1067.
1854. MS-64.
PCGS #005432.

In 1854 and 1855, for reasons that elude me, a fourth variety of the Liberty Seated quarter was created. The arrowheads by the date, introduced in 1853 to indicate that the weight of the coin had been reduced, were retained. However, the rays around the eagle on the reverse (also added in 1853) were inexplicably removed. No other changes were made, but for collectors seeking to assemble a complete type set, another variety was added to their want list.

The Liberty Seated Arrows, No Rays, variety was produced in both years at the Philadelphia and New Orleans mints and, in 1855 only, at the San Francisco Mint, which had just opened for business in the prior year. Production at the Philadelphia Mint was again huge: almost 12.4 million pieces were struck. In contrast, the total combined mintage of the other two mints in both years plus the mintage of the Philadelphia Mint in 1855 amounted to fewer than five million pieces.

Lesson 67: In building my type set, I was usually seeking the highest-quality example I could afford of each variety. This is the usual way of attacking a type set and is perfectly valid. It often means, however, that the coins you buy are among the most common of their type. Another approach, which may have greater financial potential over the long run, is to concentrate only on the rarities within each variety, without primary regard to condition. In the short Arrows, No Rays, quarter series, the two 1855 mintmarked issues (1855-O and 1855-S) have considerably lower mintages than the other three date-and-mintmark combinations. Another tempting choice might be the 1854-O, Huge O, variety. PCGS has not graded even a single example in Mint State condition, but the population of circulated coins is large enough (probably 300 to 400) that finding one should be a reasonable proposition.

Financials: Quarter, Liberty Seated, Arrows at Date, No Rays, 1854

Cost	Sale Price	Gain/Loss	Holding Period
$2,539	$3,450	+36%	4.8 years

QUARTER—LIBERTY SEATED, ARROWS AT DATE (1873–1874)

Lot 1068.
1874, Arrows. MS-65.
PCGS #005494.

Auction description: Gem Uncirculated 1874 Arrows Quarter. A satiny Gem. Rolling cartwheel luster supports a wealth of rich champagne on the obverse, with some faint champagne and rose highlights on the reverse. Somewhat prooflike, with a satiny field that tends to highlight the frosty motifs. Nicely struck for the issue with just a hint of lightness at certain obverse stars; all other details are fully delineated. PCGS Population: 9; 5 finer (all MS-66).

From the Waccabuc Collection. Earlier from Heritage's Long Beach Sale, January 2004, Lot 5756.

The fifth variety of the Liberty Seated quarter was produced in just two years—the latter part of 1873 and all of 1874. It is distinguished from the quarters immediately before and after those dates by the arrowheads placed on either side of the date. As was the case 20 years earlier, these arrowheads were added to alert the public to a change in the weight of the coins. Unlike the case in 1853, however, the weight change this time was trivial: from 6.22 grams to 6.25 grams. The arrows were removed after 1874, but the new weight was continued through the end of the series in 1891.

The 1873 and 1874 With Arrows quarters were produced in Philadelphia and San Francisco in both years and in Carson City in 1873 alone. The total mintage of this variety amounted to a little more than 2.2 million coins, about 80 percent of which were produced by the parent mint in Philadelphia. The Carson City issue is a significant rarity, with a mintage figure of only 12,462. Perhaps 50 to 75 of these survive today.

Lesson 68: A review of auction records over the past decade indicates that there's been very little change in the price of choice and gem Mint State examples of the more common 1873 and 1874 With Arrows quarters. If you want to buy one of these coins for your type set, you should do so with the expectation that you will not likely be making a good financial investment, even though you may consider the purchase a good psychic investment.

Financials: Quarter, Liberty Seated, Arrows at Date, 1874

Cost	Sale Price	Gain/Loss	Holding Period
$4,313	$4,830	+12%	3.8 years

QUARTER—LIBERTY SEATED, MOTTO ABOVE EAGLE (1866–1891)

Lot 1069.
1891. Proof-67.
PCGS #005592.

Auction description: Gorgeous 1891 Gem Proof Quarter. Vivid Iridescent Highlights. An exceptional Gem Proof quarter from the final year of the design type, one of 600 Proofs produced. Heavy cameo contrast is present, though not noted on the PCGS holder. Frosty obverse motifs and deeply mirrored fields alive with rich violet, crimson, peach, and electric blue, while the reverse is a study in faint rose and dusky neon blue. An exceptional coin that is among the half dozen finest Proofs of the date certified by PCGS. Truly beautiful. PCGS Population: 5; 1 finer within the designation (Proof-68). When all Proofs of the date are taken into consideration, including CAM examples, the population stands as six at Proof-67, with just two specimens finer, both Proof-68 CAM.

From the Waccabuc Collection. Earlier from ANR's sale of the Worthington Collection, May 2005, Lot 239.

The sixth and final variety of the Liberty Seated quarter was produced from 1866 through the end of the series in 1891. The defining feature of this variety is the addition of the motto IN GOD WE TRUST to the reverse of the coin, above the eagle.

Production of the With Motto Liberty Seated quarters was very large, particularly in the mid- to late-1870s. You will not have any difficulty finding an attractive and well-struck example for your collection. The series includes, however, several scarce and rare dates, the most famous of which is the 1873-CC issue without arrows at the date. 4,000 of these were reported to have been minted, but only four or five are known to exist today. One of these, graded PCGS MS-64, sold for $460,000 in a Stack's Bowers auction in August 2012. A more modest, but still very challenging, goal would be the 1891-O issue. This is the only Liberty Seated With Motto quarter produced at the New Orleans Mint.

Lesson 69: I took a chance with my purchase of this spectacularly beautiful 1891 quarter, and it did not work out well. I fell in love with the toning and kept my hand in the air far too long at the 2005 auction, paying almost three times the fair market price of an "ordinary" Proof-67 coin. When I sold my gem in 2007, the under-bidder from 2005 was apparently not in the audience, and the new owner only had to pay about twice the normal market value to buy this great coin. There's a difference between aggressive bidding and stupid bidding, and I was guilty of the latter in this instance.

Financials: Quarter, Liberty Seated, Motto Above Eagle, 1891

Cost	Sale Price	Gain/Loss	Holding Period
$11,500	$8,050	-30%	2.5 years

QUARTER—BARBER (1892–1916)

Lot 1070.

1900-O. MS-66.

PCGS #005626.

Auction description: Exceptional Gem Uncirculated 1900-O Quarter. A truly gorgeous Barber quarter, a coin laden with physical quality and superb aesthetic appeal. Largely brilliant centers yield to deep gold and neon blue halos. Sharply struck for the date with just a hint of lightness at certain reverse arrow feathers. A truly exceptional example of the date and grade, and a coin that deserves strong accolades. PCGS Population: 5, 2 finer (MS-68 finest). Struck from the old hub style with the tips of the eagle's wings on the reverse even with the top of the letters in the legend that they touch. Later in the year the reverse hub was touched up, and those eagle wing tips extend beyond the legends.

From the Waccabuc Collection. Earlier from Heritage's Long Beach Sale, January 2004, Lot 5772.

After more than half a century of production, the Liberty Seated quarter design was finally retired at the end of 1891. The new design, a stern, classical depiction of Miss Liberty facing right, with a laurel wreath and Phrygian cap on her head, was designed by Chief Engraver Charles E. Barber. These new quarters imaginatively came to be known as Barber quarters.

Barber quarters were produced from 1892 through 1916. Output for circulation remained large and steady for the most part through the life of this series. In addition, Proof coins were issued in each year except 1916. The type collector has many options available and has no need to hurry to make a decision. The date collector, on the other hand, faces three major stumbling blocks. The coins dated 1896-S, 1901-S, and 1913-S all had low mintages and today command high prices in all grades.

Lesson 70: My 1900-O quarter was a $5,000 to 6,000 coin when I bought it, but I paid a premium because of the superior "target" toning. Similarly, when this coin sold, the buyer also paid a modest premium over the standard MS-66 price. But I think I made one mistake that could have cost me money. When I bought this coin, it was housed in a first-generation PCGS holder, known in the trade as a "rattler" because coins in these holders had a tendency to rattle around inside the holder. The coin was also not oriented in an upright position relative to the holder but rather had rotated 120 degrees in a counter-clockwise direction inside the holder. For a small fee, I had the coin "re-holdered" by PCGS. Only later did I discover that some collectors are willing to pay extra for coins in first-generation holders. Their logic is that in the "good old days," grading standards were tougher, and many of these coins are good candidates for upgrades using today's standards. So now you know not to do what I did.

Financials: Quarter, Barber, 1900-O

Cost	Sale Price	Gain/Loss	Holding Period
$7,188	$7,935	+10%	3.8 years

QUARTER—STANDING LIBERTY, NO STARS BELOW EAGLE (1916–1917)

Lot 1071.
1916. MS-65 FH.
PCGS #005705.

Auction description: Gorgeous Gem 1916 Standing Liberty 25¢. Popular Key Date Rarity. A sparkling Gem example of this popular rare date from the first year of the series, an issue that saw a production run of just 52,000 pieces. A high degree of underlying luster supports a wealth of soft champagne, rose, and pale blue iridescence on both sides. Always in demand in all grades, with lovely Gem specimens such as the present beauty leading the list for desirable specimens. A pleasing coin that holds up well to the rigors of the Gem classification.

From the Waccabuc Collection. Earlier from Heritage's A.N.A. Convention Sale, August 1998, Lot 6521.

The extremely handsome Standing Liberty quarter, designed by Hermon A. MacNeil, was produced from late 1916 through 1930. Many collectors consider the design to be the most attractive within the quarter dollar series.

In 1916 almost 1.8 million Barber quarters were minted in Philadelphia. In December, the new Standing Liberty quarter was produced to the tune of only 52,000 coins, one of the lowest mintages of any 20th-century coin. It quickly became a favorite with collectors, and today it is expensive even in very low grades.

There are two principal varieties of Standing Liberty quarter. Variety 1 (sometimes called Type I) has a partially clothed Liberty on the obverse and a low-flying bird on the reverse. These two features were "corrected" in the middle of 1917, through the issuance of the Variety 2 (sometimes called Type II) quarter. These differences are discussed in more detail in connection with lots 1072 and 1073 below.

Lesson 71: Take a close look at the cataloger's description of this coin. The grade is listed as "MS-65 FH." The letters FH refer to "Full Head," a designation suggesting that the strike was strong enough to bring up all the details on Miss Liberty's head. But nowhere in the description of the coin does the cataloger make specific mention of the quality of the strike of this coin. In my view this is because the strike was just strong enough to qualify for the Full Head designation but was less than strong on other parts of the design, most notably on Liberty's shield: several of the rivets on the left (facing) side of the shield are barely visible, and the central part of the shield is a bit mushy. None of this is to suggest that the coin was not extremely pleasing visually—it was a great-looking example of this popular and scarce date. But it's important to know, before you buy the coin, all of the coin's strengths and weaknesses. The latter attributes are not always stressed in catalog descriptions. By the way, this identical coin reappeared in Stack's February 2008 auction, where it did not find a buyer. It's likely that an overly aggressive reserve price was the culprit.

Financials: Quarter, Standing Liberty, No Stars Below Eagle, 1916

Cost	Sale Price	Gain/Loss	Holding Period
$17,250	$34,500	+100%	9.3 years

QUARTER—STANDING LIBERTY, NO STARS BELOW EAGLE (1916–1917)

Lot 1072.
1917. MS-66 FH.
PCGS #005707.

Auction description: Deep and varied champagne hues roll easily across the intensely lustrous surfaces. Sharply struck with full shield, chevron, head, and eagle details. Undeniably Gem both aesthetically and physically.

From the Waccabuc Collection. Acquired from Heritage, June 2005.

As mentioned in the discussion of the prior lot, the Standing Liberty quarters issued in late 1916 and the first half of 1917 were different from those that followed. These Variety 1 quarters show Miss Liberty with a bare right breast on the obverse. On the reverse, the eagle is positioned below the center of the coin, and all 13 stars appear to the left and right of the bird's outstretched wings.

The 1916 issue is the key date in the Standing Liberty series. The other three Variety 1 quarters are all dated 1917 and come from the Philadelphia, Denver, and San Francisco mints. These latter three coins are all relatively common (particularly the Philadelphia issue) and probably have little financial potential because of this. Don't overpay—there will be plenty of opportunities at all grade levels.

Lesson 72: In stark contrast with the description of the 1916 quarter in lot 1071, the cataloger of the present coin wrote that my 1917 Variety 1 quarter was "sharply struck with full shield, chevron, head, and eagle details." Looking at these two coins side by side is very instructive when considering the range of striking quality that is encompassed within the Full Head designation.

Financials: Quarter, Standing Liberty, No Stars Below Eagle, 1917

Cost	Sale Price	Gain/Loss	Holding Period
$1,725	$1,610	-7%	2.4 years

QUARTER—STANDING LIBERTY, STARS BELOW EAGLE (1917–1930)

Lot 1073.
1930-S. MS-67 FH.
PCGS #005781.

Auction description: Impressive Gem 1930-S Quarter. Tied for Finest Graded by PCGS. A sparkling Gem with intense cartwheel luster and rich gold on both sides. Sharp and appealing and worthy of the assigned grade; careful examination will reveal a coin that deserves to be at the top of the PCGS Population Report. PCGS Population: 17; none finer within the designation.

From the Waccabuc Collection. Earlier from Heritage's Long Beach Sale, February 2006, Lot 1097.

Popular (though untrue) legend says that some observers complained about the partial nudity on the Variety 1 quarters, and that Mint engravers went to work and came up with a G-rated replacement design. Today we know that the change was made at the request of designer Hermon MacNeil to show the nation's military preparedness to enter World War I. Miss Liberty was clothed in chain mail. On the reverse, the eagle was moved to the center of the coin, and three of the thirteen stars were placed below the raptor.

The "new and improved" Variety 2 design was retained through the end of the series in 1930. Along the way, in 1925, a real improvement was made when the date on the Standing Liberty quarter was recessed slightly to protect it from excessive wear. Before 1925, the date was one of the first features to get worn down, and many early quarters of this type are found without any visible date at all. For the final six years of this issue, the problem was entirely eliminated.

Lesson 73: My 1930-S quarter was a "pop-top" coin—tied for finest certified in PCGS's population report. Unfortunately, it was tied with 16 other coins. Five years after the sale, the population of 1930-S quarters graded MS-67 FH had grown to 22. It's possible this number represents 22 grading events rather than 22 different coins since some of these coins may have been submitted to PCGS more than once in the hope of obtaining a better grade (a practice that is common when it comes to genuinely rare coins where a small difference in grade can mean thousands of dollars of difference in value). But either way, my "pop-top" coin didn't quite have the cachet of a finest-known coin with no or few other equals. Thus, the potential for financial gain was much more modest.

Financials: Quarter, Standing Liberty, Stars Below Eagle, 1930-S

Cost	Sale Price	Gain/Loss	Holding Period
$4,600	$4,830	+5%	1.8 years

QUARTER—WASHINGTON (1932–PRESENT)

Lot 1074.
1961. Proof-69 DCAM.
PCGS #095993.

Auction description: Tied for finest certified by PCGS. A sparkling cameo Proof of the date, a pleasing Gem with heavily frosted motifs and deeply mirrored fields. Some faint golden toning can be seen at the obverse rim. Truly exceptional and worthy of this lofty grade. PCGS Population: 41; none finer within the designation.

From the Waccabuc Collection. Earlier from Heritage's Dallas Sale, December 2004, Lot 6016.

The familiar Washington quarter, designed by John Flanagan, a New York sculptor, was first minted in 1932 and remains in production, in modified form, to the present day. It was initially conceived as a commemorative to mark the 200th anniversary of George Washington's birth.

The metallic composition of the Washington quarter was 90 percent silver and 10 percent copper through 1964. When the value of the silver in the quarter exceeded the face value of the coin, the silver content was eliminated and replaced with a copper-nickel composition.

Lesson 74: The price of modern Proof coins in high grades has been extremely volatile over the past decade. Interest has grown and ebbed and grown again. This coin, which lost half its value in the three years I owned it, would now likely cost more than my initial purchase price. The classic series of 18th- and 19th-century coins, as a general statement, are less volatile than their modern counterparts.

Financials: Quarter, Washington, 1961

Cost	Sale Price	Gain/Loss	Holding Period
$920	$460	-50%	2.9 years

QUARTER—WASHINGTON (1932–PRESENT)

Lot 1075.
1965, MS-68 SMS; 1976-S Clad, Proof-69 DCAM; 1976-S Silver, Proof-69 DCAM; 1999-S Connecticut, Clad, Proof-69 DCAM; 1999-S Connecticut, Silver, Proof-69 DCAM.

Auction description: Quintet of PCGS-certified Washington quarters: * 1965 MS-68 SMS * 1976-S Clad. Proof-69 DCAM * 1976-S Silver. Proof-69 DCAM * 1999-S Connecticut. Clad. Proof-69 DCAM * 1999-S Connecticut-Silver. Proof-69 DCAM. An exceptional group of eye-catching Washington quarters. (Total: 5 pieces)

From the Waccabuc Collection.

I bought these five common Washington quarters because I needed them for inclusion in my 20th-century type set. None qualifies as a rare coin, though all are in much finer condition than normally seen. To represent the clad and Proof Statehood quarter series, I chose examples from my home state of Connecticut. From an aesthetic standpoint, the portrait of George Washington on the quarters minted since 1999 is, to my eye, much less noble than the one used in earlier years. Nevertheless, the wide variety of reverses, commemorating the 50 states, provides a wonderful 21st-century platform for young collectors to learn about history and collecting. I have to admit that I got very little excitement from acquiring these coins, and I felt absolutely no seller's remorse when the hammer came down on this lot. As was the case with my Roosevelt dimes, I lost money on these coins. If I'd had the patience, I probably could have gotten more by selling them individually on eBay, though it hardly seemed worth the effort.

A curiosity that is loosely linked to the modern Statehood quarter series is the Statehood quarter obverse that is muled with a Sacagawea dollar reverse. (Most of us know a mule as the offspring of the union of a male donkey with a female horse. A mule in numismatic circles, not surprisingly, is a coin that mates an obverse from one series with an anomalous reverse from a different series.) These error coins are spectacular modern flubs on the part of the U.S. Mint. A dozen or more have been found so far, one of which sold in a Stack's Bowers Galleries auction in 2012 for more than $155,000.

Lesson 75: Repeating lesson 22, don't spend a lot of time or money on items you don't care about. Yes, completing the collection of modern issues was somewhat satisfying, but I rarely looked at these coins or showed them to others. This is not to say that collecting modern coins isn't worthwhile. It can be interesting, educational, and fun. But for the most part they're not rare coins, and seeking an imperceptibly finer example of a common modern coin wasn't something that gave me much of a thrill.

Financials: Quarter, Washington, 1965, 1976-S, 1976-S, 1999-S, 1999-S

Cost	Sale Price	Gain/Loss	Holding Period
$370	$184	-50%	Various

CHAPTER

12

Half
Dollars

Everyone replaces his divot after a perfect approach shot.

And everyone will tell you that you can make money by building your collection carefully and holding it for a reasonable span of years. The word *carefully* is key.

While this maxim is undoubtedly true across a large number of coins, a large number of collections, and a large number of years, you should not extrapolate that all coin purchases will yield profits with the passage of time. My collection of half dollars illustrates this point well. Among the 17 lots discussed in this chapter, 11 sold for more than their purchase prices, 5 realized losses, and 1 achieved breakeven. The details are discussed below.

Half dollars were first minted in 1794. The Flowing Hair design, similar to that used on early half dimes and silver dollars, lasted for just two years. It was replaced by another two-year issue, the famed Draped Bust, Small Eagle, design, of which a mere 3,918 pieces were minted in 1796 and 1797. After a hiatus of three years, the Draped Bust, Heraldic Eagle, format was introduced. It lasted through 1807. The Capped Bust half dollar, a workhorse coin in its time, had a 32-year run through 1839. It was succeeded by the Liberty Seated design, which, with variations, lasted for more than half a century through 1891. The Barber half followed (1892 to 1915), after which the elegant Liberty Walking design (1916 to 1947) made its appearance. The less elegant (some would say plain) Franklin half dollar was minted beginning in 1948. It remained in production through 1963, when President John F. Kennedy was assassinated. The Kennedy half appeared the next year and continues to be minted to the present day even though its usage in day-to-day commerce is limited. All of these designs are discussed in more detail on the following pages.

HALF DOLLAR—FLOWING HAIR (1794–1795)

Lot 1076.
1795. EF-45.
O-122. Rarity-5. PCGS #006052.

Auction description: Choice EF 1795 Flowing Hair 50¢. Medium golden gray with deepening toning highlights, especially on the obverse. Casual examination under low magnification reveals a scattering of tiny circulation marks, none overly deep or egregious, or worthy of individual mention. A scarce variety coupled with a pleasing coin overall, and a grand selection for those interested in assembling an early American type set.

From the Waccabuc Collection. Earlier from ANR's sale of the New York Connoisseur's Collection, March 2006, Lot 727.

In 1792, the Mint in Philadelphia turned out a few half dismes in the basement of a building near the official U.S. Mint structure, which was in the process of being remodeled and added to. The next year, some half cents and cents were struck. In 1794 they finally got around to some larger denominations.

The Flowing Hair half dollar was minted for two years—1794 and 1795. Production in the first year amounted to fewer than 24,000 pieces, of which 1,200 or so exist today. Output was ramped up to almost 300,000 in 1795, and this is the date that is usually found in type sets. Uneven striking quality and adjustment marks are the rule rather than the exception for both years. A circulated coin with some flaws is about the best you can aspire to.

Like some other early coins, the Flowing Hair half dollar does not display a denomination on either the obverse or the reverse. You have to look on the coin's "third side" (the edge) to see the inscription FIFTY CENTS OR HALF A DOLLAR.

Lesson 76: I once owned a mid-range Very Fine 1794 half dollar and earned a nice return when I sold it after five or six years. I then "traded up" for the somewhat finer 1795 half that is shown here. As noted, I lost money on this transaction after a relatively short holding period. Two years is rarely enough time to see a positive return on an investment in a coin. I would have been better off just sticking with my original purchase: I wouldn't have lost money, and I wouldn't have paid a second buyer's fee.

Financials: Half dollar, Flowing Hair, 1795

Cost	Sale Price	Gain/Loss	Holding Period
$11,500	$10,350	-10%	1.7 years

HALF DOLLAR—DRAPED BUST, SMALL EAGLE REVERSE (1796–1797)

Lot 1077.

1797. F-15.

O-101a. Rarity-4+. PCGS #006060.

Auction description: Celebrated 1797 Half Dollar. Medium to deep lilac-gray with lighter high points, evenly worn with full rim details present on both sides. Some old, shallow obverse scratches cross Liberty's portrait and the fields surrounding, though they have long since toned. From a late state of the dies with advanced obverse and reverse cracks. From a reported mintage of 3,918 pieces, a figure that includes the total for the 1796 and 1797 Draped Bust, Small Eagle half dollars. The 1796 half dollar rarity comes with 15 obverse and 16 obverse stars, while all 1797 half dollars exhibit 15 obverse stars. A greatly prized rarity in a most agreeable collector grade, and a coin with splendid eye appeal for that grade. We suspect more than the usual amount of auction activity when this favorable specimen of a classic rarity crosses the auction block.

From the Waccabuc Collection. Earlier from ANR's sale of the LaBelle Collection, July 2005, Lot 1148. From Heritage's Long Beach Sale, February 2006, Lot 1146.

An old man walked into a coin dealer's store. He said he owned a 1796 half dollar and would bring it in the next day for the dealer to look at. When the old man arrived the next morning, he proudly announced to the dealer, "Good news! My coin is even older than I thought—it's dated 1795."

I don't know if this tale is true or apocryphal, but I remember it gave me a smile when I first heard it. In the case of early half dollars, older is not necessarily better. The "new" half dollars of 1796 and 1797 have a handsome Draped

Bust obverse engraved by Robert Scot paired with a Small Eagle reverse. Fewer than 4,000 pieces were struck in total for both years. The 1796 coins are seen with both 15 and 16 stars flanking the image of Liberty, while the 1797 coins all come with 15 stars. The market values of the three principal varieties differ only marginally—all are rare and expensive. The finest known example, graded NGC MS-66, was sold in a Stack's auction in July 2008 for $1,380,000.

Lesson 77: Like most collectors, I'd always wanted to own an example of the rarest silver type coin. When my type set was nearing completion, this piece came up for sale. I took a deep breath and put in a strong enough bid to win the auction. As the cataloger pointed out, this particular coin was a "greatly prized rarity in a most agreeable collector grade." While a coin grading Fine-15 would be something to sneeze at in most other series, this is not the case when it comes to Draped Bust, Small Eagle, half dollars. In this grade it is solidly in the sweet spot of collector interest. I didn't make much money after accounting for the buyer's commission, but it was a thrill to be the custodian of this great rarity for a couple of years.

Financials: Half dollar, Draped Bust, Small Eagle Reverse, 1797

Cost	Sale Price	Gain/Loss	Holding Period
$48,875	$57,500	+18%	2.3 years

HALF DOLLAR—DRAPED BUST, HERALDIC EAGLE REVERSE (1801–1807)

Lot 1078.
1806, Pointed 6, Stem Through Claw. MS-63.
O-116. Rarity-3. PCGS #006071.

Auction description: Choice Uncirculated 1806 Half Dollar. Pointed 6, Stem Through Claw. Deep lilac-gray surfaces with richly imbedded luster supporting bright gold, sea green, neon blue, and rose iridescence. Strike substantially finer than often seen for the date but some lightness is noted on the eagle's dexter wing and at PLUR. Boldly repunched TY in LIBERTY, heavy obverse die cracks, reverse die cracks moderately heavy. An exceptional opportunity.

From the Waccabuc Collection. Earlier from ANR's C.L. Lee Sale, September 2005, Lot 397.

After the puny mintage of 3,918 half dollars in 1796 and 1797, the Mint took a three-year break. In 1801, production of half dollars was resumed with the issuance of the Draped Bust, Heraldic Eagle, design. The obverse was similar to that used on the preceding type except that the number of stars flanking Miss Liberty was standardized at 13 rather than 15 or 16. The reverse was entirely redesigned, with a large or "heraldic" eagle replacing the small eagle. The denomination was again to be found only on the edge.

Half dollars of the Draped Bust, Heraldic Eagle, type were issued in each year from 1801 through 1807, except for 1804. None of the dates is a great rarity, though the first two years of issue had the lowest mintages and are somewhat more expensive than the other dates. The most common date is the 1806, though some of the varieties created that year (particularly the one with the knobbed 6 in the date and the stem of the branch on the reverse not extending through the claw of the eagle) are decidedly scarce.

Virtually all Draped Bust, Heraldic Eagle, half dollars show signs of weak striking. This characteristic seems to have gotten worse with the passage of years. As Dave Bowers has pointed out, "Nearly all halves dated 1806 and 1807 show weakness. Even an Uncirculated specimen is apt to be very weakly defined in such areas as the rims, the obverse and reverse stars, and parts of the eagle." This is why the cataloger of my coin considered the strike to be "substantially finer than often seen," even though it was weak in several areas.

The buyer of this coin flipped it for a small profit. How do I know? I was leafing through the Stack's February 2008 catalog when I came across the photo of "my" coin on page 290. It sold for $23,000, which means a hammer price of $20,000 plus the 15 percent buyer's fee. The seller would likely have gotten something around the hammer price—a profit of $500 or so for his three-month holding period.

Lesson 78: A little study of this short series will reveal that, although no half dollars dated 1804 exist, it is possible to acquire an 1805 dollar where the 5 in the date has been punched over the numeral 4. Apparently, dies with the 1804 date were prepared at the mint, but no coins were produced. Not wanting to waste these dies, the mint engraver punched a 5 over the 4 and used the dies to produce some of the 1805 half dollars. The overdate feature is clearly visible to the naked eye and would make a delightful addition to any collection of early U.S. coins.

Financials: Half dollar, Draped Bust, Heraldic Eagle Reverse, 1806, Pointed 6, Stem Through Claw

Cost	Sale Price	Gain/Loss	Holding Period
$17,250	$19,550	+13%	2.2 years

HALF DOLLAR—CAPPED BUST, LETTERED EDGE (1807–1836)

Lot 1079.
1830, Large 0. MS-64.
O-122. Rarity-1. PCGS #006157.

Auction description: Choice Uncirculated 1830 Half Dollar. Large 0. A frosty Capped Bust half dollar that approaches Gem quality in many ways. Soft underlying luster enlivens rich sea green, peach, and pale neon blue, while the bold strike becomes an immediate focus of attention. A pleasing coin that holds up nicely to prolonged scrutiny.

From the Waccabuc Collection. Earlier from ANR's sale of the The Pevehouse and Davis Collections, October 2004, Lot 388.

John Reich was the designer of the lettered-edge Capped Bust half dollar, which was produced in every year from 1807 through 1836, except for 1816. In January of that year a fire destroyed the machinery used to make gold and silver planchets, interrupting precious-metal coin production until late 1817. As no silver dollars were produced for broad circulation between 1804 and 1840, the half dollar became the workhorse denomination in trade and commerce. Half dollars were also used for bulk transactions between banks, which probably accounts for the survival of a reasonable number of pieces in Uncirculated grades.

The Capped Bust half dollar series represents one of the most popular sets for collectors to build. The design is simple, classic, and attractive. Mintages were high—generally more than one million in each of the early years and three to six million in most years after 1823. The relatively primitive production methods in use almost two centuries ago resulted in a wide range of varieties, including many obvious overdates (1808/7, 1814/3, 1817/3, 1824 over various dates [!], and many more) and a grab-bag full of engraving blunders (the 1807 with the denomination 50 punched over an erroneous 20, the 18.11 punctuated date, the 1836 50/00, and many others). Most dates and many of the varieties are available in a wide range of grades to suit virtually all budgets. The series even has its own dedicated club: the Bust Half Nut Club (www. busthalfnutclub.org).

For type collectors, this is one coin that you do not need to buy right away. You'll see many examples in dealers' inventories and in auction catalogs. Don't rush in until you find one with excellent eye appeal and a good strike. Check for weakness on the obverse stars and on E PLURIBUS UNUM on the reverse.

Lesson 79: As noted in chapter 2, describing the color of a coin is an art form. In the Waccabuc sale, my Capped Bust half was described as "rich sea green, peach, and pale neon blue." When I bought it from American Numismatic Rarities three years earlier, it was "slate blue with brighter blue-green and rose." Whatever the words say, take a look at the coin and make sure you like it.

Financials: Half dollar, Capped Bust, Lettered Edge, 1830, Large 0

Cost	Sale Price	Gain/Loss	Holding Period
$3,450	$4,600	+33%	3.1 years

HALF DOLLAR—CAPPED BUST, REEDED EDGE, REVERSE 50 CENTS (1836–1837)

Lot 1080.
1837. MS-64.
PCGS #006176.

Auction description: Uncirculated 1837 Reeded Edge 50¢. Highly lustrous on both sides, largely brilliant at the centers with deepening blue, gold, and crimson highlights toward the rims. From the first year of mass production of the new half dollar style with reeded edge instead of lettered edge, struck to the tune of more than 3.6 million pieces—the 1836 Reeded Edge half dollar issue, made in late 1836 or perhaps even early 1837, has an estimated mintage of slightly more than 4,000 pieces. A few light hairlines and abrasions present, but no heavy surface digs or other unsightly bruises are noted. Type with reverse denomination as 50 CENTS.

From the Waccabuc Collection. Earlier from Heritage's New York Sale, June 2005, Lot 5691.

Christian Gobrecht modified John Reich's Capped Bust design to produce a similar but distinct type for the years 1836 through 1839. Steam-powered presses were used for the first time, the diameter was reduced slightly (from 32.5 mm to 30 mm), and the lettered edge was replaced with a reeded edge. In 1836 and 1837, the denomination was expressed as 50 CENTS. In the next two years (see next lot), it was changed to HALF DOL.

Almost everyone who needs an example of this variety ends up buying one dated 1837. This is understandable given the puny mintage of the 1836 (reported as 1,200 pieces but now estimated to be slightly more than 4,000) versus the mammoth production achieved in 1837 (3.6 million). In my view, the 1836 is a real "sleeper." Lightly circulated examples are not terribly expensive, especially considering the mintage, and even one of the few surviving MS-63 or MS-64 coins can be had for something like $15,000 to $25,000, though auction appearances are, admittedly, infrequent. I made a nice profit on an AU-55 example I owned for a few years, before "upgrading" to this MS-64 1837. If I had it to do again, I'd stretch for a better 1836.

Lesson 80: This 1837 half dollar is a $4,000 to $5,000 coin that I grossly overpaid for because I fell in love with the peripheral toning. While I still consider it to be an attractive coin, it's not particularly rare in MS-64— the two leading grading services have certified more than 150 coins in this grade and half as many again in higher grades. And although the toning is nice, it's not drop-dead gorgeous. The only consolation I have is that some other idiot bid almost as much as I did before he "lost" this coin to me in June 2005. I didn't do my homework before bidding on this coin. Don't fall into the same trap. Ouch.

Financials: Half dollar, Capped Bust, Reeded Edge, Reverse 50 CENTS, 1837

Cost	Sale Price	Gain/Loss	Holding Period
$8,625	$4,370	-49%	2.4 years

HALF DOLLAR—CAPPED BUST, REEDED EDGE, REVERSE HALF DOL. (1838–1839)

Lot 1081.
1838. MS-64.
PCGS #006177.

Auction description: Choice Uncirculated 1838 Reeded Edge 50¢. Chiefly brilliant centers yield quickly to deepening gold heaviest at the rims. Broadly sweeping cartwheel luster increases the eye appeal of this satiny beauty, and the bold, crisp strike is another fine highlight. Repunching seen at base of second 8. No serious marks present, pleasing for the grade. Denomination as HALF DOL.

From the Waccabuc Collection. Acquired from Larry Whitlow, January 2004.

As mentioned in the discussion of the preceding lot, the second type of Reeded Edge half dollar had the denomination expressed as HALF DOL. This version, like its predecessor, was minted for just two years—1838 and 1839.

For the first time, a branch mint was enlisted to strike half dollars. The mint in New Orleans produced 20 special strikes in 1838 (thus creating a classic rarity) and almost 179,000 regular circulation strikes in 1839. (Meanwhile, the Philadelphia Mint produced just under five million half dollars in 1838 and 1839.) The finest known example of an 1838-O half dollar sold for just under $735,000 in a Heritage auction in January 2013.

Lesson 81: It's time for another confession, similar to the one I made in connection with lot 1076. At one time, I owned an excellent example of the 1839-O Capped Bust half dollar. It had nice original toning and was graded MS-63. I made a satisfying profit when I sold it. I gained one lousy grading point when I purchased this relatively ordinary 1838 half dollar. After owning it for almost four years, I lost money in a strong coin market, even before accounting for the buyer's commission. I should not have changed horses midstream.

Financials: Half dollar, Capped Bust, Reeded Edge, Reverse HALF DOL., 1838

Cost	Sale Price	Gain/Loss	Holding Period
$5,500	$5,290	-4%	3.8 years

HALF DOLLAR—LIBERTY SEATED, NO MOTTO ABOVE EAGLE, NO DRAPERY (1839)

Lot 1082.
1839. AU-55.
PCGS #006230.

Auction description: Warm champagne hues grace the largely lustrous surfaces. Lightly circulated, but not heavily marked and choice for the grade. Some lightness of strike is seen on the dexter side of the eagle, though such is almost a given for this date.

From the Waccabuc Collection. Earlier from Heritage's C.S.N.S. Convention Sale, May 2003, Lot 6746.

Created by Christian Gobrecht, the Liberty Seated obverse design marked a sharp departure from the depictions of a bust of Miss Liberty seen up until this time on American half dollars. The basic design, which would survive for more than half a century, shows Liberty seated on a rock holding a staff in her left hand. Atop the staff is a liberty cap. Her right hand supports a shield inscribed with the word LIBERTY. The reverse is similar in general concept to that used on the Capped Bust half dollar.

For purposes of the PCGS set registry, there are six recognized varieties of the Liberty Seated half dollar. The first, as shown here, is the No Drapery type, which was minted only in 1839 and only in Philadelphia. On this variety, there is no motto (IN GOD WE TRUST was not added to the reverse until 1866), and there is no drapery hanging from Liberty's left elbow.

As a one-year type, and as the first year of issue of the Liberty Seated series, the 1839 Liberty Seated, No Drapery, half dollar is subject to steady demand from collectors. Fortunately, the mintage was large enough that there are several hundred certified coins available in the market. Prices for circulated examples are reasonable. Gems, on the other hand, are rare and expensive. An NGC MS-67 example was sold in a Heritage auction in January 2011 for $172,500.

Lesson 82: If your objective is to assemble a comprehensive type collection, you will have no choice of dates or mintmarks when it comes to the Liberty Seated, No Drapery, half dollar. The 1839 issue made in Philadelphia is your only option. Unless money is no object, look for a lightly circulated example with good color and a decent strike. You can't expect to do much better than this.

Financials: Half dollar, Liberty Seated, No Motto, No Drapery, 1839

Cost	Sale Price	Gain/Loss	Holding Period
$3,910	$4,313	+10%	4.5 years

HALF DOLLAR—LIBERTY SEATED, NO MOTTO ABOVE EAGLE, WITH DRAPERY (1839–1865)

Lot 1083.
1839. MS-64.
PCGS #006232.

Auction description: Lustrous Uncirculated 1839 Liberty Seated 50¢. With Drapery. Frosty golden gray with rich and varied champagne, peach, neon blue, and sea green highlights. Sharply struck in all areas of the design and with no serious marks that can be detected with the unaided eye. Just two examples of the date have been certified finer by PCGS than that presently offered. An exceptional example of the earliest of all Liberty Seated half dollar issues, a coin that is at once eye-catching aesthetically and of remarkable physical quality. PCGS Population: 15; 2 finer (MS-65 finest).

From the Waccabuc Collection. Acquired from Northeast Numismatics, November 2002.

The second variety of the Liberty Seated half dollar has drapery hanging from Liberty's left elbow. This new design was introduced later in 1839 and continued in use through 1865, except for the years 1853 to 1855, when the third and fourth varieties were employed (see following).

With many date-and-mintmark combinations to choose among, you will be able to find an example that fits your collection in terms of condition and budget. The Philadelphia, New Orleans, and (beginning in 1856) San Francisco mints all produced large quantities of this type of half dollar. Don't rush to buy a coin of this type: wait for one with a strong strike and great eye appeal.

Although there are a few scarcer dates or sub-varieties within this series, there is one coin that deserves special mention. The 1853-O half dollar without arrows or rays is known to exist to the extent of only four pieces. The best of these is a PCGS VF-35 example that last sold in a Stack's auction in October 2006 for $368,000. Many numismatists consider this to be the most important Liberty Seated coin of any denomination.

Lesson 83: For decades, guide books listed only three examples of the 1853-O No Arrows half dollar. But in 2012 a fourth example came to light (now graded PCGS VG-8). This is not an isolated example. Discoveries are regularly made of scarce or rare coins that are unknown to the collecting community. A friend once asked for my opinion on a few coins that he'd found in his late uncle's dresser. Most were worth very little, but one of them was a 1795 eagle in About Uncirculated condition. Hey, you never know.

Financials: Half dollar, Liberty Seated, No Motto, With Drapery, 1839

Cost	Sale Price	Gain/Loss	Holding Period
$2,900	$3,680	+27%	5.0 years

HALF DOLLAR—LIBERTY SEATED, ARROWS AT DATE, RAYS AROUND EAGLE (1853)

Lot 1084.
1853-O. MS-63.
PCGS #006232.

Auction description: Choice Mint State 1853-O Half Dollar. Arrows and Rays. Strong underlying luster supports deep golden gray and muted champagne highlights on both sides. Obverse die shattered at 2:00–3:00. Better than typical strike for the date, though some lightness is noted. Considerably scarcer, especially in Mint State, than its Philadelphia Mint counterpart. The present choice Uncirculated half dollar is among the 15 finest grading events for the date at PCGS. The Philadelphia Mint production for this date was more than 2.6 times greater than that of the New Orleans Mint, but the present writer's experience shows the New Orleans half dollar of the date to be considerably scarcer than the previously mentioned 2.6 to 1 ratio suggests. PCGS Population: 6; 9 finer (MS-65 finest).

From the Waccabuc Collection. Earlier from the Douglas L. Noblet Collection. Bowers and Merena's Rarities Sale, January 1999, Lot 112.

The third variety of the Liberty Seated half dollar in the PCGS Set Registry, known as the Arrows and Rays type, was issued only in 1853. It was produced at both the Philadelphia Mint (just over 3.5 million pieces) and the New Orleans Mint (a little more than 1.3 million pieces).

As discussed earlier, with the discovery of vast quantities of gold in California in the late 1840s and early 1850s, the value of silver rose relative to the value of gold. This meant that silver coins were hoarded or melted for their precious-metal content. To combat this, the Act of February 21, 1853, provided for a reduction in weight of most silver coins. In the case of the half dollar, the weight was reduced from 13.36 grams to 12.44 grams, with no change in fineness (90%) or diameter. To signify the change in weight, arrowheads were added on either side of the date on the obverse, and a circle of rays was attractively engraved around the eagle on the reverse.

As a single-year issue, there is considerable demand from collectors for an example of this type. Fortunately, the emission from the Philadelphia Mint was reasonably large, and today it is not difficult to find an Arrows and Rays half dollar in almost any grade desired up through MS-64. Gem and superb gem pieces (MS-65 through MS-67) are elusive and expensive. The 1853-O Arrows and Rays half dollar is somewhat scarcer than its Philadelphia cousin, but enough pieces were minted that examples are seen with some regularity at auctions.

Lesson 84: I honestly expected more from my 1853-O Arrows and Rays half dollar when it crossed the auction block. I had not overpaid for it back in 1999, I'd held it for almost nine years, and I was selling it into a generally strong coin market. I made money on the sale, but only about half as much as I was expecting. Five years after that 2007 auction, the price for a comparable coin in the same grade was unchanged from the price I achieved. Although you may feel a coin should be worth more, reality is not always so kind. Like several other Waccabuc Collection coins, this half dollar was re-consigned by its new owner to Stack's next sale in February 2008. Its reserve price was not met.

Financials: Half dollar, Liberty Seated, Arrows at Date, Rays Around Eagle, 1853-O

Cost	Sale Price	Gain/Loss	Holding Period
$4,150	$6,900	+66%	8.8 years

HALF DOLLAR—LIBERTY SEATED, ARROWS AT DATE, NO RAYS (1854–1855)

Lot 1085.
1854-O. MS-64.
PCGS #006280.

Auction description: Attractive 1854-O Arrows Half Dollar. Intense cartwheel luster supports rich and varied champagne, peach, crimson, and electric blue iridescence on the obverse, while the luster-laden reverse glows with medium champagne highlights. About as nicely struck as ever found for the date, with just a bare hint of softness. Undeniably choice for the grade both physically and visually, a coin that is destined to make a lasting impression in carefully thought out U.S. type collection.

From the Waccabuc Collection. Acquired from Larry Whitlow, March 2003.

Just as was the case for the Liberty Seated, Arrows at Date, *quarters* of 1854 and 1855, a fourth variety of the Liberty Seated half dollars was created in those same years and with the same changes. The arrowheads by the date, introduced in 1853 to indicate that the weight of the coin had been reduced, were retained. However, the rays around the eagle on the reverse (also added in 1853) were inexplicably removed. No other changes were made, but for collectors seeking to assemble a complete type set, another variety was added to their want list.

The Liberty Seated, Arrows, No Rays, variety was produced in both years at the Philadelphia and New Orleans mints and, in 1855 only, at the San Francisco Mint, which had just opened for business in the prior year. Reversing the situation that applied to quarters of this type, the New Orleans Mint, rather than the parent mint in Philadelphia, was the leading producer of half dollars in these two years, churning out about 70 percent of the total mintage. The San Francisco Mint, on the other hand, contributed only about 1 percent of the total. Most survivors are well circulated, but there's one superb gem NGC MS-67 (previously part of the magnificent James Bennett Pryor collection) that sold for $115,000 in a Stack's Bowers Galleries auction in August 2011.

Lesson 85: Most of the coins in my collection were bought at auctions, partly because the selection of different types was more extensive than most dealers' inventories, and partly because I liked the thrill of competition that the auction scene promised. However, I regularly checked the offerings of several dealers with whom I'd done business over the years. One of these was Larry Whitlow, who's had a coin business in the Chicago area for more than three decades. He sold me a premium example of the relatively common 1854-O With Arrows half dollar, with a strong strike, nice color, and excellent luster. I did well financially when I sold this coin. Don't think that auctions are the only source for rare coins at good prices. Reputable dealers won't rip you off, and you're likely to learn something about our hobby along the way.

Financials: Half dollar, Liberty Seated, Arrows at Date, No Rays, 1854-O

Cost	Sale Price	Gain/Loss	Holding Period
$3,100	$4,600	+48%	4.7 years

HALF DOLLAR—LIBERTY SEATED, ARROWS AT DATE (1873–1874)

Lot 1086.
1873. MS-64.
PCGS #006343.

Auction description: Choice Uncirculated 1873 Arrows 50¢. Warm golden gray surfaces with a glorious array of infused luster that adds vivid life to rich peach, sea green, varied golden hues, and rich carmine iridescence on the obverse; the reverse is alive with concentric rings of violet, pale gold, electric blue, and peach. Aesthetically appealing.

From the Waccabuc Collection. Earlier from Heritage's C.S.N.S. Convention Sale, May 2003, Lot 6765.

Like the Liberty Seated quarters of 1873 and 1874, the fifth variety of the Liberty Seated half dollar was produced in just two years—the latter part of 1873 and all of 1874. It is distinguished from the half dollars produced immediately before and after those dates by the arrowheads placed on either side of the date. As was the case 20 years earlier, these arrowheads were added to alert the public to a change in the weight of the coins. Unlike the case in 1853, however, the weight change this time was trivial: from 12.44 grams to 12.50 grams. The arrows were removed after 1874, but the new weight was continued through the end of the series in 1891.

The 1873 and 1874 With Arrows half dollars were produced in Philadelphia, Carson City, and San Francisco in both years. The total mintage of this variety amounted to a little more than five million coins, about 80 percent of which were produced by the parent mint in Philadelphia.

Lesson 86: The market price of a common-date Liberty Seated half dollar has not changed much over recent years. I bought mine in 2003 for about $3,000, and you didn't have to pay much more ten years later for a comparable PCGS MS-64 example. My particular example sold very well in the 2007 auction because the market was still strong at that time and the coin itself was attractive. The cataloger pulled out all the stops to describe the aesthetic appeal of this coin: "rich peach, sea green, varied golden hues, and rich carmine iridescence on the obverse; the reverse is alive with concentric rings of violet, pale gold, electric blue, and peach." Though it's hard to prove, it's my belief that catalog descriptions like this one can contribute to a strong price realization. Thank you, Stack's.

Financials: Half dollar, Liberty Seated, Arrows at Date, 1873

Cost	Sale Price	Gain/Loss	Holding Period
$2,990	$5,060	+69%	4.5 years

HALF DOLLAR—LIBERTY SEATED, MOTTO ABOVE EAGLE (1866–1891)

Lot 1087.
1885. Proof-66.
PCGS #006446.

Auction description: Gem Proof 1885 Half Dollar. Satiny, somewhat reflective fields and lightly frosted motifs exude warm, rolling luster. Both sides are graced with muted gold, rose, and violet toning. A pleasing Gem Proof of the date that is near the top of the PCGS Population Report. PCGS Population: 9; 1 finer within any designation (Proof-67). From the Waccabuc Collection. Acquired from Heritage, April 2006.

The sixth and final variety of the Liberty Seated half dollar was produced from 1866 through the end of the series in 1891. The defining feature of this variety is the addition of the motto IN GOD WE TRUST to the reverse of the coin, above the eagle.

Production of the With Motto Liberty Seated half dollars was very large, particularly in the mid- to late 1870s (peaking at 8.4 million pieces from the Philadelphia Mint alone in 1876). You will not have any difficulty finding an attractive and well-struck example for your collection.

Mintages shrank drastically after 1878 when the attention of the mints shifted to production of Morgan silver dollars. From 1879 through 1890, annual mintage figures ranged from 4,400 to 12,000. Many of these were saved at the time of issue and today are very reasonably priced despite the modest mintage figures. Standing in sharp contrast to these late-date Philadelphia issues is the 1878-S half dollar. Its mintage was 12,000, but only about 50 are believed to have survived to the present time. An example grading PCGS MS-63 sold for $184,000 in a Stack's Bowers Galleries auction in August 2011.

Lesson 87: I have to admit this 1885 Proof half dollar was one of my least favorite coins. As my type set neared completion, I was seeking extra points for my PCGS registry set ranking, and I spotted this highly graded coin in a Heritage auction. I submitted a pedestrian bid and won the coin. It wasn't exactly ugly, but it had no pizzazz. You can deduce that the cataloger was straining to find nice things to say when he wrote that the fields were "somewhat" reflective and the colors were "muted." Because of the buyer's commission, I lost a little money when I sold this coin, but I was not unhappy to see it go. Be sure you actually like the coins you buy. Then you'll enjoy owning them and showing them to others. And if you happen to lose money when you sell, you'll at least have had the pleasure of spending time with something that brought you satisfaction.

Financials: Half dollar, Liberty Seated, Motto Above Eagle, 1885

Cost	Sale Price	Gain/Loss	Holding Period
$3,220	$3,220	0%	1.6 years

HALF DOLLAR—BARBER (1892–1915)

Lot 1088.
1905. Proof-67.
PCGS #006552.

Auction description: Gem Proof 1905 Barber 50¢. Among Dozen Finest Certified by PCGS. A sparkling Gem Proof with lightly frosted motifs and richly mirrored fields. The obverse is aglow with pale peach, rose, gold, and blue iridescence, while the reverse exhibits much mint brilliance among the same varied hues. One of 717 Proofs of the date struck, and among the dozen finest examples of the date certified by PCGS. Physical quality and aesthetic beauty combine here to define the Gem grade. PCGS Population: 11; 1 finer within any designation (Proof-68).

From the Waccabuc Collection. Earlier from ANR's sale of the Kennywood Collection, January 2005, Lot 620.

After more than half a century of production, the Liberty Seated half dollar design was finally retired at the end of 1891. The new design, a stern, classical depiction of Miss Liberty facing right, with a laurel wreath and Phrygian cap on her head, was designed by Chief Engraver Charles E. Barber. These new half dollar coins imaginatively came to be known as Barber halves.

Barber half dollars were produced from 1892 through 1915. Output for circulation remained large and steady through the life of this series. The Philadelphia, New Orleans (through 1909), San Francisco, and Denver (beginning in 1906) mints all did their part. In addition, Proof coins were issued in each year.

The type collector has many options available and has no need to make a hasty decision. The only really difficult date to acquire is the 1892-O issue with a "microscopic" O. Researchers believe that an O punch intended to be used on quarter dollars was mistakenly used on a half dollar die. The error was discovered before too many pieces had been released for circulation. As a result, there are estimated to be only 75 or so examples in existence today. Auction appearances are rare: a PGCS MS-67 example sold for $97,750 in a July 2005 sale conducted by American Numismatic Rarities.

Lesson 88: In very high grades, Proof coins are often less expensive than their counterparts that were intended to be placed into circulation. The reason is that Proofs were made for collectors, and many of these coins have been well preserved over the years. Circulation strikes, on the other hand, were usually not saved in large numbers, and a very high-grade survivor is a thing of chance. My 1905 Proof-67 half dollar was a $5,000 to 6,000 coin that sold a little above that range because of its attractive toning. A Mint State–67 Barber half dollar dated 1905 would probably cost three to four times as much, if you could locate one.

Financials: Half dollar, Barber, 1905

Cost	Sale Price	Gain/Loss	Holding Period
$8,625	$7,475	-13%	2.8 years

HALF DOLLAR—LIBERTY WALKING (1916–1947)

Lot 1089.
1939. MS-68.
PCGS #006606.

Auction description: Impressive Gem Uncirculated 1939 Half Dollar. Tied for Finest Graded by PCGS. A sharply struck Gem with intense cartwheel luster and pale golden toning highlights. Each of designer Weinman's tiniest details is present here, offering an unimpeded view of the artist's great coinage master work. A superb Gem that deserves to be at the top of the PCGS Population Report. PCGS Population: 24; none finer.

From the Waccabuc Collection. Earlier from Heritage's Palm Beach Sale, March 2005, Lot 5891.

Charles E. Barber's austere design appeared on dimes, quarters, and half dollars from 1892 through 1915 (half dollars) or 1916 (dimes and quarters). Consider what followed in 1916. The new dime was graced with a stunning Winged Liberty head (the Mercury dime). The new quarter showed an elegant standing depiction of Liberty (the Standing Liberty quarter). And the new half dollar exhibited Miss Liberty striding to the west with her right arm outstretched (the Liberty Walking half dollar). The reverses of these three new coins were equally compelling. This was the Renaissance of American coinage.

The Liberty Walking half dollar was designed by Adolph A. Weinman (who also designed the Mercury dime). The motif echoes the triumphant Miss Liberty that appears on Augustus Saint-Gaudens's double eagle, considered by many to be the most beautiful of all U.S. coins. The new half dollars were produced in most years from 1916 through 1947. The mintmarks D (Denver) and S (San Francisco) were placed on the obverse below the motto in 1916 and the first part of 1917, after which they were moved to the reverse to the left of the denomination. Proofs were issued for seven years beginning in 1936. There are no great rarities in this series, but many of the dates minted prior to 1934 are scarce, in particular the mintmarked coins of 1919 and 1921.

Lesson 89: Repeating lesson 74, the price of 20th-century Proof coins in high grades has been extremely volatile over the past decade. Interest has grown and ebbed and grown again. This 1939 half dollar, despite being tied with a couple of dozen other coins at the top of its population list, lost almost a third of its value in the roughly three years I owned it. The classic series of 18th- and 19th-century coins, as a general statement, are less volatile than their modern counterparts.

Financials: Half dollar, Liberty Walking, 1939

Cost	Sale Price	Gain/Loss	Holding Period
$6,325	$4,370	-31%	2.7 years

HALF DOLLAR—FRANKLIN (1948–1963)

Lot 1090.
1962. Proof-68 DCAM.
PCGS #096703.

Auction description: Gorgeous cameo contrast exists between the heavily frosted motifs and deeply mirrored fields of this attractive Franklin half dollar.

From the Waccabuc Collection. Acquired from Heritage, December 2005.

The Benjamin Franklin half dollar (1948 to 1963) was designed by John R. Sinnock, who also designed the Roosevelt dime that debuted two years earlier. The first year of issue (1948) marked the 242nd anniversary of Franklin's birth and the 158th anniversary of his death. Neither anniversary had anything to do with the selection of Franklin as the subject for this coin. The real reason was that Mint director Nellie Tayloe Ross (the former governor of Wyoming and the first female governor of a U.S. state), who had long been an admirer of Franklin, wanted him to be honored on a U.S. coin.

The Coinage Act of 1792 required that an eagle appear on all silver and gold coins. (Dimes and half dimes were exempted from this requirement in 1837.) Usually this rule was fulfilled by making an eagle the dominant device on the reverse of these coins. In the case of the Franklin half dollar, the Liberty Bell is the dominant device. To comply with the 156-year-old act, a small eagle was placed in the field to the right of the bell.

The Mint sought comments on the new design from the Commission of Fine Arts. The Commission approved the obverse, but had unkind words about the reverse:

> The eagle shown on the model is so small as to be insignificant and hardly discernible when the model is reduced to the size of a coin. The Commission hesitates to approve the Liberty Bell as shown with the crack in the bell visible; to show this might lead to puns and to statements derogatory to United States coinage. The Commission disapproves the designs.

As history shows, the Treasury Department rejected the Commission's advisory recommendations. With the official release of the new half dollar on April 30, 1948, Benjamin Franklin became the fifth person (after Abraham Lincoln, George Washington, Thomas Jefferson, and Franklin Roosevelt) and the first non-president to be depicted on a regular-issue United States coin.

There are no even remotely scarce dates in this series. The lowest annual mintage—fewer than 2.5 million pieces—was recorded in 1955 in Philadelphia. This Franklin half sells for around $50 in MS-65 condition.

A few series of American coins have acquired special terminology to identify pieces that are especially well struck. The designations *Full Steps* for the Jefferson nickel and *Full Split Bands* for the Mercury dime are examples. In the case of the Franklin half dollar, the special designation is *Full Bell Lines*. Certain dates in the series were notoriously poorly struck. Thus, well-struck specimens of these dates command substantial premiums. For example, an ordinary

1953-S half dollar in MS-65 condition but with mushy details would sell for less than $100. In contrast, an example of the same coin in the same condition but with full bell lines sold for $25,300 in a Heritage auction in April 2012.

Lesson 90: In lessons 74 and 89, I wrote about the price volatility of modern Proof coins. Those comments clearly also apply to the miserable investment decision I made by buying this Proof Franklin half dollar. In addition, I may have made another mistake when I asked Stack's to auction my whole collection in consecutive lot listings, rather than having the coins grouped together with others of the same denomination, as is usually done. Stack's recommendation was that my half dollars, just as an example, should appear in the half dollars section of the catalog so that collectors of this denomination would be sure to see my coins. I declined, since I wanted to see all of my coins in a single section of the catalog. For my important coins, I doubt my decision made any difference. But for some of my lesser coins, it's possible that certain bidders may have missed seeing them, with the result that the prices realized were lower than might otherwise have been the case.

Financials: Half dollar, Franklin, 1962

Cost	Sale Price	Gain/Loss	Holding Period
$633	$345	-45%	1.9 years

HALF DOLLAR—KENNEDY (1964–PRESENT)

Lot 1091.
1964. Proof-69 DCAM.
PCGS #096800.

Auction description: Tied for finest certified by PCGS. Heavily frosted motifs and deeply mirrored fields form a generous cameo contrast, a relatively scarce occurrence on 1964 Kennedy half dollars. PCGS Population: 69; none finer within the designation.

From the Waccabuc Collection. Acquired from Heritage, May 2005.

Not long after John F. Kennedy's assassination on November 22, 1963, the Franklin half dollar was replaced by the Kennedy half dollar. Congress quickly approved the new design on December 30, 1963. Striking of the new coins began in January 1964, and they instantly became favorites with the public.

Huge demand for the new coins quickly exhausted available supplies in Washington, Boston, Philadelphia, and New York. Mint officials initially planned to issue 91 million Kennedy half dollars in 1964, but they soon raised this target to 141 million. As the year was drawing to a close, production of half dollars had exceeded 160 million pieces, but the coins were rarely seen in circulation, and they still sold for a premium on the secondary market. To combat this, the Mint received congressional approval to continue to strike 1964-dated half dollars in 1965. When the dust finally settled, a total of almost 430 million 1964 Kennedy halves had been struck, including about four million Proofs. Virtually every accumulation of "rare" coins that I've appraised for friends and acquaintances has included a handful or more of these coins.

With the rise in the price of silver, the Mint reduced the precious-metal content of Kennedy half dollars from 90 percent silver (the standard since 1836) to 40 percent in the years 1965 through 1970, after which half dollars struck for circulation were made of a copper-and-nickel composition. These half dollars continue to be made today, though only to the extent needed to meet collector demand. In 2014, to celebrate the coin's 50th anniversary, the Mint released a suite of collectible double-dated (1964–2014) halves, including a special gold striking.

Lesson 91: I got an extremely strong price for my "pop-top" 1964 PCGS PF-69 DCAM (deep cameo) Kennedy half dollar. I don't know why this happened, but perhaps two bidders both needed this for their PCGS registry sets. Five years later, this same coin would probably have sold for a few hundred dollars less. The gain on this coin made up for the small losses I suffered on the sale of several other modern coins. If you're too concentrated in a single area of numismatics, and if that area is out of favor when it's time for you to sell, you could lose money even if you've built your collection intelligently. As with any form of investing, it's important to diversify.

Financials: Half dollar, Kennedy, 1964

Cost	Sale Price	Gain/Loss	Holding Period
$1,495	$2,300	+54%	2.5 years

HALF DOLLAR—KENNEDY (1964–PRESENT)

Lot 1092.
1964, Accented Hair, Proof-67 CAM; 1965, MS-67 SMS; 1971-D, MS-67; 1976 Clad, MS-65; 1976-S Clad, Proof-69 DCAM; 1976-S Silver, Proof-68 DCAM; 1981-S Type I, Proof-69 DCAM; 1992-S Silver, Proof-70 DCAM.

Auction description: Selection of PCGS-certified Kennedy half dollars: * 1964 Accented Hair. Proof-67CAM * 1965 MS-67 SMS * 1971-D MS-67 * 1776-1976 Clad. MS-65. Deep yellow toning * 1776-1976-S Clad. Proof-69 DCAM * 1776-1976-S Silver. Proof-68 DCAM * 1981-S Type I. Proof-69 DCAM * 1992-S Silver. Proof-70 DCAM. (Total: 8 pieces).
From the Waccabuc Collection.

I bought these eight common Kennedy half dollars because I needed them for inclusion in my 20th-century type set. None of them qualifies as a rare coin, though the 1964 version with "accented hair" is relatively scarce, and all are in finer condition than normally seen. I have to admit that I got very little excitement from acquiring these coins, and I felt absolutely no seller's remorse when the hammer came down on this lot. How I made any money on these coins remains a mystery.

Lesson 92: Repeating lesson 22 again, don't spend a lot of time or money on items you don't care about. Yes, completing the collection of modern issues was somewhat satisfying, but I rarely looked at these coins or showed them to others. This is not to say that collecting modern coins isn't worthwhile. It can be interesting, educational, and fun. But they're not rare coins, and seeking an imperceptibly finer example of a common modern coin wasn't something that gave me much of a thrill.

Financials: Half dollar, Kennedy, 1964, 1965, 1971-D, 1976, 1976-S, 1976-S, 1981-S, 1992-S

Cost	Sale Price	Gain/Loss	Holding Period
$680	$748	+10%	Various

CHAPTER
13

Silver
Dollars

If you really want to get better at golf,
go back and take it up at a much earlier age.

As the old saying goes, the best time to plant a tree is 20 years ago; the second-best time is today. Yes, it would be magical to hop into a time machine and go back 20 (or 50) years and buy up all the rare coins you could find. But if you don't have access to such a vehicle, you can still derive a great deal of knowledge and pleasure from assembling a collection of rare coins, and you may find, as many others have, that with the passage of time you will have made a good financial investment as well.

The Coinage Act of 1792 established the mint in Philadelphia, authorized the production of various copper, silver, and gold coins, and stipulated that the dollar would be the unit of currency for the nation. The first coins issued under the provisions of the act were the 1792 half dismes, followed in 1793 by half cents and cents. In 1794 production of silver dollars (and half dollars) began.

The first design employed had a portrait of Miss Liberty with upturned face and flowing locks. This Flowing Hair design lasted for less than two years before the Draped Bust version was adopted partway through 1795. President Thomas Jefferson halted production of silver dollars early in 1804, as most were being exported. Production resumed in a small way in 1836 with the introduction of the beautiful Gobrecht dollars and in a larger way from 1840, when minting of Liberty Seated dollars commenced. The curious trade dollar (1873 to 1885), issued for circulation in the Orient, saw only limited usage within the United States and lost its legal-tender status in 1876. Much more popular, at least with the Western silver miners, was the Morgan dollar, which was introduced in 1878. Production lasted through 1904, though more were minted in 1921. That latter year saw the introduction of the final circulating U.S. dollar coin having a 90 percent silver composition. Called the Peace dollar, its production ended in 1935. The Eisenhower dollar (1971 to 1978) had a short life and was followed by several other base-metal dollar coin designs, all of which have failed to achieve wide acceptance in the channels of commerce. All of these principal designs are discussed in the sections that follow.

As noted previously, this and the subsequent chapters on gold coins include auction lot descriptions, photos, and commentary. A learning opportunity is included at the end of each lot. These lessons relate to the specific coin under discussion but are designed to have more general applicability to other series and denominations. Financial results are shown for each coin.

SILVER DOLLAR—FLOWING HAIR (1794–1795)

Lot 1093.
1795, Three Leaves. AU-50.
B-5, BB-27. Rarity-1. PCGS #006853.

Auction description: Pale to medium silver gray with champagne highlights on both sides. Strong design elements remain. No serious marks present, though low magnification reveals some tiny, scattered marks and other faint blemishes. All told, a pleasing example of this readily identifiable variety—a slip of an engraver's tool left a raised diagonal line in the field adjacent to Liberty's uppermost hair curl. A nice coin to illustrate the type.

From the Waccabuc Collection. Earlier from Heritage's F.U.N. Convention Sale, January 1999, Lot 6922.

The Flowing Hair silver dollar takes its name from Lady Liberty's flowing locks seen on the obverse of the coin. The mint in Philadelphia produced a mere 1,758 silver dollars in 1794. They were struck on a hand-turned screw press, and all were made on the single day of October 15. That press was designed for smaller coins, up to the size of a half dollar, and thus the 1794 dollars almost always show evidence of striking weakness.

Perhaps 140 examples of the 1794 dollar survive today. By far the finest of these, the Neil/Carter/Contursi specimen, changed hands in May 2010 for $7.85 million, at the time the highest price ever paid for a single coin. That same coin was sold again in January 2013 by Stack's Bowers Galleries to Legend Numismatics for a new record price of just over $10 million, reaffirming its place as the most expensive coin in the world.

Because the 1794 issue is so rare and expensive, most collectors opt for an example of the 1795 dollar to represent the Flowing Hair type. Possibly as many as 6,000 of these have survived. This coin is not cheap, but it's a more realistic goal for most.

Lesson 93: Many early coin blanks were overweight. In order to adjust their weight downward to the right standard, female Mint employees (for some reason, only women did this type of work) filed them down, leaving deep scratches on the planchets. If these marks were not obliterated through the striking process, visible blemishes would remain (these are called adjustment marks). These marks were part of the minting process and are not like damage caused by careless handling after the coins left the mint. Nevertheless, collectors will pay less for, or sometimes shun entirely, coins that have significant evidence of adjustment marks. You might be wise to do the same to avoid being stuck with a hard-to-sell coin. My 1795 Flowing Hair dollar was void of such marks and sold well.

Financials: Silver dollar, Flowing Hair, 1795, Three Leaves

Cost	Sale Price	Gain/Loss	Holding Period
$6,635	$18,400	+177%	8.8 years

SILVER DOLLAR—DRAPED BUST, SMALL EAGLE REVERSE (1795–1798)

Lot 1094.
1795, Centered Bust. EF-45.
B-15, BB-52. Rarity-2. PCGS #006858.

Although I find the Flowing Hair design appealing, it did not garner universal acclaim at the time of issue. That was probably a contributing factor in the decision to move to a new design for the silver dollar in the second half of 1795. The new motif displayed an eye-catching Draped Bust version of Miss Liberty, with a small eagle on the reverse.

The Coinage Act of 1792 specified, among other things, that silver dollars contain 89.24 percent pure silver by weight. This curious percentage was based on a study of a number of Spanish milled dollars. The feeling was that the precious-metal content of the new U.S. dollars should be equal to the average fineness of the popular Spanish dollars.

There were two problems with this. First, as was later discovered, the study was wrong: Spanish dollars were actually about 90.3 percent silver. Second, the fledgling Mint found it technically difficult to create an alloy exactly equal to 89.24 percent silver and 10.76 percent copper. With the blessing of Thomas Jefferson and Alexander Hamilton, the Mint produced Flowing Hair dollars with a fineness of 90 percent silver. The expectation was that Congress would affirm this decision.

Unfortunately, Congress did not, and so the new Draped Bust, Small Eagle, dollars were minted with the originally authorized fineness of 89.24 percent Don't you just love democracy! It was not until early 1837 that the "modern" standard of 90 percent silver and 10 percent copper was adopted for the U.S. silver dollar.

The Draped Bust design with the Small Eagle reverse survived for only four years, 1795 through 1798. However, since so many of the design elements were stamped into the dies by hand, collectors have numerous varieties to choose among. There are coins with a centered bust and others with the bust off-center to the left. There are small and large dates and small and large letters. There are 13 or 15 or 16 stars on the obverse. Among the 16-star obverses, there are sometimes 9 stars and sometimes 10 stars to the left of Miss Liberty. A comprehensive collection of Draped Bust dollar varieties is a huge challenge.

Lesson 94: I took a chance with the purchase of this Draped Bust, Small Eagle, dollar. I noticed the same thing the cataloger did: there's "an old curlicue scratch in the field before Liberty's portrait and certain stars in that area." But I bought the coin anyway because I liked the overall "look." The toning was even, not mottled (another word for *ugly* in my lexicon), the luster was decent, the strike was good, and there were no distracting adjustment marks. I didn't hit the jackpot with this purchase, but the curlicue scratch was not bad enough to overwhelm the many positive attributes possessed by this coin. With experience, you'll learn to trust your own judgment when evaluating classic coins that have some "issues."

Financials: Silver dollar, Draped Bust, Small Eagle Reverse, 1795, Centered Bust

Cost	Sale Price	Gain/Loss	Holding Period
$8,050	$10,350	+29%	3.9 years

SILVER DOLLAR—DRAPED BUST, HERALDIC EAGLE REVERSE (1798–1804)

Lot 1095.
1798, Close Date. AU-55.
B-27, BB-113. Rarity-2. PCGS #006873.

Auction description: Satiny silver gray with warm gold and lilac toning highlights. A nice degree of luster remains, especially in the protected design areas. No serious marks present, and careful examination is a treat. Nice quality for the assigned grade.

From the Waccabuc Collection. Acquired from Bowers and Merena, April 2003.

In the first half of 1798 the silver dollar's reverse design was changed from the small, perched eagle to a heraldic eagle, similar to the one seen on the Great Seal of the United States. This design was employed through early 1804.

Despite reasonably heavy mintages in 1798, 1799, and 1800, our silver dollars did not stay in circulation in the United States. Many were exported to Asia, where China, in particular, had an insatiable appetite for silver. Others were exported to the Caribbean, where they were traded for Spanish milled dollars (denominated as 8 reales, also sometimes called pieces of eight). These two coins traded at par, but the Spanish dollars were slightly heavier in weight and slightly finer in silver content. The enterprising coin merchants would then return the Spanish dollars to the Mint in Philadelphia which, by law, was required to mint new U.S. dollars without a markup. As a result, the merchants would receive an equal value of lighter, less-fine U.S. dollars *plus* some leftover silver, representing their profit.

Recognizing the futility of continuing dollar production in the face of widespread exportation and melting, President Thomas Jefferson gave the order to halt the minting of silver dollars. Output ceased in March of 1804. During the first three months of that year, 19,570 silver dollars had been produced.

So, you might ask, if almost 20,000 dollars were made in 1804, why is the 1804 dollar called the King of American Coins? The answer lies in the practice of the early Mint to continue to use dies until they were no longer serviceable, regardless of the date shown on the die. All 19,570 dollars struck in 1804 were, in fact, dated 1802 or 1803. The 15 dollars dated 1804 were produced in 1834 and later for diplomatic purposes initially, and later to meet collector demand. Several books have been written about the circumstances surrounding this fascinating coin, and I even know of one collector who couldn't afford this great rarity so he had an image of an 1804 dollar tattooed on his left ankle.[9]

Lesson 95: As the cataloger of my 1798 Draped Bust, Heraldic Eagle dollar described it, the color of this coin was "satiny silver gray with warm gold and lilac toning highlights." This is the way coins that are two centuries old should look. If you see an 18th- or 19th-century coin without toning, you can be certain it's been cleaned (or "dipped"). In my experience, most serious collectors prefer an "original" look for their old coins.

Financials: Silver dollar, Draped Bust, Heraldic Eagle Reverse, 1798, Close Date

Cost	Sale Price	Gain/Loss	Holding Period
$6,750	$10,350	+53%	4.7 years

SILVER DOLLAR—GOBRECHT (1836–1839)

Lot 1096.
1836, Plain Edge, Name on Base, Die Alignment I. Proof-62.
J-60, P-65. Rarity-1. PCGS #011225.

Auction description: Medium to deep golden gray with some slate highlights. Much luster is seen in the protected areas especially in the eagle's plumage. The strike is sharp and impressive, and except for a few faint, insignificant handling marks, the integrity of the coin is substantial for the assigned grade. America's first circulating silver dollar after 1803, struck to the tune of 1,000 or so pieces, and always desirable whether lightly circulated or nearly choice, as here.

From the Waccabuc Collection. Earlier from Teletrade's January 1998 Sale, Lot 1653.

After a hiatus of 32 years, the Philadelphia Mint recommenced production of silver dollars in 1836. The initial design, engraved by Christian Gobrecht, showed Miss Liberty seated on a rock in a starless field, and there was an impressive image of an eagle in flight (very similar to that used on the Flying Eagle cent of 1856 to 1858) on the reverse. Output was tiny (1,600 in total, with two different die alignments). Several other patterns and restrikes were made in 1836, 1838, and 1839, all of which are rare.

The Gobrecht dollar I purchased serves as an excellent example of the evolution of grading standards over the past dozen years or so. When I bought it in early 1998, PCGS's judgment was that it warranted a grade of PF-60. Like many Gobrecht dollars, it is a bit on the dark side, and there are a number of minor marks, particularly on the obverse. However, the marks didn't seem that significant to me, so in 2000, I sent this coin to PCGS for re-grading, and it came back in a holder marked PF-61.

Then in 2003 I was at a coin convention in Baltimore and was sitting at the PCGS table with a few coins I felt might have a shot at a higher grade. Sitting next to me was a dealer from New Jersey (not Legend Numismatics). At the suggestion of the representative from PCGS, I asked the dealer what he thought of my coins. He took a quick look and said, "What, are you trying to get these downgraded?" (Needless to say, I never did any business with his firm.) Undeterred, I resubmitted my Gobrecht dollar to PCGS and was very pleased to get it back as a PF-62 coin.

By 2007, in the opinion of the Stack's cataloger, "the integrity of [this] coin is substantial for the assigned grade," and it is "nearly choice." Maybe it now resides in a PCGS PF-63 holder, though I would guess not. This identical coin, still in its PF-62 holder, resurfaced in a March 2009 auction conducted by Stack's. It did not sell, probably because of a combination of the weak economy at that time and an overly optimistic reserve price. It reappeared in the Stack's November 2009 auction with the same results. I wonder where it is today.

Lesson 96: Yes, you should learn how to grade coins, especially those in the various degrees of high-grade preservation. But you also need to be aware of the gradual inflation of grading standards in the years since the grading services were established. Coins in older holders will sometimes (but not always) attract a higher grade today than they did when those coins were originally encapsulated.

Financials: Silver dollar, Gobrecht, 1836, Plain Edge, Name on Base, Die Alignment I

Cost	Sale Price	Gain/Loss	Holding Period
$7,450	$36,800	+394%	9.8 years

SILVER DOLLAR—LIBERTY SEATED, NO MOTTO ABOVE EAGLE (1840–1865)

Lot 1097.
1849. MS-64.
PCGS #006936.

Auction description: Somewhat prooflike with frosty motifs and reflective fields. Lively rose and champagne highlights evenly dispersed on both sides. An attractive Uncirculated survivor from a mintage of 62,600 pieces intended for general circulation. As with all other dates in the 1840s, Uncirculated Liberty Seated dollars of 1849 can be considered rare in any grade of MS-60 or finer. In MS-64, as here, the date becomes an unsung rarity, though we hasten to mention that Liberty Seated dollar aficionados recognize the nature of the date. Devoid of serious marks save for a few light hairlines, and impressive as such. One of fewer than 10 examples of date called MS-64 or finer by PCGS. PCGS Population: 7; 2 finer (MS-67 finest).

From the Waccabuc Collection. Acquired from Heritage, February 2007.

In 1840 production of the Liberty Seated dollar began in earnest. The figure of Miss Liberty was modified slightly from that used on the so-called Gobrecht dollars, and the glorious flying eagle on the reverse was changed to the more familiar one with its wings spread wide and with arrows in one claw (representing America's preparedness for war) and an olive branch in the other (showing our preference for peace). The first variety of Liberty Seated dollar (1840 to 1865) does not have the motto IN GOD WE TRUST on the reverse.

Once upon a time, I owned the single finest-graded 1840 Liberty Seated dollar, a beautiful, sharp example grading MS-64. Sadly, Legend Numismatics made me an offer I couldn't refuse, so I traded it to them for an MS-62 example of the same date plus a low five-figure pile of cash. I still regret that trade: it would have been fascinating to see what that "pop-top" 1840 dollar would have brought at auction.

By early 2007, I was looking to squeeze a few more ranking points out of the PCGS set-registry system before disposing of my type set. I spotted this attractive MS-64 1849 dollar in a Heritage auction and submitted a secret online maximum bid of $12,000. I was delighted to acquire the coin for just $9,200, but not nearly as delighted as I was nine months later when another buyer decided to pay three times as much for this same coin. I hope he got it re-graded as MS-65.

Lesson 97: It's not a bad strategy to look for attractive coins at reasonable prices as your sole collecting criterion (without regard to date or denomination, or type), but even this approach will not guarantee that you will double or triple your money in a short period. However, sometimes you'll get lucky, and as the old saying goes, it's better to be lucky than good.

Financials: Silver dollar, Liberty Seated, No Motto, 1849

Cost	Sale Price	Gain/Loss	Holding Period
$9,200	$27,600	+200%	0.8 years

SILVER DOLLAR—LIBERTY SEATED, WITH MOTTO ABOVE EAGLE (1866–1873)

Lot 1098.
1866. Proof-65 CAM.
PCGS #087014.

Auction description: Sparkling champagne surfaces with richly frosted motifs and re-flective fields. Boldly struck, one of 725 Proofs of the date produced in the first year of silver dollar coinage to bear our nation's motto IN GOD WE TRUST. Among the dozen finest CAM examples of the date certified thus far by PCGS. An attractive Gem that easily meets the standards of the assigned grade. PCGS Population: 9; 3 finer within the designation (Proof-68 CAM finest).

From the Waccabuc Collection. Acquired from Heritage, December 2005.

The second variety of the Liberty Seated dollar was introduced in 1866. On this version, the motto IN GOD WE TRUST has been added to the reverse of the coin, above the eagle. Production continued through 1873, primarily at the Philadelphia Mint, though the Carson City and San Francisco mints chipped in a handful of coins from 1870 to 1873. An 1870-S dollar (with an estimated mintage of 12 to 15 pieces, of which 9 are known to exist today) sold for almost $1.1 million in a May 2003 Stack's auction.

Lesson 98: In 1871 and 1872, the Philadelphia Mint produced slightly more than one million silver dollars in each year. This output dwarfed the mintages reached in earlier years, but by the standards of the Morgan dollar series that followed, these figures would be considered modest. And yet the price of Liberty Seated dollars does not, in my view, fully reflect the disparity in mintage figures and survival rates. I've always thought that the Liberty Seated dollar series represents better potential value for collectors than the Morgan dollar series. But it's important to recognize that Morgan dollars are more popular than Liberty Seated dollars, and part of that popularity derives from the fact that they are more readily available. Economics always comes back to supply and demand.

Financials: Silver dollar, Liberty Seated, With Motto, 1866

Cost	Sale Price	Gain/Loss	Holding Period
$12,650	$12,650	+0%	1.9 years

SILVER DOLLAR—MORGAN (1878–1921)

Lot 1099.
1900-O. MS-67.
PCGS #007266.

Auction description: A frosty and brilliant Gem with broadly sweeping cartwheel luster on both sides. The devices are sharply struck and the eye appeal is nothing short of fabulous. Among the nicest examples certified by PCGS of this otherwise relatively commonplace issue. PCGS Population: 29; none finer within the designation.

From the Waccabuc Collection. Earlier from the Palm Beach Collection; Heritage's F.U.N. Convention Sale, January 2004, Lot 9084.

The Fourth Coinage Act, better known as the Coinage Act of 1873, demonetized silver and effectively put the United States on the gold standard. (The gold standard was not officially made the law of the land until 1900.) Liberty Seated dollars were not produced after 1873, and trade dollars (discussed following) were produced primarily for usage overseas.

Western silver-mining interests later called the Fourth Coinage Act the "Crime of 1873." (That crime is explored in detail in the eponymous book by Robert R. Van Ryzin.) Eventually, however, they and their allies in Congress got what they wanted with the passage of the Bland-Allison Act in 1878. That act required the Mint to purchase between $2 million and $4 million worth of new (not recycled) domestic silver every month for the production of silver dollars. President Rutherford Hayes rightly saw the act as wasteful and exercised his right of veto, but Congress overrode the veto on the last day of February 1878, and the Morgan dollar was launched. It was produced in large quantities from 1878 through 1904 and again in 1921.

But the Western mining interests were not finished with their lobbying. With the price of their product declining because of worldwide oversupply, they prevailed on Congress in 1890 to pass the Sherman Silver Purchase Act, even though the silver dollars being produced were, for the most part, piling up in Mint vaults due to lack of demand. This new law required the Mint to buy an additional 4.5 million ounces of silver every month beyond the amount being purchased under the provisions of the Bland-Allison Act. The silver miners were paid in notes convertible into gold, and soon enough much of the government's hoard of gold was exhausted. President Grover Cleveland persuaded Congress to repeal the ridiculous Sherman Act in 1893, but not before the Panic of 1893 had wrought havoc on Main Street and Wall Street. A loan from a syndicate of banks under the direction of J.P. Morgan is credited with saving the nation from default.

The new dollar was designed by George T. Morgan, the Mint's assistant engraver. The story of the model he used for the image of Miss Liberty is an interesting one. Here's the version as told by Walter Breen in his *Encyclopedia*:

> Morgan's design portrayed Miss Anna Willess Williams, a schoolteacher, as Miss Liberty. Morgan, with difficulty, had persuaded her to become his model, and she sat for him five times at the home of the illustrious painter Thomas Eakins, under promise of strict secrecy. The cover story represented her head as that of "a Greek figure" at the Philadelphia Academy of Art; others noticed a resemblance to Oudine's head on French coins. Despite all precautions, some years later a newspaperman recognized her as the model, thought "Aha?" (thus exhausting his stock of bright ideas for the year), and (over protests) published the story; whereupon Miss Williams, as she had feared, did lose her job. In those days respectable ladies could not be artists' models, nor vice versa.

Other sources report that Miss Williams did not lose her job, but all researchers agree that she regretted her decision to pose. Indeed some believe that her 1896 engagement to be married was terminated after unwanted publicity about her role as the "silver dollar girl" brought her into the limelight once again.

Lesson 99: Because of the massive overproduction of Morgan dollars, they are easily available today in any grade up through superb gem Uncirculated. Examples such as the one I owned are beautiful to behold, but they are more like commodities than rare coins. Unless you want to specialize in Morgan dollars, I suggest you try to obtain one of the rare dates (such as the 1889-CC or the 1893-S or the Proof-only 1895). True rarity never goes out of fashion.

Financials: Silver dollar, Morgan, 1900-O

Cost	Sale Price	Gain/Loss	Holding Period
$5,060	$4,600	-13%	3.8 years

SILVER DOLLAR—PEACE, HIGH RELIEF (1921)

Lot 1100.
1921. MS-65.
PCGS #007356.

Auction description: A lustrous Gem with wisps of faint champagne and rose. Choice for the grade with better than typical strike; here virtually all of Liberty's obverse hair strands are delineated. Well above average for the date and grade combination.

From the Waccabuc Collection. Earlier from Bowers and Merena's sale of the Voigt and Lee Collections, March 1999, Lot 547.

After years of celebrating war on its coins through the use of arrows and shields and the fasces of rods and an axe (the last on the Mercury dime), the United States finally decided to celebrate peace following the conclusion of World War I. With impetus provided by Farran Zerbe (former president of the American Numismatic Association and founder of the Chase Manhattan Bank Money Museum), and without congressional approval (since the Morgan design had been in use for more than 25 years), the federal Commission of Fine Arts held a design competition and chose the submission of sculptor Anthony de Francisci. His design, modeled by his young wife, portrayed a left-facing head of Miss Liberty with a spiky crown reminiscent of the Statue of Liberty. The word PEACE appears below the perched eagle on the reverse.

The Peace dollar was issued intermittently from 1921 through 1935. There are no rarities in the series, though the low-mintage date of 1928, when "only" 360,649 pieces were struck, is considered scarce in all grades. The dollars were minted with high relief in 1921 (resulting in a high incidence of die breakage) and in low relief thereafter.

Lesson 100: Just over one million Peace dollars were hastily produced in 1921 in the week after Christmas. They have an attractive high-relief appearance, but most survivors are weakly struck. It makes sense to seek a better-than-average strike (like mine, which was described as "well above average for the date and grade combination"), but don't go crazy when you find one. There are enough around that you don't have to overpay, the way I did.

Financials: Silver dollar, Peace, High Relief, 1921

Cost	Sale Price	Gain/Loss	Holding Period
$2,530	$2,070	-18%	8.7 years

SILVER DOLLAR—PEACE, NORMAL RELIEF (1922–1935)

Lot 1101.
1922-D. MS-66.
PCGS #007358.

Auction description: A satiny Gem with robust cartwheel luster that supports pale sky blue and rose iridescence.

From the Waccabuc Collection. Acquired from Larry Whitlow, September 2002.

From 1922 through the end of the Peace dollar series in 1935, the Mint employed the lower-relief version of the design. Most appear "mushy" even in Uncirculated condition, and the lettering on both sides is usually weak. Sharply struck gems with strong luster are decidedly scarce.

Lesson 101: If your goal is to vault to the head of the pantheon of Peace dollar collectors, you should find an example dated 1964-D and add it to your collection. Your task will prove to be difficult. In May 1965, the Denver Mint produced more than 300,000 1964-dated Peace dollars under the Act of August 3, 1964, which provided for the issuance of up to 45 million silver dollars (primarily to benefit Nevada gambling casinos). Pressure from critics caused the Treasury and President Lyndon Johnson to countermand the authorization. All of the coins that had been minted were ordered to be recalled and melted. However, rumor has it that a few pieces were bought or taken by Mint employees. The risk of confiscation has kept these few pieces, if they exist, out of sight. But wouldn't it be a thrill to have one in your cabinet of special coins?

Financials: Silver dollar, Peace, Normal Relief, 1922-D

Cost	Sale Price	Gain/Loss	Holding Period
$1,625	$1,495	-8%	5.2 years

SILVER DOLLAR—ASSORTED MODERN

Lot 1102.

1971-D, MS-66; 1971-S Silver, Proof-69 DCAM; 1976-S Silver, Proof-68 DCAM; 1976-S Clad, Type 2, Proof-69 DCAM; 1977-S, Proof-69 DCAM; 1979-S, Type 2, Proof-69 DCAM; 2000-P, MS-67; 2000-S, Proof-69 DCAM.

Auction description: Group of PCGS-certified modern dollars: * 1971-D MS-66 * 1971-S Silver. Proof-69 DCAM * 1776-1976-S Silver. Proof-68 DCAM * 1776-1976-S Clad, Type II. Proof-69 DCAM * 1977-S Proof-69 DCAM * 1979-S Susan B. Anthony. Type II. Proof-69 DCAM * 2000-P Sacagawea. MS-67 * 2000-S Sacagawea. Proof-69 DCAM. A few pieces with faint toning highlights. (Total: 8 pieces)

From the Waccabuc Collection.

I bought these eight modern dollars because I needed them for inclusion in my 20th-century type set. Only one is worth writing about—the 2000-P Sacagawea dollar—which I found by looking through a roll of dollars purchased directly from the Philadelphia Mint. The PCGS holder cost me far more than the coin did. None of these coins is even remotely rare, though all are in much finer condition than normally seen. I have to admit that I got very little excitement from acquiring these coins, and I felt absolutely no seller's remorse when the hammer came down on this lot.

Although not part of the regular U.S. coin series, American Eagle silver dollars have been minted since 1986. These coins have a face value of $1 but are made of 99.93 percent pure silver and are primarily traded as bullion coins based on the price of silver. However, many hundreds of collectors have assembled date sets of these coins, and the PCGS set-registry system provides a forum for these collectors to compete for the designation as the finest collection of American Silver Eagles in existence. The key coin in the series is the 1995-W (for West Point) dollar, with a mintage of "just" 30,125. While PF-69 deep cameo examples typically sell for less than $4,000, one of the (then) very few PF-70 deep cameo specimens sold for a lofty $86,655 in a Great Collections auction in March 2013 and another changed hands for $90,000 in a private-treaty transaction in August 2013. One word of caution, however: in little more than a year, the population of this coin in PCGS PF-70 DC grew from 3 to 19. Other examples almost certainly are out there, waiting to be certified. In late September 2013, another "perfect" 1995-W American Silver Eagle sold for less than $56,000. Ouch. Remember the law of supply and demand.

Lesson 102: Repeating lesson 22 (for the last time), don't spend a lot of time or money on items you don't care about. Yes, completing the collection of modern issues was somewhat satisfying, but I rarely looked at these coins or showed them to others. This is not to say that collecting modern coins isn't worthwhile. It can be interesting, educational, and fun. But for the most part they're not rare coins, and seeking an imperceptibly finer example of a common modern coin wasn't something that gave me much of a thrill.

Financials: Modern dollars, 1971-D, 1971-S, 1976-S, 1976-S, 1977-S, 1979-S, 2000-P, 2000-S

Cost	Sale Prices	Gain/Loss	Holding Period
$590	$575	-3%	Various

TRADE DOLLAR (1873–1885)

Lot 1103.
1873. Proof-64.
PCGS #007053.

Auction description: Choice Proof 1873 Trade Dollar. Highly reflective golden gray fields and lightly frosted motifs encircled by rich violet and neon blue halos at the rims. A sharp and crisp Proof from the first year of trade dollar coinage, one of 865 such pieces struck. An unsung rarity in Proof, certainly far more rare than the Proof-only issues of 1879–1883, but overlooked in the rarity sweepstakes. Just a half dozen examples of the date have been certified finer than the present beauty by PCGS. An outstanding opportunity to obtain a gloriously toned and physically sound Proof trade dollar.

From the Waccabuc Collection. Acquired from Legend Numismatics, January 2001.

Silver dollars produced in the 1800s for domestic use were slightly lighter than Mexican "dollars," and they therefore traded at a discount in international trade. In China this discount could reach 15 percent, even though the weight differential was less than 2 percent. To address this problem, the U.S. Mint produced trade dollars from 1873 through 1885, primarily for use outside the United States. Their weight was 420 grains, compared to a standard silver dollar's 412.5 grains. These coins had limited legal-tender status (up to $5) domestically in their early years of production, but this status was revoked in 1876.

With new discoveries and increased production of silver (such as from the famed Comstock Lode in Nevada, which was discovered in 1859 but which reached peak production in the mid-1870s), the price of silver declined. After 1876 unscrupulous employers could buy trade dollars at their bullion value of less than 85 cents each and put them in the pay envelopes of their employees. Many merchants and banks refused to accept trade dollars except at bullion value, leaving the hapless employees in the lurch. Walter Breen, never shy about expressing an opinion, wrote in his *Encyclopedia*:

> The issue of this coin was an expensive mistake—its motivation mere greed, its design a triumph of dullness, its domestic circulation and legal-tender status a disastrous provision of law leading only to ghastly abuses, its repudiation a source of hardship for Pennsylvania coal miners and other laborers held in virtual peonage by company stores, its recall a long overdue but very mixed blessing, and its collection a source of decades of frustration.

Personally, I don't agree with all of Breen's sentiments. I find the iconography appealing, with the ocean, bales of cotton, a sheaf of wheat, and the western-facing Liberty extending an olive branch of peace to our Asian trading partners. And many collectors enjoy collecting this short series. None of the circulation-issue date-and-mintmark combinations from 1873 through 1878 are impossibly rare, and the Proofs from 1873 through 1883 are all seen with some regularity at auction. A complete set with Chinese chopmarks (symbols punched into the coins after inspection by a merchant) is also possible to assemble.

The Proof issues of 1884 and 1885 deserve special mention. Mint records show that trade dollar production ceased after 1883, but ten coins dated 1884 and five dated 1885 exist today. These were produced under shady circum-

stances at the Mint and held secretly for many years until being revealed to the numismatic world in 1908. The 1885 specimen once owned by Louis Elias-berg was reportedly sold by Heritage Galleries in a private transaction in January 2006 for $3.3 million.

Lesson 103: Records show that most of the early trade dollars were, indeed, used in export trade with Asia, and many of these acquired chopmarks from Chinese merchants. And although the Proof issues were not exported, the early Proofs also survive in smaller numbers than later issues. A well-struck and attractive example of an 1873 trade dollar, either a Proof or one minted for circulation, would make an excellent choice for a type-set collection.

Several of the coins in the Waccabuc Collection that were sold in Stack's November 2007 auction were then re-consigned to Stack's for its February 2008 sale. This 1873 trade dollar was one of those coins. As was generally the case with these re-consigned coins, it did not sell, probably because the reserve was set too high. The immediately following lot in the February 2008 sale was another 1873 trade dollar grading Proof-64, though in an NGC holder. It was fully brilliant (i.e., dipped), and it realized $4,600. Buying coins for immediate resale can be a risky business unless you're a dealer with a large customer base.

Financials: Trade dollar, 1873

Cost	Sale Price	Gain/Loss	Holding Period
$3,750	$5,520	+47%	6.8 years

Gold
Dollars

*Two longtime golfers were standing at the third tee, overlooking the
river. Just before teeing off, Lester turned to David and said,
"Look at those idiots down there, fishing in the rain."*

I've actually played golf in the rain with those two guys, David and Lester, and I'm sure some people looked at us and thought we were idiots, too. And I'm equally sure some people consider numismatists at least a little weird. But that's okay. Fishing or golfing in the rain or collecting rare coins can be enjoyable if you're prepared and know what you're doing. And in the end, isn't that all that matters?

We've now reached the realm of gold coins. The Coinage Act of 1792 contemplated gold coins with denominations of $2.50, $5.00, and $10.00. But then came the California Gold Rush, which began in 1848. This landmark event was followed, not coincidentally, by the Act of March 3, 1849, which authorized the production of $1 and $20 gold pieces.

The first version of the gold dollars, introduced in 1849, had a head of Miss Liberty on the obverse almost identical to the one that would appear on the inaugural double eagle in 1850. These so-called Type 1 gold dollars were tiny—less than three-quarters the size of a modern dime. When complaints over their small size became widespread, the Mint introduced a wider, thinner version (Type 2) in 1854. This Indian Princess, Small Head, type was succeeded in 1856 by an Indian Princess, Large Head, version (Type 3), which was minted consistently through 1889. These three varieties of gold dollars are discussed in more detail in the sections below.

GOLD DOLLAR—LIBERTY HEAD (1849–1854)

Lot 1104.
1849, Open Wreath. MS-64.
PCGS #007501.

The Type 1 gold dollar, designed by James B. Longacre (of Indian Head cent fame), was minted from 1849 through 1854. With the Treasury flush with gold from California, output of this type from the Philadelphia Mint was extremely high (more than 11 million pieces), and the New Orleans Mint chipped in with a reasonable production approaching a million pieces. Bringing up the rear were the Charlotte and Dahlonega mints, which relied on local supplies of gold. Mintages from these branch mints were puny. The newly opened San Francisco Mint contributed slightly fewer than 15,000 pieces in 1854.

Assembling a date set of Philadelphia Mint Type 1 gold dollars, even in Uncirculated condition, does not pose much of a problem. However, if you aspire to build a date-and-mintmark set, particularly in high grade, you'll run into enormous challenges. There weren't many branch-mint gold dollars to begin with, and survivors in high grade are extraordinarily elusive.

The undisputed key to this short series is the 1849-C, Open Wreath, variety, of which only four are known to survive today. The finest of these, an NGC MS-63 example, sold for $690,000 in a David Lawrence Rare Coins auction in July 2004.

Lesson 104: The 1849 gold dollar with no L (for Longacre) on the truncation of the neck was reportedly minted only to the extent of 1,000 pieces. Nevertheless, a high proportion of the output was saved, and it is estimated that as much as half the original mintage survives in Mint State condition today. Since very few collectors try to collect gold dollars by date and mintmark (most merely seek a single Type 1 gold dollar to represent the design), it's not that surprising that my "rare" 1849 No L gold dollar was relatively inexpensive. Sadly, it had gotten less expensive by the time I sold it, and more than five years later a sale price around $2,000 was typical. I'd have been better off buying a genuinely rare Type 1 gold dollar from one of the branch mints, such as the one in the following lot.

Financials: Gold dollar, Liberty Head, 1849, Open Wreath

Cost	Sale Price	Gain/Loss	Holding Period
$3,252	$2,530	-22%	3.8 years

GOLD DOLLAR—LIBERTY HEAD (1849–1854)

Lot 1105.
1849-D, Open Wreath. AU-58.
PCGS #007507.

Auction description: Bowers Gold Rush History Plate Coin. Deep yellow gold with much mint brilliance in the protected areas. Some warm honey and orange highlights have gathered on both sides. No serious digs or scrapes present, lending greatly to the overall eye appeal. One of just 21,588 gold dollars struck in Dahlonega during the first year of the denomination.

From the Waccabuc Collection. Earlier from Bowers and Merena's sale of the Mory Collection, June 2000, Lot 1143. Illustrated on page 343 of *A California Gold Rush History* by Q. David Bowers.

As can be seen, I had two Type 1 gold dollars in my collection. The one described in the immediately preceding lot was better preserved and garnered more points in the PCGS set-registry system. But I personally far preferred this lightly circulated example from the Dahlonega Mint. For me, it just had more interest, character, and pizzazz.

In 2001, Dave Bowers was working on his monumental (1,055-page) book entitled *A California Gold Rush History*, featuring the treasure from the SS *Cen-*

tral America. I was one of his many "helpers," copyediting sections of the book as they became available. (Indeed, I think I'm one of the very few people who actually read every single page of that weighty [10-pound] work.)

When I got to chapter 10 ("1849: Gold Coins and Ingots"), I saw that Dave had written himself a note to find an image of an 1849-D gold dollar to supplement the text. I immediately let him know that just such an image existed in the Mory Collection catalog—an auction conducted by his firm the year before. I knew this because I had bought that coin at the auction. And that's the story of how my 1849-D gold dollar came to be pictured in the heaviest coin book of all time.

Lesson 105: A coin with a story is more fun than one that's just another widget. Anything from the historic but little-known Dahlonega, Georgia, mint has a story to tell, and one that is also plated in a major numismatic work is even more enjoyable. If you want to learn more about the Dahlonega Mint, you should get your hands on a copy of *The Neighborhood Mint: Dahlonega In The Age Of Jackson* by Sylvia Gailey Head and Elizabeth W. Etheridge.

Financials: Gold dollar, Liberty Head, 1849-D, Open Wreath

Cost	Sale Price	Gain/Loss	Holding Period
$3,229	$4,370	+35%	7.4 years

GOLD DOLLAR—INDIAN PRINCESS HEAD, SMALL HEAD (1854–1856)

Lot 1106.
1855-O. AU-58.
PCGS #007535.

After six years of production, the diameter of the gold dollar was enlarged in mid-1854 from 13 mm to 15 mm, and the obverse design was changed from the familiar Liberty Head to the more attractive small Indian Princess Head. Only about 1.7 million of these Type 2 gold dollars were produced, with fully 94 percent being made in Philadelphia in 1854 and 1855. These are the dates that almost invariably appear in type collections. In my view, they're both over-priced. You would be well advised to wait for the appearance of one of the other four date-mintmark coins—the 1855 minted in Charlotte, Dahlonega, or New Orleans or the 1856 minted in San Francisco. These all cost somewhat more than their Philadelphia cousins, but they're all much rarer and more desirable.

Lesson 106: Many people seek to acquire first-year-of-issue coins. I was one of these people. For many series, mintage figures in the first year were high, and high-grade examples are often available since people tended to save these as novelties. For some series, however, you should consider buying a last-year-of-issue coin. The 1856-S Type 2 gold dollar is an excellent example: with a mintage of just 24,600, it is more than 30 times as rare as the 1854 Type 2 gold dollar. Two other last-year-of-issue coins with low mintages and investment potential are the 1909-S Indian Head cent and the 1912-S Liberty Head nickel.

Financials: Gold dollar, Indian Princess Head, Small Head, 1855-O

Cost	Sale Price	Gain/Loss	Holding Period
$2,760	$5,060	+83%	5.7 years

GOLD DOLLAR—INDIAN PRINCESS HEAD, LARGE HEAD (1856–1889)

Lot 1107.
1880. MS-67.
PCGS #007581.

Auction description: Satiny Gem Uncirculated 1880 Gold Dollar. A satiny beauty with intense cartwheel luster that fairly leaps from deep golden surfaces. A wealth of rich peach and fiery orange toning graces both sides of this impressive Gem. One of only 1,600 circulation strikes of the date produced, sharply struck with every small design element crisp and clear.

From the Waccabuc Collection. Earlier from Heritage's F.U.N. Convention Sale, January 2004, Lot 7348.

The image of Miss Liberty with her Indian headdress on the Type 2 gold dollars was sculpted in high relief. This resulted in chronically poorly struck coins at all mints, but most especially at the branch mints that were using older equipment. The central hair details are usually weak, and the LL in DOLLAR and even the date are often blurry.

To remedy these problems, the Large Head Type 3 gold dollars were introduced in 1856 and remained in production through the end of the series, in 1889. The enlarged and repositioned obverse design solved the striking issues, with the result that today it is not difficult to find a crisply impressed example of the Type 3 gold dollar for your type collection.

Lesson 107: Except for the years 1873 and 1874, the mintage figures for gold dollars from 1863 through the end of the series in 1889 are low. In 20 of those years, fewer than 10,000 pieces were struck. And yet many of these dates, particularly during the final decade of production, are not rare today, even in Mint State. Few of these gold dollars entered circulation, and many were saved. According to Walter Breen, most of the 1,600 gold dollars minted in 1880 went to hoarders, including Virgil Brand and, later, Charles E. Green, among others. Hundreds of choice examples appeared on the market in the 1950s and 1960s, and worn examples of this date are virtually non-existent. This kind of background information is useful in understanding the pricing of particular coins and for making a judgment about their investment potential.

Financials: Gold dollar, Indian Princess Head, Large Head, 1880

Cost	Sale Price	Gain/Loss	Holding Period
$3,752	$4,370	+16%	3.8 years

Quarter
Eagles

Every time a golfer makes a birdie, he must subsequently make two triple bogeys to restore the fundamental equilibrium of the universe.

I had no triple bogies among the seven quarter eagles in my collection. Indeed, all yielded profits, and I more than doubled my money on the coin dated 1804. For this denomination, at least, numismatics did not mirror the fundamental rules of golf.

The quarter eagle, or $2.50 gold coin, was authorized by the Mint Act of 1792. That act established the eagle, or $10 gold coin, as our largest denomination, with the half eagle and quarter eagle as our two subordinate fractional gold pieces.

The Capped Bust to Right (or sometimes called Turban Head) quarter eagles were minted in small quantities from 1796 through 1807. This design was followed by a one-year type, the Capped Bust to Left motif, which was minted only in 1808 and is scarce or rare in all grades. Next came the Capped Head to Left design, which was made from 1821 through 1834 in two sizes. Production was notably more generous for both the Classic Head type (1834 to 1839) and for the Liberty Head or Coronet type (1840 to 1907). The final quarter eagle design is the Indian Head type, produced in Philadelphia and (in three years only) Denver from 1908 through 1929. Rarities abound among quarter eagles made before 1834, but none are impossible for the collector with patience and a generous budget. All of these types are described and discussed in more detail below.

QUARTER EAGLE—CAPPED BUST TO RIGHT (1796–1807)

Lot 1108.
1804, 14 Stars Reverse. AU-58.
BD-2, B-1. Rarity-4. PCGS #007652.

Auction description: Bright and satiny yellow gold with reflective fields, frosty motifs, and exceptional remaining luster. This strike is crisp for the type, and the surfaces are free of contact marks though we note some diagonal planchet adjustment marks, as struck, in the reverse shield. An exceptional coin for the assigned grade, one that surely beckoned to Harry Bass in much the same way it will beckon to you once you cast an appreciative eye upon it.

From the Waccabuc Collection. Earlier from Stack's sale of the Bartle Collection, October 1984, Lot 1102; Harry W. Bass Jr. Collection; Bowers and Merena's sale of the Bass Collection, Part II, October 1999, Lot 266.

The Capped Bust to Right (or Turban Head) quarter eagles were first produced in 1796 without any stars on the obverse. After 963 pieces were coined, 16 stars were added to the left and right of the figure of Liberty late in 1796, after which the star count was reduced to 13 in subsequent years.

The No Stars sub-type is considered a separate design by the PCGS set-registry system, and this is one of the few types that was not represented in the Waccabuc Collection. As fewer than 90 pieces are estimated to survive today, it's not surprising that examples in all grades are expensive. The finest of these, presently housed in a PCGS MS-65 holder, sold for $1,725,000 at a January 2008 auction conducted by Heritage.

The Capped Bust to Right quarter eagles with stars on the obverse are also scarce to rare, with mintages of a few hundred to a few thousand in most years through 1807. The most elusive of these is the 1804 issue with only 13 stars on the reverse (unlike mine, which has 14 stars on the reverse). No more than a dozen of the 13-star variety survive today. The best of these, graded PGCS AU-58, sold for $322,000 in a July 2009 auction, again conducted by Heritage.

Lesson 108: Consider creating mini-collections within your main collection. This 1804 quarter eagle is one of three 1804-dated gold coins within the Waccabuc Collection (see also lots 1117 and 1125). In the early 19th century, there were only three denominations of gold coins being made in the United States—the quarter eagle, the half eagle, and the eagle. Grouped together, they make an appealing display, especially if they all bear the same date. And, of course, for coin collectors, the 1804 date resonates, because of its association with the King of Coins—the 1804 silver dollar. It's not a coincidence that the Post Office box number of the Stack's Bowers office in Wolfeboro, New Hampshire, is 1804, and the telephone number there is 866-811-1804 . . . it's a magical date for us coin nuts. (I was not paid for this publicity.)

Financials: Quarter eagle, Capped Bust to Right, 1804, 14 Stars Reverse

Cost	Sale Price	Gain/Loss	Holding Period
$18,400	$41,400	+125%	8.1 years

QUARTER EAGLE—CAPPED BUST TO LEFT, LARGE SIZE (1808)

Lot 1109.
1808. VF-35.
BD-1, B-1. Rarity-4. PCGS #007652.

Auction description: Deep honey gold with deeper orange highlights on both sides. Possibly cleaned long ago, long since re-toned to a more natural hue. No serious marks present, just wear from a somewhat lengthy stay in circulation. While not the rarest date in the U.S. gold series, the 1808 quarter eagle is the rarest design type, as it was produced in just one year and in a limited quantity of just 2,710 pieces. Of that mintage figure, it is thought that perhaps 125 to 150 or so examples of the type can be found in all grades today. The present coin is a pleasing mid-range example, one that will be within reach of many interested collectors. One of the "stoppers" in the early U.S. gold series and worthy of serious consideration.

From the Waccabuc Collection. PCGS holder marked "Troy Wiseman Collection." Heritage's Long Beach Sale, September 2006, Lot 3103.

As noted by the cataloger, the Capped Bust to Left design is a one-year-only type and is the rarest design type in the entire U.S. gold series. Demand for quarter eagles was low, and production ceased entirely for the next 12 years.

Of the fewer than 150 examples that are estimated to survive today, no more than 10 are in Mint State. One of these, which is graded PCGS MS-63, was sold by Stack's in a November 2008 auction for slightly more than half a million dollars. The finest example grades two points higher, but it has not appeared in an auction in many years.

Lesson 109: John Jay Pittman (1913–1996), the 37th president of the American Numismatic Association and one of the most astute 20th-century coin collectors, spent only about $100,000 to build his impressive collection of United States and world coins. When his collection was sold in three auctions in the late 1990s, it realized almost $40 million. It's a sign of how prices and expectations have changed that the Stack's cataloger described my moderately circulated 1808 quarter eagle as "one that will be within reach of many interested collectors." I spent more than half of Pittman's lifetime coin budget to buy this single coin, and someone else paid 16% more 14 months later to become its new owner. How times have changed!

Financials: Quarter eagle, Capped Bust to Left, Large Size, 1808

Cost	Sale Price	Gain/Loss	Holding Period
$54,625	$63,250	+16%	1.2 years

QUARTER EAGLE—CAPPED HEAD TO LEFT, LARGE DIAMETER (1821–1827)

Lot 1110.
1825. MS-61.
BD-2, B-1. Rarity-4+. PCGS #007664.

Auction description: Bright yellow gold with distinctive olive highlights. Somewhat prooflike and cameo-like in appearance, as frequently seen for the date. Some faint marks are present, these visible courtesy of the reflective fields; were the fields frosty the marks would seem less apparent. Variety with repunched 5 in date and "distant fraction" on reverse. The Dannreuther text suggests that perhaps just 80 to 100 or so examples of this variety are currently known in all grades. Another elusive design type presented here in a collectible grade.

From the Waccabuc Collection.

After a long hiatus, production of quarter eagles resumed in 1821. The new design displayed a capped head of Miss Liberty facing left on the obverse and, on the reverse, an eagle with its wings spread wide, which was very similar to the reverse design used on the preceding type.

For the new quarter eagle, engraver Robert Scot adapted the design first used for the half eagle that had been introduced in 1813. For the years 1821 through 1827, the diameter of the new quarter eagles was approximately 18.5 mm. After that date, the diameter was reduced slightly and certain design elements were refined (see following lot).

All of the "large" diameter Capped Head to Left quarter eagles are rare, with mintages of fewer than 7,000 in each year of production. The lowest mintage date is the 1826, of which only 760 were produced; perhaps 50 of these survive today.

Lesson 110: Opportunities to acquire certain type coins come along only infrequently. The Capped Head to Left quarter eagle is clearly one of these. The usual pattern is for collectors to fill the "easy" holes in their collections first, and to put off purchases of the difficult dates or types for later. A smarter strategy would be to focus on the tough coins from the start. This means spending more money early on, but the financial and psychic rewards are likely to be maximized by this approach. I didn't follow this advice here, but I still snagged a good profit when I sold this genuinely rare coin.

Financials: Quarter eagle, Capped Head to Left, Large Diameter, 1825

Cost	Sale Price	Gain/Loss	Holding Period
$29,941	$39,100	+31%	0.7 years

QUARTER EAGLE—CAPPED HEAD TO LEFT, REDUCED DIAMETER (1829–1834)

Lot 1111.
1829. AU-55.
BD-1, B-1. Rarity-4+. PCGS #007669.

Auction description: Bright and lustrous yellow gold with strong olive highlights on the frosty high points and highly reflective mirrors. Pale orange toning and frosty mint bloom is noted as well. No serious marks present, though low magnification picks up a few surface disturbances. This strike is bold and the aesthetics are all that might be hoped for at the assigned grade. Regarding this elusive design type, the Dannreuther reference notes: "Only one variety is known for each date in this type; almost no variance in die states is seen, as production was very limited." From a mintage for the date of 3,403 pieces, with an estimated 70 to 90 examples currently found in all grades.

From the Waccabuc Collection. Earlier from the Dr. Douglas Roane Collection. Heritage's Long Beach Sale, September 2003, Lot 7689.

The reduced-diameter Capped Head to Left quarter eagle was produced from 1829 through 1834. The reduction in size as compared with the preceding type was minor (18.2 mm versus 18.5 mm), but other changes were more important.

William Kneass, who succeeded Robert Scot as U.S. Mint engraver following Scot's death in 1823, modified the design by using smaller lettering and stars, adding detail to Liberty's head and the eagle, and replacing the tooth-like border with beads. Most importantly, these quarter eagles were produced using a "close collar" with a fixed diameter for the first time, assuring that the coins had a uniform size.

Lesson 111: As was the case with their large-diameter cousins, the mintages for the reduced-diameter Capped Head to Left quarter eagles were tiny—fewer than 4,600 pieces were produced in each year. All dates are of approximately equal rarity today except for the 1834 issue. In that year, the price of gold had risen so that the gold content of the quarter eagle exceeded its face value. Of the 4,000 that were made in the first half of 1834, most were melted at the mint.

No more than 15 or possibly 20 pieces avoided the melting pot, making the 1834 Capped Head to Left quarter eagle one of the great rarities in U.S. numismatics. But for some reason, the prices achieved upon the infrequent appearances of these coins at auctions do not match up with the issue's established rarity. A PCGS AU-55 example sold in an American Numismatic Rarities auction in October 2004 for "just" $35,650, multiples less than certain other more famous but also more readily available gold rarities. If you ever spot one of these for sale, take a very close look and consider making a strong bid. In my view, this is a classic "sleeper."

Financials: Quarter eagle, Capped Head to Left, Reduced Diameter, 1829

Cost	Sale Price	Gain/Loss	Holding Period
$9,775	$12,650	+29%	4.2 years

QUARTER EAGLE—CLASSIC HEAD, NO MOTTO ON REVERSE (1834–1839)

Lot 1112.
1834. MS-63.
B-6140. PCGS #007692.

Auction description: Frosty yellow gold with warm orange and olive highlights. A sharp and frosty example of the date with no serious marks present and an abundance of aesthetic appeal in place. Undeniably choice for the assigned grade. Breen-6140. "1834 Large or 'Booby' Head. Large 4 very close to curl; deep indentation curls at 2:30, thick lips, jutting jaw, eye more deeply set."

From the Waccabuc Collection. Earlier from Heritage's Central States Numismatic Society sale, May 2004, Lot 9074.

As noted in the discussion of the preceding lot, a rise in the price of gold starting in 1820 meant that quarter eagles (and other so-called "old tenor" gold coins) were being hoarded or melted. To address this, Congress passed the Act of June 28, 1834, which reduced the weight of quarter eagles from 4.37 to 4.18 grams and reduced the fineness from 0.9167 to 0.8992 gold. (The fineness was rounded up to 0.900 in 1837.)

To accompany the change in weight and fineness, both the obverse and reverse designs were changed. For the obverse, William Kneass decided on what is, in my view, an inferior version of the Classic Head design that first appeared on the large cents of 1808 to 1814 (see lot 1012). On the reverse, the scroll with the motto E PLURIBUS UNUM was removed. With these changes, the new coins could be readily identified from either side.

Lesson 112: For the first time in the quarter eagle series, mintages were generous, at least in the early years of this design type. More than 100,000 pieces were produced in 1834 and 1835, and more than 500,000 were made in 1836. Any of these more common issues would be perfectly fine in a type collection, but if you are willing to pay a premium, you should carefully consider getting one of the mintmarked dates: 1838-C, 1839-C, 1839-D, or 1839-O. Mintages were much lower, and, curiously, the mintmarks appear on the obverse of the coin, immediately above the date. One of these would be a welcome addition to any advanced collection.

Financials: Quarter eagle, Classic Head, No Motto on Reverse, 1834

Cost	Sale Price	Gain/Loss	Holding Period
$4,600	$9,200	+100%	3.5 years

QUARTER EAGLE—LIBERTY HEAD (1840–1907)

Lot 1113.
1904. MS-66.
PCGS #007856.

Auction description: A sparkling, frosty Gem with intense cartwheel luster and a bold strike. Rich orange highlights endorse both sides.

From the Waccabuc Collection. Earlier from Heritage's F.U.N. Convention sale, January 2004, Lot 7439.

The longest-running design used on the quarter eagle was the Liberty Head (also called Coronet Head) type, which was minted in Philadelphia and several branch mints from 1840 through 1907. In that 68-year period, the design remained basically unchanged, though there was some minor tinkering with the size of the reverse lettering and arrows beginning in 1859. The PCGS set-registry system does not recognize that particular modification as a separate type.

As might be expected for a long series like this one, there are several tantalizing rarities that are worth mentioning. One is the issue of 1841 from the Philadelphia Mint. Known as the Little Princess (a name probably invented by Norman Stack for a catalog description in 1954), the 1841 quarter eagle has no known mintage of circulation strikes and a surviving population of fewer than 20 pieces today. PCGS, in a 2012 change of policy, now recognizes both Proofs and circulation strikes. An NGC PF-55 example sold for just under $150,000 in a Heritage auction in April 2012. Other important dates are the 1854-S (with a mintage of just 246 pieces), the Proof-only 1863 (mintage of 30 pieces), and the 1875 (mintage of 420 pieces).

Also worth mentioning is the issue of 1848 with the abbreviation CAL. stamped on the reverse, above the eagle's head. The military governor of California, Colonel R.B. Mason, sent 230 ounces of newly discovered California gold to the secretary of War, who then turned it over to the Mint. The special CAL. mark was stamped onto fewer than 1,400 coins while they were still in the die. Today, perhaps 200 exist. A spectacular NGC MS-68 example sold in a Heritage auction in January 2008 for $345,000. That same coin had sold for $402,500 two years earlier.

Lesson 113: The first Liberty Head quarter eagle I bought was dated 1840, the first year of issue. It was a duplicate from the Harry Bass collection. The grade was PCGS MS-60. Dave Bowers was standing next to me when I made my successful bid and congratulated me on the purchase, noting that this date was genuinely rare in Mint State condition. The coin itself looked like it warranted a grade of MS-63 or better, except for one thing. There was a very noticeable scratch in the obverse field right in front of Miss Liberty's nose. With the passage of time, the only thing I could see when I looked at this coin was the scratch. So I sold it (at about the same price I'd paid) and bought the common-date gem pictured here. Since that episode I've always tried to stay away from coins with problems (scratches, blotchy toning, darkness, etc.), even if they're housed in third-party grading holders. You should enjoy the coins you own—otherwise what's the point?

Financials: Quarter eagle, Liberty Head, 1904

Cost	Sale Price	Gain/Loss	Holding Period
$1,955	$2,645	+35%	3.8 years

QUARTER EAGLE—INDIAN HEAD (1908–1929)

Lot 1114.
1908. MS-63.
PCGS #007939.

Auction description: Satiny orange gold with strong underlying luster. A choice example from the first year of Indian quarter eagle coinage.

From the Waccabuc Collection. Earlier from Kingswood Galleries' October 2002 Sale, Lot 838.

In 1905, President Teddy Roosevelt commissioned Augustus Saint-Gaudens to redesign America's gold coins. The sculptor designed only the two largest denominations before passing away on August 3, 1907. (His work on the $20 and $10 gold coins was completed by his assistant, Henry Hering.) Bela Lyon Pratt was chosen to take up where Saint-Gaudens had left off and design new images for the quarter eagle and half eagle.

Pratt's obverse design (used on both the quarter eagle and half eagle) depicts, for the first time, a true American Indian. Previous representations of Indians on coins such as the Indian Head cent and the Indian Princess $1 and $3 gold pieces were, in fact, merely versions of Miss Liberty wearing incongruous headdresses. On the reverse is a perched eagle that is reminiscent of the eagle used by Saint-Gaudens on his $10 gold piece (see lots 1129 through 1132). The redesigned quarter eagles were minted intermittently from 1908 through 1929.

There are no genuinely rare coins in the Indian Head quarter eagle series, though the 1911-D issue, with a mintage of 55,680 pieces, is considered scarce. A PCGS MS-66 example sold for $172,500 in a Heritage auction in March 2010. All other coins in the series are easily available in circulated grades, though considerably less so in choice or gem Mint State.

Lesson 114: More remarkable than the features of the new motif was the fact that Pratt's Indian Head quarter eagle and half eagle had designs that were incuse or inset below the surface of the coin (except for the D mintmark on the coins produced in Denver). This "sunken relief" means that the first part of the surface of these coins to acquire marks and wear was the field rather than the design elements. For this reason, the Indian Head quarter eagles and half eagles are notoriously difficult for collectors to grade. I strongly recommend you stick to professionally graded slabs when buying these two issues. But never forget to make up your own mind as to whether the coin meets your own standards for eye appeal.

Financials: Quarter eagle, Indian Head, 1908

Cost	Sale Price	Gain/Loss	Holding Period
$892	$1,495	+68%	5.1 years

$3 Gold
Pieces

Never try to keep more than 300 separate thoughts
in your mind during your swing.

The Act of March 3, 1851 is known in numismatic circles because it authorized the silver three-cent piece. Less well known is the fact that the same act reduced the postage cost of a prepaid letter from five cents to three cents.

Speculating that the public would want a convenient way to buy 100-stamp sheets of three-cent stamps, Congress helpfully authorized the issuance of a gold $3 coin via the Act of February 21, 1853. Mintage commenced in the following year and continued through the end of the series in 1889. As it turns out, there is scant evidence that $3 gold pieces were used to purchase stamps, particularly in the South and West. Nevertheless, production of this curious, and now popular (in collecting circles), denomination continued for more than three decades.

Although PCGS only recognizes a single design for this denomination, there actually are two. The first was used only in 1854, where the word DOLLARS was inscribed in small letters on the reverse. In all subsequent years, the word DOLLARS appears in large letters.

THREE-DOLLAR GOLD PIECE—INDIAN PRINCESS HEAD (1854–1889)

Lot 1115.
1854. MS-62.
PCGS #007969.

Auction description: A high degree of luster swirls broadly across rich honey gold surfaces. Hints of rich rose brilliance can be found in the protected areas. Devoid of serious marks and choice for the assigned grade.

From the Waccabuc Collection. Earlier from Heritage's F.U.N. Convention Sale, January 2004, Lot 7554.

Although many dates in the $3 gold series are scarce, there's one coin that is a true numismatic landmark. In 1870, the superintendent of the San Francisco Mint discovered that the $3 die shipped from the parent mint in Philadelphia had not had an S mintmark stamped into it. The Mint director in Washington ordered that the die be returned to Philadelphia. Before complying with this directive, the coiner in San Francisco cut an S into the die and struck a total of two pieces, according to Walter Breen. One was supposedly placed in the cornerstone of the new San Francisco Mint (the famed Granite Lady), and the second was kept by the coiner, whose name was J.B. Harmstead. Most current numismatic researchers believe that only a single 1870-S $3 gold piece was produced. Whatever the case, the coin that Harmstead once owned was eventually purchased by Louis Eliasberg for $11,500 in 1946. When the gold portion of the Eliasberg collection was sold in 1982, the 1870-S $3 gold piece achieved a staggering price of $687,500, a record for a gold coin at that time.

Lesson 115: With the exception of the coins made in Philadelphia in 1854, 1874, and 1878, mintage figures for $3 gold pieces are generally low. Fully 25 of the date-mintmark combinations had production totals of fewer than 5,000 pieces. Choosing one of these dates for your type set can add some special allure to your collection. One particularly appealing choice could be the 1854-D, which has the multiple attractions of being from the Dahlonega Mint, representing the first year of issue of the denomination, and having a mintage of only 1,120 pieces.

Financials: Three-dollar gold piece, 1854

Cost	Sale Price	Gain/Loss	Holding Period
$3,220	$5,290	+64%	3.8 years

$4 Gold
Pieces (Stellas)

A couple met at the Kiawah Island resort in South Carolina and fell in love. They were discussing how they would continue the relationship after their vacations were over.

"It's only fair to warn you, Stella," Bob said. "I'm a golf nut. I live, eat, sleep, and breathe golf."

"Well, since you're being honest, so will I," Stella said. "I'm a hooker."

"I see," he said. Then, brightening, he smiled. "It's probably because you're swinging too much from the inside and not getting your clubhead square to the ball at the point of impact."

There's no way a U.S. type collection should contain a $4 gold coin (a.k.a. Stella, based on the large star that dominates the reverse). All of these coins, regardless of design or metallic composition (gold, copper, aluminum, or white metal—an alloy containing antimony and copper or tin), were produced as patterns in Proof format. Nevertheless, by numismatic tradition, Stellas are listed in all major coin guides (including the *Red Book*) between the sections on $3 gold pieces and $5 half eagles, and PCGS has seen fit to require both design types among the coins needed to assemble a complete type set.

Charles E. Barber was the designer of the Flowing Hair Stella, while George T. Morgan (of Morgan dollar fame) crafted the Coiled Hair design. Both coins were made in 1879 and 1880. Except for the 1879 Flowing Hair variety in gold, mintages were tiny—probably no more than a dozen or two of each date and type. The 1879 Flowing Hair, on the other hand, had a reported mintage of 425, though Dave Bowers has suggested that the number could have been as high as 700. A significant percentage of these have survived and are held in high-value collections around the world.

No Stellas were ever used in circulation, though a number of survivors show clear signs of wear. These "impaired Proofs" reportedly include coins that were given to madams and ladies of the night who sold their services to Washington, D.C., legislators toiling away far from home. *Plus ça change, plus c'est la même chose.*

The Waccabuc Collection did not contain any Stellas. Over the years I bid (unsuccessfully) on several of the "off-metal" (non-gold) patterns. Finally, in 2010, I acquired a copper example of the 1880 Coiled Hair Stella. It's one of the "stars" of my modest collection of pattern coins. If you want a "common" 1879 Flowing Hair Stella for your collection, you'll need to spend a low- to moderate-six-figure amount. One of the very rare Coiled Hair patterns in gold will likely set you back $500,000 or more, assuming you can find one. The finest known example of the 1880 Coiled Hair Stella changed hands in a Bonhams auction in September 2013 for $2.6 million.

1880 Coiled Hair Stella, copper—not part of the Waccabuc Collection.

CHAPTER
18

Half
Eagles

Nonchalant putts count the same as chalant putts.

H alf eagles, or $5 gold pieces, were the first gold coins minted in the United States. Production of this denomination, authorized by the Mint Act of 1792, lasted from 1795 through 1929. A little-known fact about the half eagle is that it is the only denomination minted at eight different mints. Many numismatists can come up with seven: Philadelphia, Charlotte, Dahlonega, New Orleans, San Francisco, Carson City, and Denver. The eighth is West Point, which began minting $5 one-tenth-ounce bullion gold coins in 1986.

The design motifs employed on half eagles over the decades generally parallel those used for quarter eagles. One major exception to this is the first type, which pairs a Capped Bust to Right obverse with a Small Eagle reverse that was never used on any quarter eagle (though it did appear on contemporary $10 gold pieces). In 1798, the design was changed when the small eagle on the reverse was replaced with a large (or heraldic) eagle. (Confusingly, coins of this second type exist with the dates 1795 and 1797, but these are thought to have been minted in 1798.) The Capped Bust to Left design (1807 to 1812) followed, but it, too, was soon replaced. The Capped Head to Left design was produced with a "large" diameter from 1813 through 1829 and then with a reduced diameter from 1829 through 1834. The Classic Head type (1834 to 1838) made a brief appearance before being succeeded by the long-lived Liberty Head or Coronet type (1839 to 1908). The final type of half eagle employed the Indian Head design from 1908 through 1929. All of these types are described in more detail in the sections that follow.

HALF EAGLE—CAPPED BUST TO RIGHT, SMALL EAGLE REVERSE (1795–1798)

Lot 1116.
1795. AU-55.
BD-7, Breen 5-E. Rarity-7. PCGS #008066.

Auction description: A highly elusive variety from the first year of half eagle production. Lustrous medium yellow gold with abundant remaining reflective character, particularly on the reverse. A lovely example, showing no more than the usual assortment of light contact marks. A tiny nick is noted between IB of LIBERTY, thin scratch over the left wing, some vestiges of adjustment marks above star 10 and in the low spot at absolute central obverse. Well detailed, typically struck for one of these. Excellent visual appeal for the assigned grade.

An interesting die variety, struck from an obverse die with a boldly recut 5 in the date that was later used to produce a very rare 1795 Heraldic Eagle variety in 1797. John Dannreuther and Harry W. Bass Jr. call this marriage Rarity-7 in their recently published, masterfully prepared reference book. It remains one of the most elusive die combinations of this first half eagle issue, giving the variety importance above and beyond that of a normal 1795 $5 in Choice About Uncirculated.

Our census for the variety, based on a survey of more than 1,000 major auction sales several years ago, is as follows. The specimen offered here appears to be different from the following:

1) Kagin's. November 1974, Mid-Atlantic, Lot 1611, Uncirculated.

2) Stack's, April 1967, Copeland, Lot 1630, Extremely Fine; Stack's, October 1973, Scanlon, Lot 2249, Extremely Fine; Superior, May 1989, Lot 1853, Extremely Fine; Superior, October 1989, Heifetz, Lot 4302, About Uncirculated.

3) New England, November 1977, Devonshire, Lot 922, Extremely Fine.

4) Mid-American, January 1988, FUN, Lot 1973, Extremely Fine; Bowers and Merena, September 1990, Rusbar, Lot 496, Extremely Fine.

The Harry W. Bass Jr. specimen was purchased from Stanley Kesselman in October 1972. It is illustrated in the *Harry W. Bass Jr. Museum Sylloge* prepared by Q. David Bowers of our staff in 2001.

Another appearance, possibly identical with one of those listed above: Kreisberg, September 1973, Lot 1155, Extremely Fine.

From the Waccabuc Collection. Earlier from the Allison Park Collection. ANR's New York Connoisseur Sale, March 2006, Lot 1552.

Robert Scot's Capped Bust to Right (or Turban Head) design with the Small Eagle reverse was minted from 1795 through 1798. The so-called turban is, in fact, a liberty or freedman's cap, with a misplaced strand of hair creating the suggestion of a turban.

Only 18,512 pieces were minted of all dates and varieties. The 1795 is the most common date, but even this coin is considered very scarce. The rarest date by far is the 1798, of which perhaps 100 were minted with leftover dies. Only seven examples are known to exist today. As of this writing, a 1798 half eagle of the Small Eagle type had not appeared in a major auction since 1999.

Lesson 116: It was a real eye-opener for me to read the cataloger's description of this coin. I'd bought it less than two years earlier in an American Numismatic Rarities auction. The description in that March 2006 auction was repeated almost word-for-word in the November 2007 catalog. That didn't surprise me—after all, ANR had merged its business into the Stack's operation, so it was natural that ANR's work product would be used by Stack's. What did surprise and impress me was the census that Stack's had developed, which showed only four other auction appearances for this variety in more than 1,000 recent major auctions. I really appreciated this additional research and felt that it contributed to the strong price realized for this coin. Very few potential buyers would have had this kind of information available to them at their fingertips.

Financials: Half eagle, Capped Bust to Right, Small Eagle Reverse, 1795

Cost	Sale Price	Gain/Loss	Holding Period
$52,900	$69,000	+30%	1.7 years

HALF EAGLE—CAPPED BUST TO RIGHT, HERALDIC EAGLE REVERSE (1795–1807)

Lot 1117.
1804, Small 8 Over Large 8. AU-58.
BD-5, Breen 1-E. Rarity-6+. PCGS #008086.

Auction description: Brilliant and satiny. A superlative example, and one of the very finest survivors of the die combination known to us. A few trifling marks are noted under magnification, but nothing sufficient to dim our enthusiasm in the slightest. We had the privilege to offer this beauty in our Bareford Collection Sale back in 1978 where we described it as: "The obverse mostly prooflike, the reverse frosty. An extremely attractive coin and very sharp even though it was struck from cracked dies." The reverse die state is advanced, with a bisecting die crack, closely matching the specimen illustrated in the Bass-Dannreuther early gold reference, a feature that probably explains why the die combination was so short lived. Although we hold the recently published Bass-Dannreuther reference in the highest regard, our research experience compels us to quibble a bit with their assigned rarity rating of Rarity-6+. We're of the opinion that it's actually Rarity-7, but we are always eager to see any evidence to the contrary. We were able to account for just a handful of examples, in all grades, when we conducted a survey of more than 1,000 auction sales several years ago; our resulting census for the die combination is presented below. PCGS Population: 11; 20 finer within the designation [a category that includes all three 1804 Small/Large 8 die varieties, BD-5, 6, and 7] (MS-64 finest).

Our census for the BD-5 variety, based on a survey of more than 1,000 major auction sales several years ago, is as follows:

1) Geiss-Bareford-Bass example. The specimen offered here, with fuller pedigree presented at the bottom of this description.
2) Stack's, November 1955, Farish-Baldenhofer, Lot 1213; Bowers and Merena, October 1987, Norweb, Lot 750, Uncirculated; Harry W. Bass Jr. Collection; Illustrated in the *Harry W. Bass Jr. Museum Sylloge*.
3) Stack's, October 1994, Stack, Lot 1043, Uncirculated.
4) Mid-American, September 1985, San Diego, Lot 1147, Extremely Fine.
5) Paramount, July 1984, Auction '84, Lot 892, Very Fine; Krueger, November 1987, Hansen, Lot 2850, Extremely Fine; Krueger, April 1988, Michigan, Lot 1060, Extremely Fine.

From the Waccabuc Collection. Earlier from B. Max Mehl's sale of the Geiss Collection, February 1947, Lot 1658. Stack's sale of the Harold Bareford Collection, December 1978, Lot 155; Harry W. Bass Jr. Collection; Bowers and Merena's sale of the Bass Collection, Part II, October 1999, Lot 756.

The Capped Bust to Right, Heraldic Eagle reverse, half eagle was designed by Robert Scot and minted from 1798 through 1807. (As mentioned earlier, there are coins of this type dated 1795 and 1797, but these are thought to have been struck in 1798.) All dates are scarce, and the 1795 and 1797 pieces are rare.

This is another example of an outstanding AU-58 coin. I confess that I twice re-submitted this coin to PCGS because I thought it warranted a Mint State classification. Obviously I was wrong, but to this day, I cannot understand why. Maybe there's a touch of friction on Liberty's cheek that interrupts the luster, but if so, it's extremely hard to discern.

Not noted by the Stack's cataloger, but commented upon in the 1999 Bass catalog description, are the heavy clash marks seen primarily on the reverse. The clash marks are sufficiently distinct that one can read the date on the lower reverse. This was one of my favorite coins to scrutinize with a magnifying glass—clash marks, die cracks, and the prominent small 8 over large 8 in the date.

Lesson 117: I've mentioned earlier that AU-58 is my favorite grade for classic American coins. At this grade level, all the original design features are readily visible, and much of the luster remains. And not insignificantly, these coins almost invariably cost quite a bit less than their moderate Mint State counterparts. What I haven't mentioned is my least favorite grade. It's MS-60. Coins graded at the minimum Mint State level may technically not show any signs of actual circulation, but they always have some visible problem—usually a plethora of bag marks or some scratches that are just not quite severe enough to cause the coin to be ungradeable. In my view, this is a grade you can generally avoid without regret.

Financials: Half eagle, Capped Bust to Right, Heraldic Eagle Reverse, 1804, Small 8 Over Large 8

Cost	Sale Price	Gain/Loss	Holding Period
$9,200	$31,050	+238%	8.1 years

HALF EAGLE—CAPPED BUST TO LEFT (1807–1812)

Lot 1118.

1807. AU-58.

BD-8, Breen 5-D. Rarity-2. PCGS #008101.

Auction description: Deep yellow gold with strong honey highlights and a whisper of olive here and there. Nicely struck with rich underlying luster and much mint bloom in the protected areas. No serious marks present and worthwhile as such. A popular half eagle design type in a popular collector grade.

From the Waccabuc Collection. Acquired from Heritage, December 2001.

John Reich designed a new Capped Bust to Left half eagle in 1807 to replace the earlier Robert Scot–designed coins. The design remained in use through 1812. The popular reception was mixed, with one newspaper describing the new depiction of Miss Liberty as "the artist's fat mistress," according to Walter Breen. For the first time for this denomination, the value of the coin was added, expressed as "5 D." below the eagle on the reverse.

By comparison with the prior two types, mintages of the Capped Bust to Left half eagles were generous, peaking at more than 100,000 in 1810 and approaching that mark again in 1811. However, survival rates are low since many early half eagles were melted when their gold value exceeded their face value.

Lesson 118: There are no great rarities in this short series. I chose a first-year-of-issue coin (1807) to represent the Capped Bust to Left half eagle, but any of the others would be equally desirable. I was pleased to find an attractive example in my favorite grade for early U.S. coins: AU-58. Once again, this strategy resulted in a satisfying return over the roughly six years I owned this coin.

Financials: Half eagle, Capped Bust to Left, 1807

Cost	Sale Price	Gain/Loss	Holding Period
$4,210	$9,775	+132%	5.9 years

HALF EAGLE—CAPPED HEAD TO LEFT (1813–1834)

Lot 1119.
1813. MS-64.
BD-2, Breen 1-B. Rarity-4. PCGS #008116.

Auction description: Frosty olive-gold with intensely imbued luster that seemingly glows from within. Sharply struck and aesthetically appealing, and as fresh and new under low magnification as it is to the unaided eye. An exceptional example from the first year of this rare design type, and one of the few dates of the design type that can be found readily in Uncirculated grades. An exceptional example of the date, one that has been topped in the PCGS Population Report by just three other specimens. PCGS Population: 52; 3 finer (MS-66 finest).

From the Waccabuc Collection. Earlier from Kingswood Galleries' March 2002 Sale, Lot 969.

John Reich modified his Capped Bust half eagle in 1813. The result was the Capped Head design, which was minted from 1813 through 1834. There are two varieties of the Capped Head half eagle: the large diameter (25 mm), which was minted through 1829, and the small diameter (23.8 mm), which appeared from 1829 through 1834. These coins are affectionately called "Fat Head $5s" in the trade.

Although mintages were generally modest to moderate by the standards of the era, many pieces (particularly of the small-diameter variety) were melted for their bullion value. According to Walter Breen in his *Encyclopedia*, 99 percent of all pre-1834 half eagles had been melted by the mid-1840s.

Rare and expensive coins abound in this series, but one date stands head and shoulders above the rest. That is the 1822, of which only three pieces are known to exist. Two of these are owned by the Smithsonian Institution. The third example, graded EF-45, last changed hands in 1982 at the sale of the gold portion of the famed Louis Eliasberg collection. The price was a whopping $687,500. Several serious numismatists consider this to be the most valuable of all American coins and have speculated that if it were to appear for sale now, it would cost more than $10 million.

Lesson 119: I made a wonderful profit on my 1813 large-diameter Capped Head half eagle, but I never bought the variety with the small diameter. The reason was price. These coins rarely appear for sale, and when they do, they often run into six figures. A representative specimen was the 1833 NGC PF-61 example that was offered for sale by Harry Laibstain Rare Coins in a fixed price list in 2012. The price was a breathtaking $175,000.

Financials: Half eagle, Capped Head to Left, 1813

Cost	Sale Price	Gain/Loss	Holding Period
$15,238	$47,150	+209%	5.7 years

HALF EAGLE—CLASSIC HEAD, NO MOTTO (1834–1838)

Lot 1120.
1834, Plain 4. MS-62.
B-6501. PCGS #008171.

Auction description: Deep yellow gold with rich orange and honey highlights at the rim. The fields are reflective and the devices lightly frosted, affording an exceptional example of the date and grade combination. Nicely struck as well. Breen-6501. "1834 First Head; Large Plain 4. Truncation markedly curved, its end broad and rounded. Center stroke of 8 thick; with large knob to 3."

From the Waccabuc Collection. Acquired from Alpine Numismatics, January 2003.

Rising gold prices in the early 1830s meant that half eagles (and other so-called "old tenor" gold coins) were being hoarded or melted. To address this, Congress passed the Mint Act of June 28, 1834, which reduced the weight of half eagles from 8.75 to 8.36 grams and reduced the fineness from 0.9167 to 0.8992 gold. (The fineness was rounded up to 0.900 in 1837.)

The mint in Philadelphia anticipated that a flood of old half eagles would be turned in, to be coined into the new, smaller half eagles, with a little gold left over for the depositor. The flood materialized, and more than 650,000 of the new Classic Head half eagles were produced in 1834. Output remained high through the end of the series in 1838, though the production at the branch mints in Charlotte and Dahlonega (1838 only) was very modest.

To accompany the reduction in the weight and fineness of half eagles, both the obverse and reverse designs were changed. For the obverse, William Kneass decided on what is, in my view, an inferior version of the Classic Head design that first appeared on the large cents of 1808 to 1814 (see lot 1012). On the reverse, the scroll with the motto E PLURIBUS UNUM was removed. With these changes, the new coins could be readily identified from either side.

Lesson 120: I made a decent return on my "common" Mint State first-year-of-issue Classic Head half eagle and have no complaints about that. But I had earlier owned an AU example of the 1838-D issue, which, to me, had far more sex appeal. It had a mintage of a little more than 20,000; it was minted in Dahlonega, Georgia; it had its mintmark on the obverse, right above the date; and I earned a comparable profit when I sold it. As mentioned in lesson 112, discerning collectors would do well to consider buying one of the branch-mint issues of the Classic Head quarter eagle and half eagle series.

Financials: Half Eagle, Classic Head, No Motto, 1834, Plain 4

Cost	Sale Price	Gain/Loss	Holding Period
$3,350	$8,050	+140%	4.2 years

HALF EAGLE—LIBERTY HEAD, NO MOTTO ABOVE EAGLE (1839–1866)

Lot 1121.

1856. AU-58.

PCGS #008266.

Auction description: Bright and lustrous honey gold with much mint bloom in the protected areas.

From the Waccabuc Collection. Earlier from Heritage's F.U.N. Convention Sale, January 2004, Lot 7652.

In 1839, Christian Gobrecht redesigned the half eagle—the seventh design change for this denomination in just 43 years. The new Liberty Head (or Coronet) half eagle had a completely fresh profile of Miss Liberty on the obverse, with her hair in a bun, and a "healthier and less moth-eaten" eagle on the reverse (according to Ron Guth and Jeff Garrett in *United States Coinage: A Study by Type*). This design survived for seven decades with just a single important change—the addition of the motto IN GOD WE TRUST on a scroll on the reverse, above the eagle. A minor reduction in diameter (from 22.5 mm to 21.6 mm), without any change in weight or fineness, took place in 1840. This change is not normally considered a separate design type.

There are many common dates in this series, particularly those from the Philadelphia Mint. There are also a number of scarce and rare date-and-mintmark combinations. In this regard, the 1854-S issue is notable, with an original mintage of just 268 pieces. Only three pieces are known to survive, one of which resides in the Smithsonian Institution. The finest piece (graded

AU-58) last appeared in an auction in October 1982 where, as part of the sale of the Eliasberg Collection, it reached a price of $187,000. That coin would certainly be a seven-figure star of any auction held today.

The original mintage of the 1841-O half eagle (reported to be 50 pieces, although this was probably a bookkeeping error) was even lower than that of the 1854-S. No survivors are known in any collection.

Lesson 121: My purchase of a lightly circulated (AU-58), common-date (1856), high-mintage (almost 200,000 pieces), non-mintmarked No Motto Liberty Head half eagle as a placeholder in my type collection was a complete blunder. There are so many better choices I could have made—for example, a high-grade Mint State coin of one of the relatively available dates or an appealing circulated example of one of the many scarcer date-and-mintmark combinations. I always intended to seek an upgrade, but I never got around to it. You should not follow my example when building your own collection.

Financials: Half eagle, Liberty Head, No Motto Above Eagle, 1856

Cost	Sale Price	Gain/Loss	Holding Period
$851	$633	-26%	3.8 years

HALF EAGLE—LIBERTY HEAD, MOTTO ABOVE EAGLE (1866–1908)

Lot 1122.
1906-D. MS-64.
PCGS #008414.

The Mint Act of March 3, 1865, promulgated near the end of the Civil War, provided for the addition of the motto IN GOD WE TRUST on all coins that were large enough. In practice, this meant all silver coins larger than the dime and all gold coins larger than the quarter eagle.

The Liberty Head (or Coronet) With Motto half eagle was minted from 1866 through the end of the series in 1908. As a type, these half eagles are extremely common—there are 15 date-and-mintmark combinations with mintages of more than one million pieces and 38 others with mintages numbering in the hundreds of thousands. And yet for collectors who seek coins with a degree of prestige, there are several appealing varieties to choose among. In 1875, for example, a mere 200 circulation strikes and 20 Proofs were made. An NGC-55 example of the 1875 half eagle sold for slightly less than $150,000 in a November 2010 auction conducted by Bowers and Merena. Another delicacy was created in 1887 when 87 Proofs and no circulation strikes were produced. One of these, grading PCGS PF-65, sold for slightly less than $100,000 at a Heritage auction in October 2012.

Lesson 122: Be careful when buying common gold coins such as the 1906-D half eagle pictured here. I almost doubled my money in a little over four years, but that was because I was lucky: the price of gold increased and the numismatic spread (the premium above the intrinsic value of the coin) widened between 2003 and 2007. The buyer of my coin, if he still held it five years later, had a chuck of gold worth about $1,200. Genuinely rare coins are far less volatile in price than numismatic material that is traded as an alternate form of bullion.

Financials: Half eagle, Liberty Head, Motto Above Eagle, 1906-D

Cost	Sale Price	Gain/Loss	Holding Period
$901	$1,725	+91%	4.3 years

HALF EAGLE—INDIAN HEAD (1908–1929)

Lot 1123.
1908. MS-63.
PCGS #008510.

Auction description: Frosty honey gold with attractive olive highlights and rich, effusive luster that seemingly glows from within. Sharp and appealing, just the way Bela Lyon Pratt intended his unique incused design to look.

From the Waccabuc Collection. Earlier from Kingswood Galleries' October 2002 Sale, Lot 869.

As noted earlier, President Teddy Roosevelt commissioned Augustus Saint-Gaudens to redesign America's gold coins. The sculptor only completed his work on the two largest denominations before passing away on August 3, 1907. Bela Lyon Pratt was chosen to take up where Saint-Gaudens had left off and design new images for the quarter eagle and half eagle.

Pratt's obverse design (used on both denominations) depicts, for the first time, a true American Indian. Previous representations of Indians on coins such as the Indian Head cent and the Indian Princess $1 and $3 gold pieces were, in fact, merely versions of Miss Liberty wearing incongruous head-dresses. On the reverse is a perched eagle that is reminiscent of the eagle used by Saint-Gaudens on his $10 gold piece (see lots 1129 through 1132). The redesigned half eagles were minted from 1908 through 1916 and then again in 1929.

Most of the coins in the Indian Head half eagle series are easily available in circulated grades, though considerably less so in choice or gem Mint State.

For those looking to assemble a complete collection of these half eagles, there are two difficult dates. The first is the low-mintage 1909-O, of which only 34,200 pieces were made. The sole MS-66 example of this date sold in a Heritage auction in January 2011 for a remarkable $690,000.

The most challenging issue in circulated grades is the 1929, though in high grades it is seen more frequently than the 1909-O. The 1929 had a generous original mintage of 662,000. Most of these remained stored in bags at the mint until 1933, when the United States went off the gold standard. At some point thereafter, probably in the mid- or late 1930s, the coins remaining at the mint were melted. Today, survivors number in the hundreds. A PCGS MS-65 example crossed the Heritage auction block in January 2011 at a price of $86,250.

Lesson 123: As mentioned in lesson 114, more remarkable than the features of the new motif was the fact that Pratt's Indian Head quarter eagle and half eagle had designs that were incuse or inset below the surface of the coin (except for the mintmarks on those coins produced at branch mints). This "sunken relief" means that the first part of the surface of these coins to acquire marks and wear was the field rather than the design elements. For this reason, the Indian Head quarter eagles and half eagles are notoriously difficult for collectors to grade. I strongly recommend you stick to professionally graded slabs when buying these two issues. But never forget to make up your own mind as to whether the coin meets your own standards for eye appeal.

Financials: Half eagle, Indian Head, 1908

Cost	Sale Price	Gain/Loss	Holding Period
$1,006	$4,600	+357%	5.1 years

CHAPTER

19

Eagles

Golf can best be defined as an endless series of tragedies obscured by the occasional miracle.

The miracle in this chapter is discussed below, in lot 1125. It was unexpected, but then I guess all miracles are. First, however, a few words about this majestic but defunct denomination.

The eagle, or $10 gold piece, was authorized by the Mint Act of 1792 as our country's highest-denomination coin and the unit of measurement among gold coins. The $2.50 quarter eagle and $5 half eagle gold pieces were designated as fractional parts of the eagle. It was not until two years after the discovery of vast quantities of gold in California in 1848 that the larger $20 double eagle made its public appearance.

Robert Scot modeled the first eagle after the half eagle he had designed earlier in 1795. It depicted Miss Liberty wearing a cap that resembles a turban, giving rise to the frequently seen sobriquet, Turban Head eagle. The reverse has a small eagle perched on a palm branch with a wreath in its beak. This design survived for only three years (1795 to 1797). Its replacement, introduced in 1797, had a new reverse with an imposing heraldic eagle, suggestive of the Great Seal of the United States.

Production of gold eagles ceased after 1804 due to extensive melting and exporting of these coins. The denomination did not reappear for more than three decades. The Liberty Head eagle was introduced in 1838. A slightly modified version was adopted in the middle of the next year, and then the motto IN GOD WE TRUST was added to the reverse in 1866. The basic design, however, lasted through 1907. Augustus Saint-Gaudens's novel design, showing Miss Liberty wearing an Indian headdress, appeared in 1907. The various varieties of the Indian Head eagle (with and without periods and without and with a motto on the reverse) were minted through 1933. All of these coins are discussed and illustrated in the sections that follow.

EAGLE—CAPPED BUST TO RIGHT, SMALL EAGLE REVERSE (1795–1797)

Lot 1124.
1796. AU-55.
BD-1, T-6, Breen 1-A. Rarity-4. PCGS #008554.

Auction description: Bright yellow gold with warm honey and orange highlights. Intense mint bloom glows broadly within the protected design areas. Lightly circulated with rub on the high points, but devoid of marks that draw the viewer's eye. One of an estimated 3,500 to 4,146 examples of the date struck; the *Guide Book* gives the latter figure, while the Bass-Dannreuther text gives the estimated figure just quoted. An exceptional opportunity to begin an early U.S. gold cabinet, or simply to add a pleasing coin to already extensive holding.

From the Waccabuc Collection. Earlier From Charles E. Green, April 1954; Stack's Brooklyn Sale, March 2007, Lot 1617.

Fewer than 14,000 examples of Robert Scot's Turban Head eagle with Small Eagle reverse were produced in the three years (1795 through 1797) of the inaugural design. Perhaps 500 of these survive today, making all dates and varieties scarce or rare.

The rarest variety is the 1795 issue with a palm frond on the reverse sporting only nine leaves, instead of the usually seen thirteen leaves. A PCGS MS-61 example of this coin sold in a Spink/Smythe auction in May 2011 for slightly less than $380,000. The half-million-dollar barrier has been breached a couple of times by high-grade (MS-64 and MS-65) examples of the 13-leaf variety of the 1795 eagle.

When you have a moment of leisure, perhaps right now, take a close look at the cap perched atop Miss Liberty's head. It is, indeed, just a liberty cap, not a turban at all. But there's a major strand of her hair that, defying gravity, has somehow grown upwards and wrapped itself around the cap in a way that makes the cap appear to be a turban. Strange, isn't it?

Lesson 124: The cataloger's write-up suggests that I bought my 1796 eagle at a Stack's sale in March 2007. This is not true. Someone else was the buyer at that sale, at a price of $80,500. He or she quickly sold the coin, probably at a small profit, to Legend Numismatics. Legend then sold the coin to me on August 8, 2007 for $93,500. I had by that time already consigned my collection to Stack's, but I wanted to be one rare coin closer to having a complete type set. At the November 2007 sale of the Waccabuc Collection, someone paid $103,500 for a coin that would have cost $23,000 less just eight months earlier. The lesson is that in numismatics, just as is the case when investing in stocks, timing can be critically important. The March 2007 price looks sensible, but by November 2007 the price had run up too far and too fast. I don't know if this particular coin has changed hands again, but I do know that a somewhat nicer example grading NGC MS-61 sold at a Heritage auction in January 2013 for slightly less than $97,000. My guess is that that will prove to be a sensible purchase for the new owner.

Financials: Eagle, Capped Bust to Right, Small Eagle Reverse, 1796

Cost	Sale Price	Gain/Loss	Holding Period
$93,500	$103,500	+11%	0.3 years

EAGLE—CAPPED BUST TO RIGHT, HERALDIC EAGLE REVERSE (1797–1804)

Lot 1125.
1804, Crosslet 4. AU-58.
BD-1, T-31, Breen 1-A. Rarity-4+.PCGS #008566.

The Capped Bust, Large (or Heraldic) Eagle design for the $10 gold pieces was used from 1797 through 1804, except for 1802. The most commonly seen dates by far are 1799 and 1801, but even these are now expensive as the demand for these coins is high and the survival rate low. At the end of 1804, President Thomas Jefferson ordered the discontinuance of production of both the silver dollar and the gold eagle due to exportation of these large coins to Europe and their extensive melting by bullion dealers. Neither denomination would be seen again for more than three decades.

This is the last of my three 1804-dated gold coins (see lots 1108 and 1117). I bought them all within a few months of one another in late 1999. My purchase price of over $18,000 for this early eagle was one of the highest prices I had paid for a single coin up to that time, but I kept my nerve since I guess I was expecting to receive a decent bonus that year.

Fast forward to the night of the Waccabuc Collection auction in November 2007. I was sitting at home, listening to the auction over a phone line manned by a representative from Stack's. I knew that the top pre-sale bid visible on the Stack's Web site was $39,000, but I secretly hoped that this coin would realize more than $50,000 at the live auction. That figure was quickly surpassed, and the bidding proceeded steadily in $10,000 increments all the way to $120,000. With the 15% buyer's fee (which was almost equal to my original purchase price), someone had paid $138,000 for this wonderful coin. To this day, I have a photo of the obverse of this classic eagle as the background on my computer desktop.

It would be remiss in any discussion of 1804 eagles to omit mention of the Plain 4 variety. On the rare occasions when you find an 1804 eagle for sale, it will almost always have a "crosslet" 4 in the date—displaying a short perpendicular line at the right end of the horizontal line in the digit. However, there are four 1804 eagles—all Proofs—with a plain 4 in the date. These were struck in 1834 for inclusion in diplomatic presentation sets. An astonishingly complete and entirely enjoyable discussion of the events that led to the production and distribution of these exceedingly rare coins (one sold for $5 million in 2007) and of their silver dollar cousins is included in Dave Bowers's 1999 book *The Rare Silver Dollars Dated 1804 and the Exciting Adventures of Edmund Roberts*. I was one of the copyeditors of that book, so all typos are my fault.

Lesson 125: In May 2010, an 1804 eagle grading AU-58 (by NGC) sold at a Heritage auction for $51,750, a discount of more than 60% as compared with the price realized by my coin. Only part of the price differential can be explained by the difference in grading services and a softening in coin-market conditions. Looking at the excellent photographs on the Heritage Web site, it is evident that the strike on the NGC-graded coin is inferior to my example (in particular, many of the stars are mushy), and there are a few adjustment marks evident on Liberty's cap. Three months later, a different 1804 eagle (also graded AU-58 but by PCGS) sold at another Heritage auction for slightly less than $72,000. This one is much better struck, but the adjustment marks on the obverse are more obvious than on the May 2010 example. You should avoid buying early gold and silver coins with adjustment marks (filing done at the mint to reduce the weight of blank planchets) and seek examples that possess boldly struck details.

Financials: Eagle, Capped Bust to Right, Heraldic Eagle Reverse, 1804, Crosslet 4

Cost	Sale Price	Gain/Loss	Holding Period
$18,418	$138,000	+649%	8.2 years

EAGLE—LIBERTY HEAD, NO MOTTO ABOVE EAGLE, LARGE LETTERS (1838–1839)

Lot 1126.
1838. AU-58.
PCGS #008575.

Auction description: Bright and lustrous yellow gold with warm honey and olive highlights. Strong mint luster is in full bloom across both surfaces, marks are at a minimum, and the strike is crisp in all places. From the first year of Gobrecht's Liberty Head / eagle design type, and the first of just two years with this artistic rendering of Liberty in place; late in 1839 her bust and profile details were changed, giving a more erect appearance that remained with the series through the end of its appearance in 1907. From a modest mintage for the date of just 7,200 pieces, with very few specimens able to meet the quality offered here. PCGS Population: 4; 3 finer (MS-63 finest).

From the Waccabuc Collection. Earlier from Abe Kosoff's October 1968 Sale, Lot 1631; Harry W. Bass Jr. Collection; Bowers and Merena's sale of the Bass Collection, Part II, October 1999, Lot 1314.

After a hiatus of 34 years, production of eagles began again in 1838. Christian Gobrecht, most famous for his eponymous dollars, designed the Liberty Head (or Coronet) eagle. The first type, more aesthetically pleasing than its successors in my view, lasted for only two years. It is most easily distinguished from the later types by the slightly forward-leaning pose of Miss Liberty and the right point of the neckline being positioned between stars 12 and 13. A more prosaic upright depiction of Liberty was used for the rest of the series through 1907. This is the first $10 gold piece to show its value: TEN D. appears on the reverse directly below the eagle.

With only two years to choose from, the 1838 and 1839 Large Letters (or Type of 1838) eagles are seen only infrequently in auctions. Their modest mintages contribute to their scarcity: only 7,200 pieces were made in 1838 and slightly more than three times as many in 1839.

Lesson 126: The population of certified Variety 1 Liberty Head eagles roughly parallels the mintage figures of the two dates—there are about 2.5 times as many 1839s housed in plastic holders as there are 1838s. However, the difference in prices between the two dates is typically quite modest in most grades. If you find an appealing-looking 1838 example, buy it. I made a decent profit on mine, and I suspect the new owner will do well if he holds it for a comparable period of years. In fact, he may have gotten a real bargain. *Flash*: This exact coin changed hands again in March 2009 at a Stack's auction, where the price realized was $54,625. I still think this is a bargain.

Financials: Eagle, Liberty Head, No Motto, Large Letters, 1838

Cost	Sale Price	Gain/Loss	Holding Period
$23,000	$48,300	+110%	8.1 years

EAGLE—LIBERTY HEAD, NO MOTTO ABOVE EAGLE, UPRIGHT LIBERTY (1839–1866)

Lot 1127.
1847. AU-53.
PCGS #008597.

Auction description: Medium yellow gold with some orange highlights. Strong luster present, with a few scattered marks noted for accuracy. A decent early Liberty eagle.

From the Waccabuc Collection. Earlier from Heritage's Long Beach Sale, January 2004, Lot 7142.

The Variety 1 Liberty Head (or Coronet) eagles, with the upright figure of Liberty but without the motto IN GOD WE TRUST on the reverse, were minted from 1839 through 1866 (in the final year at San Francisco only). There are no classic rarities in this series, but there are 13 date-and-mintmark combinations with mintages of fewer than 10,000 pieces.

The puniest mintage was recorded in the war year of 1863, when a mere 1,248 eagles were minted in Philadelphia. It is estimated that fewer than 40 circulation strikes exist today. The best of these, graded PCGS MS-63, was owned by Harry W. Bass. He paid more than $100,000 for this coin in August 1991, and then some lucky buyer got it for just $52,900 when the Bass Collection was sold by Bowers and Merena in November 2000. What a bargain!

Lesson 127: It can be educational and satisfying to collect common coins in average grades, but the rewards are likely to be mostly psychic. Except for acknowledged rarities, you should not expect to achieve a financial windfall from a collection of mid-range coins—even if the collection is held for many years. My common, circulated, "decent" (the cataloger worked hard to come up with this adjective) 1847 No Motto Liberty Head eagle was a filler, and my financial return, or lack thereof, reflects the ordinariness of this coin.

Financials: Eagle, Liberty Head, No Motto Above Eagle, Upright Liberty, 1847

Cost	Sale Price	Gain/Loss	Holding Period
$518	$552	+7%	3.8 years

EAGLE—LIBERTY HEAD, MOTTO ABOVE EAGLE (1866–1907)

Lot 1128.
1900. MS-63.
PCGS #008745.

Auction description: Frosty honey gold with strong luster and excellent eye appeal for the grade.

From the Waccabuc Collection. Earlier from Heritage's Long Beach Bullet Sale, January 2004, Lot 1876.

The Variety 3 Liberty Head (or Coronet) eagle has the motto IN GOD WE TRUST on a scroll on the reverse above the eagle. This variety was minted from 1866 through the end of the series in 1907. Mintage figures were generous in many years, and in the four decades of production, a total of more than 37 million eagles of this type entered circulation. In Mint State condition, the most common date is the 1901-S. Several thousand of these exist in MS-65 condition, and you shouldn't have to pay more than about $4,000 to obtain one.

At the other end of the spectrum, there are 26 date-and-mintmark combinations prior to 1890 with mintages of fewer than 10,000 pieces. Five of these issues had mintages of fewer than 1,000 pieces. The rarest of all is the 1875 eagle, of which only 100 circulation strikes were made (plus 20 Proofs). With a surviving population of perhaps 8 or 10 circulation strikes and a similar number of Proofs, the 1875 eagle is an under-appreciated rarity in American numismatics. Stack's Bowers Galleries sold one of the finest, a PCGS AU-53 example, for $345,000 in an August 2011 auction.

Lesson 128: Lesson 122 bears repeating. Be careful when buying common gold coins such as the 1900 eagle pictured here. I doubled my money in a little less than four years, but that was because I was lucky: the price of gold had increased and the numismatic spread (the premium above the intrinsic value of the coin) widened between early 2004 and late 2007. The buyer of my coin, if he still held it five years later, had a chuck of gold worth about $1,200. Genuinely rare coins are less volatile in price and possess greater potential for appreciation than numismatic material that is traded as an alternate form of bullion.

Financials: Eagle, Liberty Head, Motto Above Eagle, 1900

Cost	Sale Price	Gain/Loss	Holding Period
$805	$1,725	+114%	3.8 years

EAGLE—INDIAN HEAD, NO MOTTO ON REVERSE, WITH PERIODS (1907–1908)

Lot 1129.
1907, With Periods, Wire Rim. MS-62.
PCGS #008850.

Auction description: Sparkling yellow gold with satiny, matte-like surfaces and frosty luster. One of a reported 500 examples struck with periods before, among, and after the legend UNITED STATES OF AMERICA on reverse; the type without periods was produced later in the year in a quantity approaching a quarter million pieces. As Breen noted about this popular rarity: "The very first of these are the only available $10s showing the Saint-Gaudens conceptions anywhere near their pristine splendor." An ever-popular scarcity that belongs in your collection if a truly complete gold type collection is part of your plan.

From the Waccabuc Collection. Earlier from Heritage's Long Beach Sale, February 2007, Lot 4807.

President Teddy Roosevelt had strong opinions on many topics. One of his strongly held beliefs was that the designs of U.S. coins were "atrociously hideous." Seeking to remedy this situation, he called on the country's most famous sculptor, Augustus Saint-Gaudens, to redesign America's coinage.

Before succumbing to cancer in August 1907 at age 59, Saint-Gaudens, an American of French-Irish parentage, worked closely with Roosevelt to redesign our two highest-denomination coins, the gold eagle and double eagle. For the eagle, Saint-Gaudens designed an obverse with a profile of a young Miss Liberty (looking very much like the Greek goddess Nike) wearing an Indian headdress. As Walter Breen wrote in his *Encyclopedia*, "At President Roosevelt's insistence, and for no other reason, Saint-Gaudens gave this head a nationalistic character by the absurd addition of a feathered warbonnet, such as neither Ms. Liberty nor any Native American woman would ever have worn." For the reverse, Saint-Gaudens produced a proud, powerful image of a perched eagle, though birders have pointed out that the bald eagle's legs are unnaturally large and long. A review of several hundred images on the Internet supports this ornithological criticism.

The two earliest versions of Saint-Gaudens's $10 gold piece were minted in limited quantities. Both had small dots or periods on the reverse, between and at the ends of each word. The first, with a mintage of about 500 pieces, had a wire edge that made stacking impractical. This version is illustrated here. The second, of which all but 50 were melted at the mint, had a rounded rim, and is known as the Rounded Rim or Rolled Edge variety. The Waccabuc Collection did not have one of these great rarities.

Lesson 129: As the time approached for me to dispose of my type collection, I tried to fill some of the few remaining holes in my set. The PCGS set registry called for an example of both With Periods Indian Head eagles, but I knew this wasn't going to happen. In early 2007, I spotted this Wire Rim specimen in a Heritage auction and decided I would buy it. I didn't consult any price guides. Unfortunately, there was an under-bidder who was almost as determined as I was. Sadly, he did not reappear when I sold this coin in November 2007. My hubris and lack of research cost me about $13,000 after the auctioneer's fees. I overpaid for this coin, and it was entirely a self-inflicted wound. For coins that make reasonably regular appearances at auctions, it's unwise to ignore recent auction results.

Financials: Eagle, Indian Head, No Motto on Reverse, With Periods, 1907, Wire Rim

Cost	Sale Price	Gain/Loss	Holding Period
$43,125	$34,500	-20%	0.8 years

EAGLE—INDIAN HEAD, NO MOTTO ON REVERSE, NO PERIODS (1907–1908)

Lot 1130.
1907. MS-64.
PCGS #008852.

Auction description: A frosty specimen with exceptional eye appeal and unyielding cartwheel luster. Pale peach and rose highlights adorn the satiny honey gold surfaces. Undeniably choice for the grade.

From the Waccabuc Collection. Acquired from Superior Galleries, August 2000.

In 1907 and the first part of 1908, almost 500,000 lower-relief eagles were struck without the motto IN GOD WE TRUST. The design was fundamentally the one conceived by Augustus Saint-Gaudens, but the engraving was done by Charles E. Barber, who had the thankless task of transforming Saint-Gaudens's stunning but impractical sculpture into a product that could more easily be struck and stacked. Barber reduced the relief, removed the periods from the reverse, and made other minor changes. The coins became stackable, but striking quality was not significantly improved.

Many 1907 No Periods eagles were saved at the time of issue. Accordingly, it is easy to locate Mint State examples, and even gems are not particularly elusive. A few superb gems exist, including a PCGS MS-68 example that sold in a January 2009 Heritage auction for $149,500.

Lesson 130: I use a 1908 Indian Head eagle as a pocket piece and as a ball marker when playing golf. It's a beautiful and impressive coin to show friends, but in circulated condition it's not worth much more than its intrinsic gold value. Some of my golf buddies with good eyes have noticed that the edge of this coin does not have the reeding that's typically found on most gold and silver coins. Instead, the edge is decorated with a bunch of tiny raised stars. If you ask a friend to guess how many stars, the young ones may speculate that the number must be 50 for the 50 states in the Union, while most cagey baby boomers, who recall that Alaska and Hawaii were added as states within their memories, will announce 48 as their answer. The truth is that from 1907 through 1911, the Indian Head eagle had 46 stars on its edge. It was only after the admission of New Mexico and Arizona to the Union in January and February 1912 that Indian Head eagles sported 48 stars on their edges.

Financials: Eagle, Indian Head, No Motto on Reverse, No Periods, 1907

Cost	Sale Price	Gain/Loss	Holding Period
$2,450	$6,900	+182%	7.3 years

EAGLE—INDIAN HEAD, MOTTO ON REVERSE (1908–1933)

Lot 1131.
1908. AU-58.
PCGS #008859.

Auction description: Highly lustrous with rich rose iridescence. Visibly as fine as many coins given higher grades by PCGS.

From the Waccabuc Collection. Acquired from Bowers and Merena, September 2002.

The Coinage Act of 1890 did not require the motto IN GOD WE TRUST to be included on U.S. coins, and therefore, Augustus Saint-Gaudens left it off of his designs. This decision was very much in accord with Teddy Roosevelt's views—he felt the inclusion of the motto was a sacrilege. But the God-fearing public did not share the president's views, and Congress responded by mandating the inclusion of the motto after the middle of 1908.

The Indian Head, With Motto, eagle was minted from 1908, with interruptions, through 1933. The key to the series is the 1933. Its original mintage of more than 300,000 pieces would, under normal circumstances, make this just a typical date—one not worth special attention. But 1933 was not a year of normal circumstances. The economy and the banking system were in trouble (yes, history repeats itself), and President Franklin Roosevelt took the United States off the gold standard and ordered its citizens to turn in their gold coins (except for established collectibles). Most of the 1933 eagles were melted at the mint before they could be distributed to the public. It is estimated that only 40 or so escaped destruction. A spectacular NGC MS-66 example sold for $718,750 at a Stack's auction in October 2004.

Lesson 131: I bought this coin because it caught my eye at a lot-viewing session before an auction in 2002. I thought it looked like a choice Mint State coin, with outstanding luster, even though the slab only admitted to a grade of AU-58. I never got around to resubmitting the coin to see if PCGS would grant it a higher grade, but it's clear the cataloger saw what I saw when he wrote, "Visibly as fine as many coins given higher grades by PCGS." If I hadn't been so lazy, and instead had taken the time to see if this coin warranted a Mint State grade, I might not have needed to spend the money I did to purchase the coin in the next lot.

Financials: Eagle, Indian Head, Motto on Reverse, 1908

Cost	Sale Price	Gain/Loss	Holding Period
$419	$633	+51%	5.2 years

EAGLE—INDIAN HEAD, MOTTO ON REVERSE (1908–1933)

Lot 1132.
1910-D. MS-65.
PCGS #008866.

Auction description: A frosty, matte-like Gem with a rich array of peach, rose, and yellow toning highlights on the lustrous surfaces. A popular branch-mint issue in an outstanding state of preservation.

From the Waccabuc Collection. Earlier from ANR's sale of the Richard C. Jewell Collection, March 2005, Lot 800.

This 1910-D Indian Head eagle is of the exact same type as the coin in the preceding lot. I bought it solely in order to have a higher-quality example in my collection. The word *popular* as used by the cataloger is often a euphemism for *high mintage*. The 1910-D eagle had the second-highest mintage (after the 1932 issue) of all Indian Head eagles.

Lesson 132: A common adage in numismatics is to buy the best coin you can afford. The corollary is not to buy a low-quality coin and then upgrade later—you may well not make money on the first purchase, and you'll definitely pay the auction or dealer's fee twice. Indeed, I've offered this exact advice elsewhere in this book. Nevertheless, sometimes things work out anyway. I bought a low-grade (AU-58) eagle first and then upgraded to an MS-65 gem, and yet I made a profit on both transactions. Both coins, however, were extremely attractive for their grades, and both times I sold into a strong market for Indian Head eagles.

Financials: Eagle, Indian Head, Motto on Reverse, 1910-D

Cost	Sale Price	Gain/Loss	Holding Period
$4,600	$6,670	+45%	2.7 years

CHAPTER
20

Double
Eagles

Don't buy a putter until you've had a chance to throw it.

G olfers have been known to express anger by throwing their clubs when they become frustrated with the way they've played the game. Well, in 1848 Mexico certainly had reason to throw a figurative golf club. The Treaty of Guadalupe Hidalgo, signed on February 2, 1848, marked the end of the Mexican-American War. Among other spoils of war, the United States acquired California from Mexico. Nine days earlier, on January 24, 1848, James Marshall, a foreman working in partnership with mill-owner John Sutter, had found gold in the American River about 35 miles northeast of Sacramento. Sutter and Marshall were unsuccessful in their efforts to keep the discovery quiet, and by March the news spread to San Francisco and elsewhere. The California Gold Rush was underway. You can read all about it in Dave Bowers's superb volume, *A California Gold Rush History*.

With the discovery of vast quantities of gold, Congress authorized the production of $20 gold pieces, called double eagles. These were similar in size and intrinsic value to Latin American gold doubloons and certain other foreign gold coins. They were made in only two basic designs, the Liberty Head type and the Saint-Gaudens type, though there are several important varieties within each type. These are discussed in more detail below.

As noted previously, this and earlier chapters include auction lot descriptions, photos, and commentary. A learning opportunity is included at the end of each lot. These lessons relate to the specific coin under discussion but are designed to have more general applicability to other series and denominations. Financial results are shown for each coin.

DOUBLE EAGLE—LIBERTY HEAD, NO MOTTO ON REVERSE (1849–1866)

Lot 1133.
1851. MS-61.
PCGS #008904.

Liberty Head double eagles, designed and engraved by James B. Longacre, were minted from 1850 through 1907. The first variety of this type, without the motto IN GOD WE TRUST on the reverse, was produced from 1850 through 1866. Large quantities were made in most years at the Philadelphia Mint and, beginning in 1854, at the San Francisco Mint. Production at the New Orleans Mint, which ceased for several years after the Civil War year of 1861, was much more modest. In five different years, New Orleans output failed to reach 10,000 pieces, with a low-water mark of 2,250 in 1856. Not surprisingly, the 1856-O is a prized rarity. An example graded NGC SP-63 sold at a Heritage auction in May 2009 for more than $1.4 million.

Another interesting coin in this series is the 1861-S double eagle with a reverse design by Anthony Paquet. As the Mint's assistant engraver, Paquet had the assignment to improve the design of the reverse. He attempted this by using taller, narrower letters for the wording around the perimeter. Many observers found the modification attractive, but when physical production began, it was soon discovered that without a protective rim around the outside of the coin, the design elements were immediately subject to wear and abrasions. The San Francisco Mint struck 19,250 pieces using the new dies before they were taken out of service. No Uncirculated examples are known to exist today, but an NGC AU-58 piece sold for $184,000 at a Heritage auction in January 2012.

The rarest of all regular-issue double eagles is the Philadelphia version of the 1861 Paquet-reverse coin. An unknown number of these were struck, but almost all went into the melting pot before being released to the public. Today, only two are known to have survived. One of these, graded PCGS MS-61, sold at a Heritage auction in August 2006 for just over $1.6 million. The other example, the Boyd-Noweb specimen (with an estimated grade of MS-67), has not appeared at a public auction for more than a quarter of a century.

If you're seeking a Mint State example of a No Motto Liberty Head double eagle, you'll probably have greatest luck finding a coin dated 1857-S or 1865-S. In 1857, the SS *Central America* sank in the Atlantic with a cargo of gold coins and gold bars. In 1865 another side-wheel steamer, the SS *Brother Jonathan*, met its demise near Crescent City, California. It, too, was carrying a large supply of gold coins. In recent decades both sunken treasures have been recovered, and the known population of Uncirculated No Motto double eagles has multiplied. The tragic and compelling stories of these two shipping disasters are told in Dave Bowers's marvelous books, *A California Gold Rush History: Featuring the Treasure from the S.S. Central America* and *The Treasure Ship S.S. Brother Jonathan: Her Life and Loss 1850–1865.*

Lesson 133: Many numismatic reference books, including the *Red Book* and Walter Breen's *Encyclopedia*, make reference to the No Motto Liberty Head double eagle as having been produced beginning in 1849, rather than in 1850. That's because pattern dies, with higher relief, were made in 1849 and an unknown (but small) quantity of this pattern issue was struck. Most numismatic scholars believe only one 1849 double eagle exists today—the one that resides in the National Numismatic Collection at the Smithsonian Institution. It would almost certainly become the most expensive coin in the world if it ever were consigned to an auction. (A second example might exist. It would make an excellent subject for a numismatic mystery—maybe this will be my next writing project.)

Many other patterns are almost as rare as the 1849 double eagle but sell for far, far less because so few collectors focus on this area of American numismatics. You can add interest and variety to your own collection by including a pattern or two with a connection to your main area of collecting interest.

Financials: Double eagle, Liberty Head, No Motto on Reverse, 1851

Cost	Sale Price	Gain/Loss	Holding Period
$5,750	$5,060	-12%	2.7 years

DOUBLE EAGLE—LIBERTY HEAD, MOTTO ABOVE EAGLE, VALUE TWENTY D. (1866–1876)

Lot 1134.
1867. MS-61.
PCGS #008951.

Auction description: A frosty and lustrous Type II double eagle, a pleasing coin for the grade with swiftly moving unbroken cartwheel luster on both sides.

From the Waccabuc Collection. Earlier from ANR's sale of the Old Colony Collection, December 2005, Lot 1697.

In 1866 the design of the reverse of the Liberty Head double eagle was modified to include the motto IN GOD WE TRUST above the eagle. (As you know from reading this far, all U.S. coins larger in size than the cent were similarly updated after the conclusion of the Civil War.) This With Motto or Variety 2 design was produced at the Philadelphia, San Francisco, and (beginning in 1870) Carson City mints from 1866 through 1876. Mintage figures were generally generous, particularly from the San Francisco facility. Production at the new Carson City Mint, however, began slowly, and the 1870-CC double eagle is one of the stars of the whole $20 gold series. One of the finest, graded NGC AU-55, sold at a Bowers and Merena auction in March 2009 for $414,000.

Lesson 134: My 1867 Variety 2 double eagle was a low-end Mint State specimen, but its surfaces had fewer distractions than are often seen on an MS-61 coin. Over the years, I found that one of the best ways to learn to grade Mint State coins was at lot-viewing sessions held prior to most auctions. As you go through the boxes of coins, try holding your thumb over the grade shown on the slab and just look at the coin itself. Make a quick judgment as to the grade and then take a look at what PCGS or NGC or ANACS has decided. Your confidence in your own grading abilities will grow quickly, and you'll occasionally spot coins that are strong for the stated grade.

Financials: Double eagle, Liberty Head, Motto Above Eagle, Value TWENTY D., 1867

Cost	Sale Price	Gain/Loss	Holding Period
$4,485	$6,325	+41%	1.9 years

DOUBLE EAGLE—LIBERTY HEAD, MOTTO ABOVE EAGLE, VALUE TWENTY DOLLARS (1877–1907)

Lot 1135.
1901. MS-65.
PCGS #009039.

Auction description: Broadly sweeping cartwheel luster supports pale rose and peach iridescence on both sides. A sharply struck Gem with strong eye appeal.

From the Waccabuc Collection. Earlier from Heritage's Dallas Sale, November 2005, Lot 4601.

In 1877 the reverse design of the Liberty Head double eagle was again tweaked, this time when the denomination was changed from TWENTY D. to TWENTY DOLLARS. The new design continued through the end of the series in 1907. In general, mintages continued to be high, peaking at more than 6.2 million pieces at the Philadelphia Mint in 1904. These and other common-date examples sell for modest premiums over their melt value (except in the higher levels of Mint State preservation).

Nevertheless, there are a number of scarce and rare dates among Variety 3 double eagles. One curiosity is the 1879-O issue, the only Variety 3 double eagle produced at the New Orleans Mint. Only 2,325 pieces were made, and auction appearances are infrequent. The Philadelphia Mint produced fewer than 1,500 pieces for circulation in each of four years: 1882, 1885, 1886, and 1891. At a January 2007 auction conducted by Heritage, an 1882 double eagle grading PCGS MS-60 brought a price of $138,000.

In three other years—1883, 1884, and 1887—the Philadelphia Mint produced no circulation strikes at all, just Proofs. The coins dated 1884 are generally considered to be the scarcest of these. A PGGS PF-64 example sold for $208,000 in an October 2008 Heritage auction. The exact same coin fell drastically in value when it crossed the auction block a little more than two years later. In January 2011 at another Heritage auction, the price realized for this rarity dropped to $103,500. This latter price is more in line with Proof double eagles of comparable mintages.

Lesson 135: After gold ownership by American citizens became illegal in 1933, many gold coins, especially double eagles, found their way into Swiss and other European banks. When the gold-ownership restrictions were lifted in 1974, many of these European holdings made their way back to the United States. As a result, a very large number of Mint State double eagles are available to collectors today. Even my slightly scarcer 1901 double eagle (with a mintage of 111,526) has a gem Mint State population of 400 pieces or so. I got caught by a shrinking numismatic premium for MS-65 Liberty Head double eagles and consequently lost money on this investment. As is almost always the case, coins with foundational rarity are better investments than high-grade examples of common coins.

Financials: Double eagle, Liberty Head, Motto Above Eagle, Value TWENTY DOLLARS, 1901

Cost	Sale Price	Gain/Loss	Holding Period
$5,750	$4,600	-20%	2.0 years

DOUBLE EAGLE—SAINT-GAUDENS, HIGH RELIEF (1907)

Lot 1136.
1907, High Relief, Wire Rim. MS-63.
PCGS #009135.

Auction description: A sparkling example of one of the most beautiful coinage designs ever brought to fruition in America, a satiny specimen with expansive cartwheel luster supporting faint olive and gold toning highlights. Plenty of mint bloom resides in the deep recesses of the Saint-Gaudens design. Exceptional quality overall, especially within the confines of the assigned grade.

From the Waccabuc Collection. Acquired from Bowers and Merena, March 1998.

The story of the conception and creation of the Saint-Gaudens double eagle and the relationship between President Theodore Roosevelt and the sculptor Augustus Saint-Gaudens is told in Roger W. Burdette's extensively researched book *Renaissance of American Coinage 1905–1908*, and in Michael Moran's *Striking Change: The Great Artistic Collaboration of Theodore Roosevelt and Augustus Saint-Gaudens*. I've included just a few highlights here to give you a taste of this fascinating story.

Two days after Christmas in 1904, President Roosevelt wrote a letter to Treasury Secretary Leslie Mortier Shaw: "I think our coinage is artistically of atrocious hideousness. Would it be possible, without asking permission of Congress, to employ a man like Saint-Gaudens to give us a coinage that would have some beauty?"

Less than a month later, Roosevelt wrote directly to Saint-Gaudens: "It appears that under the law, the silver coinage cannot be changed until 1917, and the five cent nickel piece cannot be changed until 1908. The gold coins and the one cent piece are the only ones that can be changed now without act of Congress. But I suppose the gold coins are really the most important. Could you make designs for these; what would be the expense?"

After visiting the Smithsonian Institution in November 1905 and viewing examples of ancient Greek coins, Roosevelt again wrote to Saint-Gaudens: "How is that gold coinage design getting along? I want to make a suggestion. It seems to me worthwhile to try for a really good coinage, though I suppose there will be a revolt about it! I was looking at some gold coins of Alexander the Great today, and I was struck by their high relief. Would not it be well to have our coins on high relief, and also to have the rims raised?"

Throughout 1906, Saint-Gaudens worked on the designs for the $10 and $20 gold pieces, though his physical condition worsened as he suffered from the effects of colon cancer. When Roosevelt finally saw large design models of the double eagle in December 1906, he wrote to Saint-Gaudens: "Those models are simply immense—if such a slang way of talking is permissible in reference to giving a modern nation one coinage at least which shall be as good as that of the ancient Greeks. I have instructed the Director of the Mint that these dies are to be reproduced just as quickly as possible and just as they are. It is simply splendid. I suppose I shall be impeached for it in Congress; but I shall regard that as a very cheap payment!"

Saint-Gaudens worked with Mint officials to move the project along, but there were obstacles, both practical (the difficulty in striking high-relief coins) and intangible (the professional jealousy of Mint employees toward the private-sector sculptor Saint-Gaudens). When Saint-Gaudens died on August 3, 1907, he had seen some pattern pieces of both the $10 and $20 denominations, but no coins had yet been produced for circulation. At Roosevelt's insistence ("Begin the new issue, even if it takes you all day to strike one piece!"), the Mint produced more than 11,000 high-relief double eagles late in 1907. America's most beautiful coin was finally a reality.

70 to 80 percent of the original mintage of high-relief Saint-Gaudens double eagles survives today in various gradations of Mint State. A superb example, grading PCGS MS-69, changed hands at a Heritage auction in November 2005 for $575,000. An example of the very rare extremely high-relief pattern double eagle sold for almost $3 million at the same auction.

Lesson 136: In March 1998 I was in Baltimore for the American Numismatic Association convention being held there. At one point, I sat down at the Bowers and Merena table and asked to look at the glistening 1907 high-relief double eagle I saw on display. Mark Borckardt handed it to me and said he had just purchased it from another dealer on the floor of the convention. On the back of the slab that other dealer's sticker described the coin as "choice for the grade and a candidate for an upgrade." I didn't ask Mark his opinion of this assessment, but just went ahead and bought the coin.

Thinking I might be able to get an upgrade, I cracked the coin out of its PCGS MS-63 holder and sent it to PCGS to be re-graded and encapsulated. Imagine my surprise and disappointment when PCGS returned the coin in a holder marked MS-62. I spoke with a senior PCGS official and told him my tale of woe. He asked me to send him the coin in its new holder along with the original MS-63 insert, which (fortunately) I'd kept. A few weeks later, my coin came home to me in its brand-new PCGS MS-63 holder. That was the last time I pretended to be a crack-out artist.

Financials: Double eagle, Saint-Gaudens, High Relief, 1907, Wire Rim

Cost	Sale Price	Gain/Loss	Holding Period
$10,500	$20,700	+97%	9.7 years

DOUBLE EAGLE—SAINT-GAUDENS, WITHOUT MOTTO, ARABIC NUMERALS (1907–1908)

Lot 1137.
1907, Arabic Numerals. MS-64.
PCGS #009141.

Augustus Saint-Gaudens died in August 1907, and this event gave Mint engraver Charles E. Barber the opportunity to modify Saint-Gaudens's stunning but hard-to-strike high-relief design. Barber's low-relief Without Motto double eagles are not unattractive coins, but they seem pedestrian when compared with Saint-Gaudens's original concept. Besides lowering the relief to improve the efficiency of production, Barber also changed the date from Roman numerals to Arabic (i.e., normal) numerals.

As with the early Saint-Gaudens eagles, the Without Motto double eagles did not include the words IN GOD WE TRUST. President Teddy Roosevelt was a religious man, but he strongly believed in the separation of Church and State and, according to Walter Breen, felt that "inscribing the deity's name on coins which might be used for criminal purposes was blasphemy." Congress, possibly stirred up by unhappy members of the clergy, objected, and production of Without Motto double eagles ended in 1908.

A total of 5.3 million Without Motto double eagles were made. These bear dates of 1907, 1908, and 1908-D. The coins minted in Philadelphia in 1908 are by far the most often seen, particularly in gem grades. I chose a decent 1907 because I liked first-year-of-issue coins. The excellent financial results I achieved with this coin had more to do with the increase in the value of gold during this period than with any brilliance I had in buying this particular coin.

Lesson 137: Up through MS-64 there's only a slight difference in cost between the very common 1908 Without Motto double eagles and the distinctly scarcer 1907 and 1908-D coins. If you're looking for an MS-65 or better example, the 1908 is the only practical choice, but if a less-lofty grade will fit your collection, you'd be well advised to pick one of the other two dates.

Financials: Double eagle, Saint-Gaudens, Without Motto, Arabic Numerals, 1907

Cost	Sale Price	Gain/Loss	Holding Period
$1,043	$2,300	+121%	5.0 years

DOUBLE EAGLE—SAINT-GAUDENS, WITH MOTTO (1908–1933)

Lot 1138.
1928. MS-66.
PCGS #009189.

Auction description: 1928 MS-66 (PCGS). A frosty Gem with superb eye appeal that easily matches the intense cartwheel luster. Wisps of pale rose and olive grace both sides. From the Waccabuc Collection. Earlier from the Allison Park Collection; ANR's C.L. Lee Sale, September 2005, Lot 1426.

The With Motto Saint-Gaudens double eagle was minted from 1908 through the end of the series in 1933. Almost 65 million coins of this design were produced, and though millions were melted, there are still many hundreds of thousands of Uncirculated examples available in PCGS and NGC holders. The most common gems are dated 1924 and 1927, with the 1928 not far behind. Not long ago, with gold priced at about $1,350 per ounce, I received an email from a major coin dealer offering up to 125 Saint-Gaudens double eagles graded by PCGS or NGC at the MS-65 level for $2,100 each. Even at the gem level, common-date Saints are just *commodities*, not rare coins.

At the other end of the spectrum are a handful of scarce and rare dates, most of which are hard to find today not because of low mintages but rather because so many were melted following the abolition of gold coinage in 1933. 180,000 double eagles were produced at the Denver Mint in 1927, but specialists believe that only 12 remain in existence (three of which are in the Smithsonian). A superb gem example (PCGS MS-67) of the 1927-D double eagle was sold in a Heritage auction in 2005 for slightly less than $1.9 million. Because of the size, beauty, and metallic content of Saint-Gaudens double eagles, many collectors are tempted to build a collection of these coins. Completion, however, requires a seriously thick wallet.

Although the PCGS set registry does not recognize it, there was a design change in 1912. Early in that year, New Mexico and Arizona were added as the 47th and 48th states. From 1908 through 1911, the With Motto double eagles (like their Without Motto predecessors) had 46 small stars around the periphery of the obverse. In 1912, two additional stars were added to the lower right of the arc. You can amaze many experienced collectors with this factoid.

Lesson 138: Type-set collectors who opt for a common-date With Motto double eagle should recognize that the market price of gold will have a great deal to do with the price they pay and the return they achieve when the coin is sold. These coins move up and down in price in close relation to changes in the price of gold. Less well known is the fact that the numismatic premium (that is, the price above the melt value of the coin) also expands and contracts over time. The reasons for this are not always clear, but demand in the market (for example, from telemarketers) certainly plays a role. Experienced dealers and traders try to buy common gold coins when the numismatic premium is low and then benefit, if all works out as planned, from both an increase in the price of gold and a widening of the numismatic premium. To me, this is not coin collecting, but it's important to be aware of this feature of the gold-coin market.

Financials: Double eagle, Saint-Gaudens, With Motto, 1928

Cost	Sale Price	Gain/Loss	Holding Period
$2,185	$2,530	+16%	2.2 years

The Joy of Golf

A Dream?

Grace, Penny, Starr, and I reached the 152-yard, par 3, 17th hole of the Vale do Lobo (Valley of the Wolf) Ocean Course, in the Algarve region of southern Portugal, as the afternoon shadows of a mid-November day lengthened across the green landscape. Before me I saw a fairway sloping gently upward to an elevated green, well guarded in front by a gaping bunker. Needing a high shot but with enough distance, I selected a five-iron and perched my ball way up on its peg.

I clipped the ball cleanly, and as it soared high in the air, I said to myself, "Bob, you were well balanced on that shot." We saw the ball bounce once, before losing sight of it beyond the steep wall of the front bunker. Grace, a 14-handicapper from Vancouver, spoke my thoughts when she remarked, "That should be close."

Grace's and Starr's shots found the umbrella pine tree to the left of the green. Penny batted a dribbler down the middle, and after two more bats, she'd advanced her ball to the left-hand fringe. She then joined me at the right-side of the green to watch Grace and Starr chip their balls on.

I hadn't yet spotted my ball but didn't want to say anything. Penny, however, also noticed that the green wasn't sporting any white orbs and said, "Maybe it's in the hole."

Together, we watched Grace and Starr hit indifferent approach shots, and then we cautiously approached the pin. And there, nestled at the bottom of the cup, was my Wilson Hyper-Titanium ball. I raised my arms in triumph and relief (relief that I hadn't embarrassed myself by checking the hole first before seeing if my shot had scooted over the green and into the rough), while Penny announced to the stunned gallery of two that I had shot a hole-in-one!

No, it was not just a dream: on November 15, 2004, I shot my first and only ace.

Appendices, Notes, Bibliography, Credits, and Index

The 19th Hole
—When It's Time to Sell

*All things that are
Are with more spirit chased than enjoy'd.*

The Merchant of Venice, *Act II, Scene 6*

William Shakespeare was being cynical, but sadly truthful, when he wrote these words about the relationship of a man toward a woman. And his observation applies with complete veracity with respect to many other aspects of life.

In numismatics, the chase is the thing. It was satisfying as a kid to find a Lincoln cent that filled a hole in your Whitman folder. And as an advanced collector, it's equally satisfying to snag a scarce or rare coin that brings you closer to completion of a PCGS set-registry collection.

But eventually, the chase ends. There can be many reasons. Perhaps you completed the collection. Or perhaps you completed as much as your budget allowed, as was the case for me. Or maybe you needed the money for something else, or you simply lost interest. Or, as happens to all of us eventually, maybe you died.

With the passage of time, every coin collection gets sold. We are all merely temporary custodians of the rare coins we own. When the time comes, someone else will own and enjoy the coins that used to be ours. If you've built your collection wisely and held it for a period of years, you may be rewarded with a worthwhile financial gain. But the coins themselves are never consumed—they just take their place in someone else's cabinet until it's time for the new owner to sell (or, occasionally, donate) them to someone else.

● ● ●

There are three ways for you to sell your rare coins:

You can sell them privately yourself;
You can hire someone else to sell them privately on your behalf; or
You can consign them to an auction house.

I've had some success with each of these avenues, and there's no rule that says you have to stick to just one approach for your whole collection. Your own circumstances will often dictate which route you'll take. Do you have the experience and self-confidence to sell your collection yourself? Do you need the money right away, or can you wait for three to six months to get paid? Do you know a dealer you can trust to act on your behalf? Do you understand the rules and fees involved in consigning coins to an auction? These are the kinds of questions you need to answer when it comes time to sell your collection. Let's now explore each of the three main options.

SELLING YOUR COINS YOURSELF

There are many attractions to selling your coins yourself. You have complete control. You don't have to pay a fee to someone to sell your coins on your behalf. You can get your money quickly.

Often this route really is the best way to go. If you've developed a good relationship with one or several dealers, they will almost always be more than happy to make a bid for your full collection. You should avoid dealers who offer to buy just your best coins, leaving you with the task of disposing of the rest.

I've sold groups of coins to dealers through the mail, and I've sold or traded coins with dealers and other collectors in person at coin shows. I've always been pleased with the results. But this approach only works if you have a clear idea of what you expect to receive for your coins.

When you offer coins to a dealer, he will typically ask you what you want to get. As with any negotiation, the party that speaks first is giving information to the other side. If you can, try to parry the dealer's question by saying, "I'm trying to get your best price. What are you willing to offer?" But no matter who begins the discussion, you really do need to know in advance the least amount of money you will accept and at what point you will say, "Thanks, but no thanks."

Online portals also offer you an avenue to sell your coins directly. I just checked eBay and found more than 600,000 United States coins for sale. Clearly this is one of the most active forums for selling (and buying) coins. I've sold about a dozen coins on eBay without encountering any problems, and I met some interesting people in the process. The coins I've sold on eBay have all been valued at less than $1,000 each, but a number of higher-priced coins change hands in this marketplace every day. As I write this, there were more than 1,200 coins listed for sale with "Buy Me Now" prices above $10,000.

Selling on eBay is not hard, but you do have to know and follow their rules. You have to write a description of what you're offering, upload some photos, and be prepared to package and ship your coins promptly after an auction closes. Beth Deisher has some good tips on selling coins on eBay in her book *Cash in Your Coins: Selling the Rare Coins You've Inherited.* Indeed, all collectors should keep a copy of this book with their collection. If you happen to die before you've sold your coins, your heirs will appreciate Deisher's unbiased roadmap.

CHOOSING AN AGENT TO SELL YOUR COINS

If you're not in a hurry to get your money, and if your goal is to get the best possible price for each and every coin in your collection, you may want to hook up with a trusted dealer who will sell your coins for you. Certain dealers will, for a commission, offer your coins to their clients alongside their own inventory. This is a way for you to reach the retail audience that will, in theory, be prepared to pay the highest prices.

Of course, there's no assurance of when or how many of your coins will actually be sold, and you may find yourself still the owner of part of your collection after the passage of many months. If this happens, the unsold coins are likely to be those that are the most difficult to sell to a dealer or other prospective buyer and are probably of the least interest to an auction house.

To protect yourself, you may want to try to negotiate a floor price for your entire collection, to be received within some specified period of time, with a sharing arrangement for proceeds above the floor. Since any consignment arrangement like this involves an element of trust, you will only want to enter into a pact of this type with a dealer you know and have complete confidence in. This is probably the most important consideration of all.

CONSIGNING YOUR COINS TO AN AUCTION

If you have a modest-sized collection, or if you own coins that have a tight bid-ask spread (such as many Morgan silver dollars and common-date gold coins), either of the selling approaches outlined above should work very well for you. However, if your collection is broad and varied and contains some rare or unusual pieces, you will probably want to give serious consideration to consigning your coins to one of the leading auction firms.

One of the biggest advantages of auctioning your coins this way is the breadth of the pool of potential buyers that will have a chance to bid on your coins. Competition is always a good thing when you're the seller. Also, unlike private transactions, auctions are conducted in the glare of public gaze, so you can have complete confidence in the fairness of the transaction. And your interests are aligned with those of the auction house—the more you get for your coins, the more the auctioneer earns.

There are several numismatic auction houses to choose among. The two largest and best-known are Heritage Auction Galleries and Stack's Bowers Galleries. One or the other (and sometimes both) of these companies always seems to be chosen by the American Numismatic Association to host the sales that are held in conjunction with the ANA's major conventions. They both have excellent reputations and research capabilities and produce world-class catalogs. And both have industry-leading online lot-viewing and bidding technology, with Heritage probably holding a small edge in this area as of this writing.

I chose Stack's (now Stack's Bowers Galleries) to sell the Waccabuc Collection. I'm sure Heritage would also have done an excellent job, but I had a closer personal relationship with the principals at Stack's, and so I went with that firm.

After negotiating the consignment agreement, I arranged for John Pack, executive director of consignments at Stack's, to drive down from Wolfeboro, New Hampshire, to pick up my coins for cataloging and sale. John appeared at my home on the appointed morning. I'd laid out my coins on a felt-covered table—they made an impressive display. He and I looked at each coin individually and checked them off against my inventory list. It was a long, bittersweet farewell. After an al fresco lunch at a local eatery, John packed up my coins and drove away. The Stack's insurance policy covered my coins as soon as that firm took possession of my collection.

You're very likely to have an excellent experience selling your coins through either Heritage or Stack's Bowers. Collectors and dealers alike follow the offerings of these two firms, and your coins will have wide exposure to the market. Choosing between them will in large part be based on the personal relationship you've developed over time with the principals of one or the other of these firms as you built your collection. To some extent, however, the terms of the deal you strike when you negotiate the consignment agreement may influence your decision. More on this below.

There are other prominent auction firms. The family-owned company Ira and Larry Goldberg Auctioneers conducts a regular series of auctions each year and has offered some of the finest collections of copper coins to appear on the market. The owners of the firm have many decades of numismatic experience, and this is reflected in the company's motto, "A family tradition since 1931."

Teletrade, established in 1986, was the first online auction house that offered only certified coins and currency in its weekly sales. As a general statement, its auctions included a higher percentage of lower-priced coins and modern coins than Heritage, Stack's Bowers, or Goldberg. Following a recent reshuffling of ownership (a common occurrence in the numismatic world), Teletrade is now part of the Stack's Bowers family and has been rebranded as Stack's Bowers iAuctions.

GreatCollections is another online auction firm. Its president, Ian Russell, co-founded the company in 2010. Previously he had been the president of Teletrade.

Legend-Morphy Rare Coin Auctions was established in 2012. It combines the high-end rare-coin expertise of Laura Sperber and Legend Numismatics with the auction experience of Dan Morphy and Morphy Auctions. After Sperber and Dan Morphy parted ways in 2014, the company was rebranded as Legend Rare Coin Auctions.

Bonhams, the privately owned British auction house, traces its heritage back to the late 1700s. It has a well-respected coin-and-currency department that conducts regular auctions in London, New York, and Los Angeles.

The famous global auction firms Sotheby's and Christie's are not active in the coin-auction business. To the extent that I have seen coins offered in their catalogs, they seem to be a small part of some larger consignment of non-numismatic material.

If you inherit a collection of rare coins and want to dispose of them, you won't go far wrong by dealing with one of the two or three leading numismatic auction firms. If you've built your own collection, however, you will meet a number of dealers and the principals of several auction houses as your collection grows. With the passage of time, you will come to know which firms give you the best service and with which individuals at those firms you feel the most amity. These relationships will serve as your surest beacons when the time arrives to decide how to dispose of your coins.

NEGOTIATING THE CONSIGNMENT AGREEMENT

In chapter 2, I discussed the terms and conditions that govern the activity of bidding on coins at an auction. If you want to bid at an auction, you must agree to be bound by the auction firm's terms and conditions. There isn't any practical way to negotiate the terms of the contract—either you agree to the company's terms, or you won't be permitted to bid. This ensures that everyone participating in the auction will be playing by the same rules.

When you consign your coins to an auction firm, on the other hand, there's a little more wiggle room. The firm will have relatively standard rates that apply to a broad spectrum of "average" consignments. However, each consignment is different and therefore, at each end of this broad spectrum, there is room for negotiation. Naturally, the higher the value of the consignment, or the higher the value of the individual items therein, the more appealing it is to the auction house to secure it. On the other hand, consignments that are highly time-consuming or complex might require higher fees in consideration of the time the auction house will require to present the material properly. Knowing this, you should read the proposed agreement carefully and decide which parts may be crafted to be more in your favor before you sign on the dotted line.

Let's now take a look at the provisions contained in a typical auction consignment agreement, with a focus on the parts that may be subject to negotiation.

Seller's Commission: The consignment agreement will say that the consignor shall pay to the auctioneer a commission, which will typically be 5% (or sometimes up to 10%) of the total "hammer price" of all coins sold. This is entirely appropriate in certain circumstances. For example, if a seller walks in off the street with one or a few low-value, uncertified coins, he won't be in a strong position to negotiate the seller's commission. Similarly, if your consignment consists of material that requires extensive research, attribution, and authentication (such as certain tokens, medals, or ancient coins), a robust seller's fee may be apposite. But if you're offering a high-value collection of certified coins, the standard seller's commission is definitely subject to discussion with your friendly auction house. Whatever your circumstances, always remember that you'll get what you pay for. If you beat up the auction house too much on the commission, they may need to compensate by devoting less space in their catalog to your coins (smaller photos or shorter descriptions) or by choosing other coins to feature in their advertising and promotion activities.

In a competitive market, the seller's commission might be negotiated down from 5% to 2.5% or even 0%, depending on the quality and value of the coins being offered. As noted above, other factors may influence the level of the commission, including research and promotion costs. Auction firms understandably do not like to talk about this, but I am aware of a few instances when the owners of particularly choice collections of very significant value have been able to achieve negative seller's commissions—in other words, they receive the full hammer price *plus* a sliver of the auction firm's buyer's commission. It never hurts to ask. The consignment agreement I signed with Stack's prohibits me from disclosing the seller's commission that applied to the sale of the Waccabuc Collection. I will say, however, that I did not pay 5%.

Grading Costs: Auction firms will usually pick up their own costs for catalog preparation, mailing, photography, promotion and other typical auction-process expenses. But they will not automatically pay to have the consignor's raw coins graded by an independent third-party certification service. These fees, which will typically be in the range of $30 to $50 per coin, can add up quickly. But if your raw coins are particularly valuable, you may be able to get the auctioneer to absorb the cost of certification, particularly if you didn't spill any blood in your negotiation of the seller's commission.

Reserves: In auction parlance, a reserve is the price below which the auction house agrees not to sell a coin. At first blush, you may be tempted to try to negotiate reasonable reserve levels for all the coins in your consignment so that no coin will be sold below the price you think is acceptable. However, this is not always a good strategy, for several reasons.

First, auction firms do not like reserve prices, particularly if the reserves are set near or at the level of the coins' retail values. The reason is obvious: if a coin goes unsold, then the firm earns no buyer's commission.

In order to discourage sellers from setting reserve prices, auction firms will charge a fee, sometimes known as a reacquisition fee, against any coins that do not reach their reserve price. The consignment agreement might say something like "In lieu of the buyer's commission, the consignor shall pay the auctioneer a fee of 10% of the reserve amount for any coin that fails to attract a bid equal to or greater than the reserve amount."

Second, even if you are able to negotiate a reduced reacquisition fee, it's worth asking yourself if you really want to continue to own the coins in your collection that do not reach their reserve prices. Let's say you own 100 coins and you negotiate reserve prices on all of them, and at the end of the auction 20 of the coins have not met the reserve prices. After paying the 10% (or some other) reacquisition fee, thereby reducing the proceeds you receive from the sale of the other 80 coins, what are you going to do with the coins returned to you by the auction house? Your cost basis is now effectively 10% (or so) higher than it was before the auction, and if the coins are at all unusual, active participants in the market will know that they did not sell the first time around.

Third, if you choose to negotiate hard on reserves, you may have less leverage to negotiate on the seller's commission. Since, in my view, the seller's commission is a more important factor in the ultimate financial success of your sale than the reacquisition fee, this is the area you should focus your energies on.

And fourth, reserve prices are difficult to set accurately and need to be realistic to serve their purpose. Even coin-market experts can, at best, only make an educated guess about how much a specific coin will realize at an auction being conducted at a future date. If the reserve is set too low, it serves no real purpose. And if it's set too high, it will probably prove to have been an expensive mistake in the long run.

So how do you protect yourself against selling your coins too cheaply at an auction? The best protection is provided by choosing a firm that has a proven track record in handling the type of collection you're seeking to sell. The major auction houses all do an outstanding job cataloging and showcasing a broad range of numismatic material, and they have the capabilities to present this material to the appropriate audience. The smaller and more specialized firms, on the other hand, may do very well in their own areas of expertise, but there are many segments of numismatics with which they may have only limited experience.

If you have a particular concern about the prospective selling price of a few items within your collection, you should by all means discuss these concerns with your consignment director. After consultation, you may decide to establish a reserve for one or a few coins.

Alternatively, you may simply want to understand the level at which the auction house intends to open bidding for these special coins. The opening bid serves as a "free" reserve for you: if the opening bid is not met, the coin will be returned to you without the imposition of a reacquisition fee. See, for example, lot 1034 in chapter 7.

After discussion with John Pack of Stack's, I decided not to establish any reserve prices for the coins in my collection. Although, as disclosed in prior chapters, I lost some money on a number of the coins I sold, I fully believe the prices I achieved, even for these "losers," were fair. The one coin that gave me pause was my 1907 Wire Rim eagle (lot 1129 in chapter 19). As mentioned, I lost about $13,000 on this coin. But even six or seven years after the auction, I doubt I would have gotten close to the actual price realized back in 2007. This particular coin sold well—I just bought it badly.

Pre-auction Advance: Although I have not tried this myself, I know that most auction houses are willing to make an advance to their consignors, to be repaid via receipt of the proceeds of the auction. Just to be clear, an advance of this type is simply a short-term loan secured by your coin collection. The amount of the loan will typically be 50% (or sometimes more) of the value the auction house expects the collection to realize. The interest rates I've seen are reasonable, and are probably not negotiable. The consignment agreement, and any separate loan or note agreement, will state that if the proceeds from the sale of the coins are insufficient to repay the advance, the consignor will still be liable to repay the shortfall. In other words, the loan is made with full recourse to you as the borrower if there is not enough value realized from the sale of your coins to extinguish the loan.

Other Provisions of the Consignment Agreement: There are many other provisions in a typical consignment agreement, and I strongly recommend you take the time to read the full contract before signing it. To give you a sense of what else is covered in the agreement, here are some common topics:

The consignor provides several representations and warranties, including that he owns the material being auctioned, that he will not pledge the coins to anyone else, that the material is authentic, and that he will hold the auctioneer harmless from any claims relating to the consignment.

The auctioneer will pay the consignor the net proceeds of the sale 45 days after the close of the sale. However, if the buyer of a coin or coins is in default, the auctioneer will not be obligated to remit any proceeds until the buyer has paid. It's worth noting that although this provision is contained in the contract to protect the auctioneer, it is extremely infrequently invoked. I am not aware of any consignor who has not been paid in full after the prescribed 45 days by any of the leading auction houses.

The consignor is required to review all lot descriptions and report any inaccuracies to the auction firm. This is simply a commonsense provision that benefits both the consignor and the auction house.

The auction house reserves the right to offer coins individually or to group them into lots, to describe the coins as it deems fit, to provide photographs or not, to accept returns from bidders (though this right is rarely exercised), and to hold the auction when and where it chooses. In practice, most or all of these decisions will be made in consultation with the consignor.

The consignor commits not to withdraw any coins from the auction for any reason. If, upon written request, the auction house agrees to a withdrawal of any material, the consignor will incur a fee equal to 20% of the fair market value of the material, as determined by the auction house in its sole discretion.

Although the consignor is not strictly prohibited from bidding on his own coins, this activity is discouraged. If the consignor is the winning bidder on one of his own coins, he will be subject to the buyer's commission (even though he's already the owner of the coin), as well as the seller's commission. Although you might be tempted to bid on your own coins in the hope of driving up the price, this stratagem can easily backfire. It is not a sensible practice.

The auctioneer retains the right to postpone the auction for a reasonable period of time due to an act of God or certain other significant events, as defined in the agreement.

There's one final intangible advantage of liquidating your collection of coins via an auction rather than through a private sale. After the auction has closed and you have received your check, your coins will be gone, but you will still have the catalog as a memento of the collection you assembled. When I sold the Waccabuc Collection, I negotiated with Stack's Bowers to have the name of the collection included on the cover of the catalog and to have all of the lots grouped together in a discrete section of the catalog rather than having them disbursed throughout the catalog with other coins of similar type or denomination. Since the conclusion of the sale in late 2007, I have on many occasions gotten enjoyment from flipping through the pages of that catalog and admiring the coins for which I served as temporary custodian. Those coins are gone from my collection, but they're not forgotten.

Finances
—The Final Scorecard

Fast payers make fast friends.

After a round of golf, the players head for the 19th hole. There, drinks are ordered, and, before the drinks arrive, bets are settled. Thus the adage, "Fast payers make fast friends." Your scorecard and your wallet will give you instant feedback on how well you've played the game.

In coin collecting, there are price guides, past auction results, and appraisals that can give you a sense of how your collection is performing financially. But there's no way to know precisely how you've done until you sell your coins. The day of reckoning will likely come many years after you begin building your collection.

In chapters 3 through 20, I've shown the financial results for the individual coins that made up the Waccabuc Collection. In those chapters, I showed my actual purchase price and the actual price the coin sold for—including the buyer's commission. In this appendix, I'll discuss my aggregate financial results. Here, all commentary about gains and losses will be with reference to the money I actually received after deduction of all commissions.

There are lots and lots of numbers in this appendix. But before we get to them, I want to stress one point. I did not invest in the rare-coin market with the intention of earning a profit. Rather, I built a collection of rare coins with the twin objectives of enjoying the challenge of the chase and appreciating the history and beauty of the objects themselves.

Having said that, I was acutely aware that my coin-collecting activity was diverting funds away from the realm of traditional investment options (stocks, bonds, real estate, etc.). I did not want to lose money on my hobby, and so, with a few exceptions, I was careful in my selection of coins and prudent in my bidding at auctions. My hope was that I would at least break even, and as we will see below, my modest expectations were exceeded. The title of this book is *Pleasure and Profit*. My focus was on *Pleasure* first. *Profit* was a secondary motivator.

COINS VS. STOCKS

Compared with stocks and bonds, the market for rare coins is small, shallow, and illiquid. A really big auction of thousands of coins at a national convention of the American Numismatic Association might generate total sales of $50 million. Compare this with the value of Bank of America common shares traded January 31, 2014, on the United States stock exchanges: more than $1 billion. Or to look at it another way, the two leading numismatic auction houses had total auction sales of $342 million in 2013 ($237 million at Heritage and $105 million at Stack's Bowers Galleries). In comparison, more than $70 billion of Exxon Mobil shares changed hands in the same time period.

And while you'll pay a commission of $10 or less to trade a block of shares through an online broker such as Fidelity (where the bid-ask spread might be a few cents per share), the vigorish in a typical rare-coin transaction will be 10 to 20% or sometimes even more, with little or no transparency. Rare coins are not an appropriate vehicle for people with short investment horizons or a potential need for ready funds. However, if you have room in your investment portfolio for some long-term, hard assets, and if you enjoy the beauty, history, and romance of rare coins, then by all means take a flyer.

Although I would never recommend that anyone invest his or her entire retirement nest egg in a portfolio of rare coins, it is instructive to look at how rare coins have fared as investments over time. Since 2005, *Coin World* has published a measure of rare-coin values called the "Classic U.S. Rarities Key-Date Investment Index." This index is made up of 82 rare, high-grade coins: 15 copper coins, 5 copper-nickel coins, 39 silver coins, and 23 gold coins. Since the index was first calculated in 2005, the value of the basket of coins has risen from $7.7 million to $13.9 million. This represents a total gain over the eight-year period of 80.5% and a compounded annual return of 7.7%.

By way of comparison, the Dow Jones Industrial Average (DJIA) ended 2005 at 10,718 and had risen to 16,577 by the end of 2013. Excluding dividends, this represents a total gain over the eight-year period of 54.7% and a compounded annual return of 5.6%. These figures, however, mask the substantial volatility experienced in the stock market during that period. The DJIA hit a closing low of 6,547 in March 2009 (a drop of close to 40% from the end of 2005), and then rebounded sharply to more than 16,500 by the end of 2013 (a gain of more than 150%).

In the chart below, you can see that the *Coin World* index was generally less volatile than the DJIA from 2006 to 2013. Other coin indices I've seen show similar patterns. In addition, it's worth noting that there is little apparent correlation between the investment performance of stocks and rare coins. From 2006 through 2008, you would have done much better in coins than in stocks. But from the spring of 2009 to the end of 2013, stocks have far outperformed coins.

INVESTMENT RETURNS	Dow Jones Industrial Average	Coin World Rare-Coin Index
2006	19.1%	15.8%
2007	8.9%	31.9%
2008	-31.9%	8.8%
2009	22.7%	-7.9%
2010	14.1%	8.3%
2011	8.4%	5.0%
2012	10.2%	-0.5%
2013	29.7%	2.5%

Sources: The *Wall Street Journal* and *Coin World*. Note that the annual returns for the DJIA as computed by the *Wall Street Journal* include dividends.

These statistics support the oft-repeated aphorism that a carefully built collection of rare coins, held for a number of years, will more often than not generate a satisfying profit for the collector. While I do believe this is true, I nevertheless recommend that your primary focus be on the psychic rewards of building a collection of rare coins. Let yourself be pleasantly surprised if you find you've made some money at the end of the day.

WHAT ABOUT THE WACCABUC COLLECTION?

So how did I do when I sold my collection? I spent just a tad more than $1 million over a period of roughly 10 years to buy the coins that made up the Waccabuc Collection. My purchases each year were not done in equal amounts—I spent less in the early years as I was learning the ropes and more in the later years as my knowledge and confidence grew. I owned some coins for more than 10 years. Others I purchased only months before the auction. My weighted average holding period (i.e., the average amount of time I owned each coin, adjusted to reflect the value of each coin) was 3.4 years.

When I sold the collection in November 2007, I received net proceeds, after commissions, of $1,405,136. This represented a total gain of 39.4% and an annual compounded return of 10.2%.[10] (These numbers would have been closer to 55% in total and 15% per annum before the auction commissions.) But readers of the preceding chapters will know that these numbers hide a lot of noise. The results achieved by individual coins varied drastically.

BIGGEST LOSERS

Fully 52 of the 138 lots in the sale of the Waccabuc Collection generated losses. Granted, many of these losses were minor. Often they arose when coins sold for an amount near my purchase price: after deduction of the auction house's fees, the proceeds received by me were less than what I had originally paid.

But a handful of my losses were doozies. The "Biggest Losers" were these:

Lot Number	Description	Purchase Price	$ Loss	% Loss
129	1907 eagle, MS-62	$43,125	$12,225	28%
80	1837 half dollar, MS-64	$8,625	$4,711	55%
69	1891 quarter, MS-67	$11,500	$4,290	37%
11	1796 large cent, AU-58	$8,625	$3,218	37%
9	1793 Liberty Cap large cent, VF-20	$46,000	$2,740	6%

All of these coins were attractive—indeed, the 1891 Liberty Seated half dollar was one of the prettiest coins in my collection. Two of the coins were genuinely rare—the 1907 eagle with periods and the 1793 Liberty Cap large cent. My holding periods on these coins were generally short—ranging from nine months to a little more than three years. That's part of the lesson. But the biggest fault was that I fell in love with these coins and stubbornly ignored the price lists when I arrived in the auction room. The original auctioneer and consignor loved me; my accountant did not.

BIGGEST WINNERS

At the other end of the spectrum, about 62% of the lots generated gains, and some of these were spectacular. The biggest winners were:

Lot Number	Description	Purchase Price	$ Gain	% Gain
125	1804 eagle, AU-58	$18,418	$105,182	571%
119	1813 half eagle, MS-64	$15,238	$26,993	177%
96	1836 Gobrecht dollar, MS-62	$7,450	$25,510	342%
7	1793 Chain large cent, VF-25	$9,775	$21,125	216%
126	1838 eagle, AU-58	$23,000	$20,260	88%

So what did these coins have in common? First, all five coins had what Dave Bowers calls "foundational" rarity—low mintages and low survival rates. Second, they were well-preserved and attractive relative to their counterparts. Third, each coin was special in some way and had a story to tell. And fourth, although I paid full market prices for each of these coins, I owned all of them for more than five years, and three of them for more than eight years. When my accountant saw these results, he rejoiced.

RESULTS BY DENOMINATION

I'm a retired banker and have always been a "wanna-be" mathematician. Since I'd already entered all the financial results into an Excel spreadsheet for recordkeeping purposes, I decided to look at the results through several different lenses.

In this section, I've broken down the numbers by denomination. In the following four sections I've massaged the numbers by age, metallic composition, grade, and holding period. While certain insights may be gained by studying these numbers, I caution the reader that the sample sizes are small, and it would not be wise to extrapolate too broadly from these specific results.

Among the 17 denominations from half cents through double eagles, four showed strong gains: quarters, silver dollars, half eagles, and eagles. Far less satisfying results were achieved from most of the lower denominations (two-cent pieces through dimes) and from the half dollars.

Looking first at the 16 quarters and the one 20-cent piece in my collection, only a single coin (the above-mentioned 1891 Liberty Seated quarter) generated a significant loss. More than offsetting that disappointment were three quarters that more than doubled in value, the one coin that tripled in value (the 1875-CC 20-cent piece), and the one coin that vaulted six-fold in value (the 1806 Draped Bust quarter). Among these last five coins, only one had a holding period of less than five years.

The 82% gain shown by my 11 silver dollars was driven by three coins: the 1795 Flowing Hair dollar, the 1836 Gobrecht dollar, and the 1849 Liberty Seated dollar, all of which more than doubled in value. I held the first two of these for more than eight years, but the third coin was a fluke, with a holding period of only nine months.

Chart 1—Results by Denomination				
Denomination	Number of Lots	Purchase Price	$ Gain or Loss	% Gain or Loss
Half cent	6	$22,723	$9,414	41%
Large and small cent	16	$99,118	$35,987	36%
Two- and three-cent piece	5	$6,812	$374	6%
Nickel	8	$17,750	$378	2%
Half dime	9	$56,709	$8,573	15%
Dime	14	$72,747	$2,429	3%
Twenty-cent piece and quarter	17	$93,924	$69,599	74%
Half dollar	17	$133,227	$3,653	3%
Silver dollar	11	$64,290	$52,512	82%
Gold dollar	4	$12,994	$1,632	13%
Quarter eagle and $3	8	$123,408	$33,358	27%
Half eagle	8	$87,656	$66,381	76%
Eagle	9	$186,835	$118,385	63%
Double eagle	6	$29,713	$7,470	25%

Seven of my eight half eagles showed gains, and five of these more than doubled in value. The eagles also performed well, led by the stunning result achieved by the 1804 Capped Bust specimen.

The biggest disappointment for me was the roughly $200,000 I invested in 31 dimes and half dollars that generated a loss of about $6,000 after an average holding period of about 3-1/4 years. Nine of the 14 dimes showed losses, and none of the 5 gains was significant. The gains and losses among the 17 half dollars were about evenly split (9 losses and 8 gains), and again, there were no big winners. While it's tempting to blame the "short-ish" holding period, I doubt the results would have been much different if I'd sold these coins five years later. Perhaps the lesson is that even a group of just nice (but not spectacular) coins may not, in fact, appreciate in value over relatively long periods of time.

RESULTS BY CENTURY

As shown in chart 2, most of the increase in value of my collection was derived from the 78 coins minted in the 19th century. While the modest performance of my 20th-century coins was not a surprise to me, since very few of these are genuinely rare, the lackluster results posted by the score of 18th-century coins was a revelation when I added up the numbers.

Chart 2—Results by Century				
Century	Number of Lots	Purchase Price	$ Gain	% Gain
18th century (1700s)	20	$379,560	$67,717	18%
19th century (1800s)	78	$471,129	$318,222	68%
20th century (1900s)	40	$157,216	$11,292	7%

Several factors contributed. First among these was the relatively short average holding period of 2.3 years for my 18th-century coins, which compares unfavorably with the 4.3 years for my 19th-century coins and the 3.8 years for my 20th-century coins. In effect, I waited too long to buy some of the rarer and more expensive early-dated coins needed in a type collection.

In addition, my three most expensive 18th-century coins (the 1793 Liberty Cap large cent, the 1797 half dollar, and the 1796 eagle) all showed only small gains or losses and therefore skewed the overall results downward. And the one big winner, the 1793 Chain cent, which more than tripled in value, was not enough by itself to influence the overall results materially.

RESULTS BY METALLIC COMPOSITION

As is apparent in chart 3, the gains were more or less evenly divided among the base and precious metals. The slightly better results shown by the gold coins can be attributed both to the big gains shown by the 1804 eagle and a few other stars, and to the generally rising value of gold during the period I was building my collection.

Chart 3—Results by Metallic Composition				
Metallic Composition	Number of Lots	Purchase Price	$ Gain	% Gain
Base metal (copper, nickel)	32	$141,898	$47,076	33%
Silver	71	$425,402	$122,929	29%
Gold	35	$440,605	$227,226	52%

RESULTS BY GRADE

A couple of numbers in chart 4 jump right out and grab you. First and foremost is the 179% gain achieved by the dozen AU-58 coins. As mentioned in the text, this is my favorite grade for classic rare coins, since it combines the luster, detail, and eye appeal of many Uncirculated coins without the price premium usually associated with those more highly graded cousins.

Included in the AU-58 bucket is the by-now-familiar 1804 eagle. But I also doubled or tripled my money on three other gold coins with AU-58 grades: the 1804 quarter eagle, the 1804 half eagle, and the 1838 eagle. All four coins had holding periods of six to eight years.

Chart 4—Results by Grade				
Grade	Number of Lots	Purchase Price	$ Gain or Loss	% Gain or Loss
Fine and Very Fine	6	$177,445	$42,460	24%
Extremely Fine	5	$34,510	$8,853	26%
About Uncirculated 50–55	10	$201,990	$23,734	12%
About Uncirculated 58	12	$92,850	$165,814	179%
Mint State 60–62	10	$111,469	$22,225	20%
Mint State 63	12	$83,018	$19,364	23%
Mint State 64	23	$99,986	$74,887	75%
Mint State 65	15	$53,954	$22,060	41%
Mint State 66	10	$29,058	$12	0%
Mint State 67–70	12	$42,156	$8,629	21%
Proof 63–70	17	$78,957	$27,287	35%

The MS-64 bucket also performed well, with a gain of 75%. Of the 23 coins in this category, 18 (78%) generated profits, and there was a good mix of denominations represented. Rare-coin investors often shun the MS-64 grade in favor of "gem" coins graded MS-65 or above. As a result, some excellent values can be found in the less-competitive MS-64 category.

Not so impressive were the results coming from coins graded MS-66 and above. I lost money on 15 of these 22 high-grade coins, and several of the "profitable" coins showed only minimal gains. Not included in this category were the six multiple-coin lots that were comprised of low-value modern coins.

These lots were, by their nature, made up of high-grade coins, and their performance was equally woeful—I lost money on five of the six lots, and the overall loss was 24% on my (fortunately modest) investment of $2,413.

RESULTS BY HOLDING PERIOD

I was stunned when I compiled the numbers shown in chart 5. I spent more than half of my total numismatic budget in the three years before the November 2007 auction and only achieved breakeven financial results from those coins. Yes, there were some successes, most notably the 169% gain on the 1849 Liberty Seated dollar. But I lost money on 23 of the 41 lots. The best that can be said is that, in aggregate, I almost covered the auction companies' buyer's fees.

Chart 5—Results by Holding Period				
Holding Period	Number of Lots	Purchase Price	$ Gain or Loss	% Gain or Loss
0–3 years	41	$549,676	$789	0%
3–5 years	53	$215,174	$31,233	15%
5–8 years	28	$99,396	$102,052	103%
More than 8 years	16	$143,659	$264,736	184%

The coins that I held for three to five years generated a positive return, though nothing to write home about. These coins had a weighted per annum yield of less than 4%.

At the long end of the holding-period spectrum, I spent a little less than 25% of my coin budget on coins I held for more than five years. These coins generated 92% of my profits. Among coins I held for five to eight years, I more than doubled my money (103% gain), and for those held for more than eight years, I almost tripled my money (184% gain).

• • •

In summary, it is definitely possible to make money by building a sensible collection of rare coins. As an investment, coins are not particularly liquid, and they are not, in my view, appropriate for investors without knowledge and patience.

But if you've been bitten by the coin bug, there is no reason not to allocate a portion of your investment portfolio to rare coins. For my part, I had better financial results from quarters, silver dollars, half eagles, and eagles minted in the 19th century, particularly those graded AU-58 and MS-64, and generally those held for five years or more. My gold coins showed better appreciation than my silver or base-metal coins, though the run-up in gold prices contributed to this outcome.

Your own financial results will be different from mine—better or worse. But if you derive as much enjoyment, and gain as much knowledge, as I did from the process of building your collection, then your reward will be great, indeed.

● ● ●

"Looking back, of course, it was irresponsible, mad, forlorn, idiotic, but if you don't take chances then you'll never have a winning hand, and I've no regrets."

—Bernard Cornwell, 2005, not speaking about coin investments
but rather about writing his first book

1. For my non-golfing readers, a *bogey* is a score on a hole of golf that is one stroke worse than the accepted standard (or par) for that hole. A double bogey is one stroke worse than a bogey. A snowman is a score of 8, which is really bad.

2. If there are any golfers still reading this, let me explain some of the lingo. S-74 is a designation assigned by Dr. William H. Sheldon (thus the "S") to a lettered-edge variety of the 1795 large cent. Sheldon's book on large cent varieties minted from 1793 through 1814, *Early American Cents*, was published in 1949 and subsequently updated and reissued as *Penny Whimsy* in 1958. Initials such as AG, EF, and AU are abbreviations for grades indicating the extent of wear on a coin's surfaces. AG means About Good, but if you saw a coin in this grade, you'd think that AG meant About Gone, since a coin in this condition has had almost all its design detail worn away. EF means Extremely Fine—a very nice-looking coin—and AU means About Un-circulated, which is slightly better than EF.

3. Another footnote for golfers who haven't yet become numismatists: The 1877 In-dian Head cent is considered a key date because of its low mintage—only 852,500 pieces, while other coins in the series had mintages that numbered in the tens of millions. A PCGS holder is a sonically sealed, tamper-evident, inert plastic case used by the Professional Coin Grading Service, of Newport Beach, California, to encapsulate a coin. Collectors and dealers often refer to these holders as *slabs*. PCGS (like other similar grading companies) includes an insert inside its holders, identify-ing the coin and providing an opinion of its grade. A "raw" coin is a coin that is not housed in a third-party grading service's holder.

4. The first U.S. mint was established in Philadelphia in the last decade of the 18th century. Coins from this parent mint generally do not have a mintmark to show where they were made. (Nickels made in Philadelphia during World War II, and most modern coins, are the exceptions to this rule.) The spread of commerce and the discovery of precious metals led to the creation of branch mints in ensuing de-cades. Coins minted at branch mints have mintmarks to indicate their origin: C for Charlotte, North Carolina; CC for Carson City, Nevada; D for Dahlonega, Geor-gia; D for Denver (which opened in 1906, 45 years after the Dahlonega Mint closed); O for New Orleans; S for San Francisco; and W for West Point, New York.

5. Die clashing, as the term suggests, occurs when the obverse and reverse dies come together without a coin blank in between them. When this happens, a bit of the design from the obverse die is punched onto the reverse die, and vice versa. Coins minted after an instance of die clashing will show traces of this form of die damage.

6. A *Guide Book* variety refers to a coin type or design that is listed in the *Red Book* (the annually issued *Guide Book of United States Coins* by R.S. Yeoman). Guide Book va-

rieties often command a premium over varieties that haven't been considered by the editors of the *Red Book* to be of sufficient significance for inclusion in their reference book.

7. S-V.D.B. is shorthand for the 1909 cent minted in San Francisco (S), with the designer's initials (V.D.B., for Victor David Brenner) appearing in small letters on the lower reverse.

8. My 1792 half disme:

9. That tattoo is seen here:

10. In November 2013 the auction of part II of the Eric P. Newman collection had just been concluded. Worldwide publicity was given to the huge gain generated by the sale of Mr. Newman's 1,800 coins. According to reports, Newman spent about $7,500 in the late 1930s and early 1940s to acquire the coins that realized a little over $23 million in the sale. If we assume that his weighted average holding period was 73 years, then his annual compounded return was 11.6%. This is an excellent result, of course, but not as dazzling as some commentators would have you believe.

Bowers, Q. David. *A Guide Book of United States Type Coins*. Atlanta, GA: Whitman Publishing, 2005.

———. *American Coin Treasures and Hoards*. Wolfeboro, NH: Bowers and Merena Galleries, 1997; Atlanta, GA: Whitman Publishing, 2015.

———. The *Rare Silver Dollars Dated 1804 and the Exciting Adventures of Edmund Roberts*. Wolfeboro, NH: Bowers and Merena Galleries, 1999.

———. *The Expert's Guide to Collecting and Investing in Rare Coins*. Atlanta, GA: Whitman Publishing, 2005.

———. *The Treasure Ship S.S. Brother Jonathan: Her Life and Loss 1850–1865*. Wolfeboro, NH: Bowers and Merena Galleries, 1999.

———. *A California Gold Rush History, featuring the Treasure from the S.S. Central America*. Newport Beach, CA: The California Gold Marketing Group, 2002.

Breen, Walter. *Walter Breen's Complete Encyclopedia of U.S. and Colonial Coins*. New York, NY: Doubleday, 1988.

Burdette, Roger W. *Renaissance of American Coinage 1905–1908*. Great Falls, VA: Seneca Mill Press, 2006.

Deisher, Beth. *Cash In Your Coins: Selling the Rare Coins You've Inherited*. Atlanta, GA: Whitman Publishing, 2014.

Doty, Richard. *America's Money, America's Story: A Chronicle of American Numismatic History*. Atlanta, GA: Whitman Publishing, 2008.

Frankel, Alison. *Double Eagle: The Epic Story of the World's Most Valuable Coin*. New York, NY: W.W. Norton, 2006.

Guth, Ron, and Jeff Garrett. *United States Coinage: A Study by Type*. Atlanta, GA: Whitman Publishing, 2005.

Head, Sylvia Gailey, and Elizabeth W. Etheridge. *The Neighborhood Mint: Dahlonega in the Age of Jackson*. Alpharetta, GA: Gold Rush Gallery, 2000.

Mihm, Stephen. *A Nation of Counterfeiters—Capitalists, Con Men, and the Making of the United States*. Cambridge, MA: Harvard University Press, 2007.

Moran, Michael. *Striking Change: The Great Artistic Collaboration of Theodore Roosevelt and Augustus Saint-Gaudens*. Atlanta, GA: Whitman Publishing, 2008.

Newman, Eric P. and Kenneth E. Bressett. *The Fantastic 1804 Dollar, Tribute Edition*. Atlanta, GA: Whitman Publishing, 2009.

Sheldon, William H. *Penny Whimsy*. New York, NY: Harper & Row, 1958.

Stack, Norman. *United States Type Coins*. New York, NY: Stack's, 1986.

Van Ryzin, Robert R., *Crime of 1873*. Iola, WI: Krause Publications, 2001.

Yeoman, R.S. *A Guide Book of United States Coins*, published annually. Atlanta, GA: Whitman Publishing.

Credits and Acknowledgments

For Gayle, my muse.

Many individuals provided assistance in the creation of this book. The following were of particular importance. Gayle Beyer encouraged and supported me in my efforts, always gave me the space to write, and motivated me to finish this project. Q. David Bowers provided unsolicited discounts on coin purchases when I re-entered the hobby in the mid-1990s, allowed me to be a "helper" on six of his books, and offered up the Stack's Bowers Galleries photos and lot descriptions used in the text. He reviewed the entire manuscript and suggested many important improvements and corrections. He also wrote the very generous foreword. Dave is a treasured resource to the hobby and an inspiration to me. John Pack handled the consignment of the Waccabuc Collection seamlessly from start to finish and reviewed extensive parts of the manuscript. My brother (and onetime editor) Richard Shippee reviewed the manuscript in detail and made many valuable suggestions. My daughter Starr Shippee provided insightful copyediting suggestions on a large portion of the manuscript. The associates of Whitman Publishing showed early confidence in my work and turned it into a much improved final product. The photographs of my 1792 half disme were provided courtesy of Heritage Auctions. The errors that remain in this book are mine and mine alone.

I would also like to acknowledge two online resources that were particularly useful in the preparation of this book. Heritage Auctions' Past Auction Archives is an outstanding source for recent and historical auction prices realized and has outstanding photos. The Professional Coin Grading Service's CoinFacts portal has an abundance of information about every U.S. coin minted from colonial times to the present. It includes record-setting sales and also has excellent photos. In addition, I benefited from years of reading the weekly numismatic newspaper *Coin World*, sometimes while sipping a Laphroaig and smoking a Davidoff cigar. Time well and enjoyably spent!

About the Author

Robert W. Shippee is a semi-retired, international banker, a lifelong coin collector, and a 13-handicap golfer. His credentials as a writer are meager—a dozen annual Christmas letters that only rarely are rejected as spam by family and friends plus, of course, many thousands of tedious emails and memoranda generated in his 37 years as a banker. This is his first book. He does, however, have a hole-in-one to his credit.

Index